A terrifying look into what happens when backs are turned, the Constitution forsaken, and religious fundamentalism takes over in violent and unfathomable ways.
—**ROBERT O. "BOBBY" MULLER**, 1997 Nobel Peace Prize, Co-Founder of the International Campaign to Ban Landmines, and President of Veterans for America

In the name of Jesus, how low can some stoop? An attempted coup in America? A scheme to subsume our nation's military? In these pages duplicity, intimidation, chicanery, undermining, death threats, subversion and bullying, all in the name of Jesus, meet a two-fisted response from a man who will yield no ground as he defends religious freedom for those who serve our country.
—**MIKE FARRELL**, best known as B.J. Hunnicutt of M*A*S*H, and the author of *Just Call Me Mike: A Journey to Actor and Activist* and *Of Mule and Man*

Right now America is engaged in a tough argument over what kind of country this is, and is going to be. Mikey Weinstein believes the armed forces of our country belong to us all, and value us all, from *every* religious background...and *none*. Love him (as many do) or hate him (as many do), Mikey's an American Original. This book will introduce you to his bare-knuckled style and the work of the Military Religious Freedom Foundation. Prepare to have your preconceptions about religious freedom and American pluralism challenged, and reconsidered.
—**RAY SUAREZ**, author of *The Holy Vote: The Politics of Faith in America* and Senior Correspondent, PBS NewsHour

Mikey Weinstein is a passionate, articulate, forceful, stunningly courageous, and occasionally confrontational advocate for the separation of church and state in the United States Armed Forces. One could wish his work unnecessary. Certainly I do. Yet it is compelling, even crucial. The American military, as an arm of the federal government, is required to accommodate all religions, and to favor none. Tragically, that simple lesson is apparently not understood, or it is patently ignored, by too many who wield power in our armed forces.
—**GENE NICHOL**, Boyd Tinsley Distinguished Professor of Law University of North Carolina and President Emeritus, College of William & Mary

Often one man's experience can highlight a crisis. Rarely, however, does that same man intervene to right the wrong. Mikey Weinstein and his family challenge the pervasive ultra-conservative Christian domination of our armed services and the harm it has done to service personnel. Weinstein's goal is protecting religious freedom for all Americans but especially those in the military who risk their lives defending the Constitution – only to be denied their own right to private religious conviction. Whether one is Christian, Jewish, Muslim, other believer or non-believer, this family's courageous and compelling story is a "must read" for everyone who loves the Constitution and cherishes freedom of faith and conscience.
—**ELIZABETH SHOLES**, Director of Public Policy, California Council of Churches IMPACT

Fearless and bombastic, Mikey Weinstein is one of the country's fiercest champions of religious pluralism. He is defending us all from fundamentalists who seek to turn the U.S. armed forces into their own sectarian Christian army, a project conflagration ever more likely. It's heroic, invaluable work.

— **MICHELLE GOLDBERG**, Senior Contributing Writer for *The Daily Beast/Newsweek*, author of the *New York Times* bestseller *Kingdom Coming: The Rise of Christian Nationalism*

No snowflake in an avalanche ever feels responsible.
—Voltaire

ALSO BY
MICHAEL L. "MIKEY" WEINSTEIN AND DAVIN SEAY

WITH GOD ON OUR SIDE
One Man's War Against an Evangelical Coup in America's Military

NO SNOWFLAKE
IN AN AVALANCHE

THE MILITARY RELIGIOUS FREEDOM FOUNDATION,
ITS BATTLE TO DEFEND THE CONSTITUTION,
AND ONE FAMILY'S COURAGEOUS WAR AGAINST
RELIGIOUS EXTREMISM IN HIGH PLACES

MICHAEL L. "MIKEY" WEINSTEIN
AND **DAVIN SEAY**

This is A Vireo Book
An imprint of Rare Bird Books

Copyright © 2012 by Michael L. Weinstein

Distributed in the U.S. by Cameron + Company, Inc.

Printed in the United States of America.

For information and inquiries, address Rare Bird Books, 453 South Spring
Street, Suite 531, Los Angeles, CA 90013.

Design by Tamra Rolf
Set in Goudy Old Style

Cataloging-in-Publication Data for this book is available from the Library
of Congress.

ISBN-13: 978-0-9839255-3-8
ISBN-13: 978-0-9839255-6-9 (ebook)

Rare Bird Books are available at special discounts for bulk purchases in the
U.S. by corporations, institutions, and other organizations. For more
information, please contact Cameron + Company, 6 Petaluma Blvd.
North, Suite B6, Petaluma, CA 94952 or email info@cameronbooks.com.

10 9 8 7 6 5 4 3 2 1

Printed in the United States of America

This book is dedicated to those exceptional and heroic human beings—those brilliant lions of virtue and moral and ethical strength—who abjectly refuse to be "snowflakes in an avalanche," thus possessing the uncommon courage to speak truth to power. Chiefly among them are my wonderful wife Bonnie and my beautiful children, Casey, Amanda, Curtis, and Amber. Ah, but there are more lions still. This book is likewise dedicated to all Military Religious Freedom Foundation staff, advisory board and board members, supporters, donors, and especially our thousands of soldier, sailor, marine, airman, cadet, midshipman, and armed forces veteran clients around the world. They show us all that we CAN and MUST stand up and fight boldly against the unconstitutional wretchedness of bigotry and prejudice and religious predators. Indeed, One Day as a Lion is all that may ever be needed to summon the fortitude to fight back against this brutal intolerance. But one never knows when that day will beckon. —M.L.W.

TABLE OF CONTENTS

INTRODUCTION

Books are written for many reasons.

Some have a story to tell. Some have a score to settle or a lesson to teach. Some have an agenda all their own.

This book has been written to save lives.

It may sound like an outsized claim for what seems, on its surface, an account of the struggle for a lofty Constitutional principle. To many, that principle may be nothing more than legal abstraction, a dense argument revolving around the arcane niceties of freedom of expression as defined by the Founding Fathers.

It is anything but.

For the sake of those principles, real people are being ruthlessly persecuted. They are suffering deprivation, degradation and despair. Their most basic rights, as human beings no less than as American citizens, are being systematically suborned, subverted and smothered. Their hopes and dreams are being shattered, their families destroyed, their lives ruined.

But it goes even deeper than that: much, much, deeper. Real tears are being shed. And real blood. The lives of real people are in real danger. Their existence is shadowed by the specter of sudden, savage violence, of unreasoning hatred, of a clear and of present danger to everything they hold dear.

That danger extends far beyond the metastasizing threat to many of the freedoms we most cherish and often take for granted; past the illegal and immoral outrages being perpetrated against those with little recourse and no power to fight back; further, even, the treasonous sedition that this virulent threat to our national security represents.

This book is not about an issue or a problem. It is not about winning an argument or settling a dispute. It is about saving lives. And the lives it saves may be more than just a handful of helpless, hapless victims. It may be the lives of our friends and neighbors and family. It may be the life of our nation, our society, our civilization.

It may be, in the end, our own lives.

No one knows this better than Michael L. "Mikey" Weinstein. In 2005, Weinstein founded the Military Religious Freedom Foundation (MRFF), an organization formed in response to a persistent and pervasive pattern of religious intolerance, coercive attempts at conversion and an intolerable abuse of the chain of command within the nation's armed services, the most powerful and lethal military force in the history of mankind. In the course of a wide ranging and ever expanding investigation, Weinstein had positively and conclusively identified the perpetrators as hardcore fundamentalist Christian elements within every branch of the military, intent on creating nothing less than an army of zombie zealots prepared to fight and die in order to usher in the dispensational reign of Jesus Christ on earth.

He has, ever since, dedicated every waking hour to rolling back this floodtide of fundamentalist fervor with an unremitting defense of the U.S. Constitution's crucial Establishment Clause, guaranteeing complete freedom from any religious test. But that was only part of Weinstein's tireless efforts. He has also provided direct assistance in the form of legal and occasionally even financial aid to the victims of this shocking intolerance and persecution within the ranks of the armed forces, men and women who, in many cases, had nowhere else to turn.

This isn't the first time Mikey Weinstein had sounded the clarion call, bringing global attention to this horrific crisis and its life threatening consequences. His scathing exposé of egregious and illegal religious abuses in the military was detailed in his 2006 book, *With God On Our Side*, which in part told the gripping story of Weinstein's own encounter with visceral anti-Semitism while a cadet at the United States Air Force Academy.

Weinstein's Military Religious Freedom Foundation represents the interests of over 25,000 clients in all branches of the military; the Army, the Navy, the Air Force, the Marines, the Coast Guard and the Merchant Marines, along with all their respective veteran, Guard and Reserve units. Each and every one of them, he wrote in an early MRFF mission statement, had "requested personal guidance and assistance in confronting unconstitutional religious prejudice and discrimination." It was a revealing fact that, among them, the vast majority, approximately ninety-six percent, were self-professed practicing Christians who, while discharging their sworn military duties, had been subjected to belligerent harassment and persecution by fundamentalists, who were often their own superior officers, as well as non-commissioned officers. But the foundation has also come to the aid of what Weinstein characterized as a "veritable rainbow of other faith traditions including, but not limited to, Muslims, Buddhists, Hindus, Jews, Sikhs, Native American spiritualists, as well as agnostics and atheists."

Along with providing timely and effective help to those in the crosshairs of fundamentalist Christian terror tactics, the MRFF has also spearheaded a raft of historic lawsuits to bring the religious criminals to heel. An accomplished and experienced attorney, Weinstein also taps the expertise of top lawyers, litigators and legal scholars from some of the most prestigious firms in the country, all of them inspired to give of their time and talent on a pro bono basis. Small wonder Mikey has come under intense fire both from the enemies he confronts and those who urge a more measured and cautious approach for fear of upsetting the powerful interests arrayed against him.

"Since I started the foundation, I've been called a lot of things," Weinstein remarks with a defiant grin. "Among the kinder epithets that have been hurled my way is that I'm an intemperate firebrand and an irresponsible whistleblower. It's true that I don't deal in nuance. I'm not interested in 'constructive dialogue' with those who are perpetrating these unconstitutional outrages. Desperate times call for desperate measures. When others complain that I can't keep my mouth shut, I'm reminded of a quote from Dr. Martin Luther King to the effect that, in the end, we remember not the words of our enemies but the silence of our friends. There comes a time when silence is betrayal. That time is now.

"But I'm not the only one who understands what's at stake for our military if we let the forces of fundamentalist dominionist religious extremism run amok," he continues, his words echoing the certainty with which he fearlessly expresses his bedrock convictions. "When we invaded Iraq, General Tommy Franks, Commander of the United States Central Command, overseeing armed forces operations in a twenty-five nation region, issued what was known as General Order 1A. Its actual title was 'Prohibited Activities for U.S. Department of Defense Personnel Present within the United

States Central Command Area of Responsibility.' The purpose of the order was, and I quote, '*To identify and regulate that conduct which is prejudicial to the maintenance of good order and discipline of forces.*' The order was applicable to 'All United States Military Personnel.'

"Suffice it to say, this order didn't deal in nuance or fine distinctions either. There was nothing ambiguous in its description of prohibited activities. Purchase, possession or distribution of alcohol within the theater of operation was forbidden. So were drugs and pornography and gambling. And then, right there in this long list of prohibitions, item 'K' to be exact, was a single line, banning 'proselytizing of any religion, faith or practice.'"

He pauses for a long moment to let the words, and their significance, sink in. "Look," he says at last, "there is a compelling reason why our soldiers aren't supposed to be trying to convert the very people in whose territory we're fighting a war against jihadist extremists. A major part of winning that war is winning the hearts and minds of the population, to convince them that we're not just the latest incarnation of the Crusaders, or that we're intent on extinguishing their faith or trampling on their traditions. The commanders of our armed forces, deployed in a volatile and hostile part of the world, understand that. They couldn't have made the distinction between our actual mission there and the fevered dreams of Christian fundamentalists in uniform any more clearly. Our job is not to usher in the millennial rule of Jesus Christ on earth. Our job is to defeat the enemy and go home, leaving these people to live their lives and determine their destiny as best they can.

"But that same principle extends beyond the battlefield. It applied to the homeland, as well. The real impact of General Order 1A, later redesignated as General Order 1B, is inherent in its purpose, which is worth repeating: 'To identify and regulate that conduct which is prejudicial to the maintenance of good order and discipline of forces.' That holds for 'All United States Military Personnel,' and I take that at face value to mean both here and abroad. Religious proselytizing has absolutely no place in military life. It says so in the Establishment Clause of the Constitution and it's never been truer than it is today, when we are fighting an enemy who uses religion to justify acts of terror and mass murder. We can't stoop to their level, using some skewed interpretation of an ancient text to justify barbarism and conquest.

"I respect the fact that the Bible tells Christians to win converts to Christ. "Go into all the world and preach the gospel to all creation," Jesus says in Mark 16:15. In Matthew 28:19 he tells the disciples to "Go therefore and make disciplines of all the nations." That's part of the call of every Christian's faith. But there are distinctions that must be made if we want to live in a free society. Those distinctions are evident in the radically different approaches to witnessing to your faith, depending on whether you're an evangelical or a fundamentalist. An evangelical will seek converts, but only in the proper time, place and manner as is laid out in the foundational documents of our nation. Fundamentals have no such restraints, either legally or morally. They think and act as if the whole world was their mission field. It's un-American, it's inhuman and it's a throwback to a time, not so long ago, when an entire people's religious heritage was enough to get them exterminated by the multiple millions."

Weinstein makes no apologies for his inflammatory language. "There's no use mincing words," he asserts. "As a nation we are at a crossroads. In President Eisenhower's Farewell Address to the nation on January 17, 1961, he famously warned his fellow countrymen of the dangerous rise of what he called the 'Military-Industrial Complex.' With apologies to Ike, I would contend that we are facing a far more serious threat today with the rise of what I call the Fundamentalist Christian Para-Church, Military, Corporate, Proselytizing Complex. It took us years to figure out the nature of the beast, to fully understand that it's immense and multi-tentacled and is run by the individuals who would joyfully point the way to Armageddon in the twisted belief that it would usher a heaven on earth. But, of course, entry to the pearly gates is only for the born again believer. Which makes us all a target for 'conversion,' whether we like it or not. 'Turn or burn' is the phraseology of choice. These fucking people have infiltrated into some of the highest circles of government and operate directly out of the Pentagon, or what I like to call the 'Pentecostal-gon'. Nowhere, in fact, is their influence more pervasive and dangerous than in the military. It's only within the armed forces of America that the power actually exists to destroy the world. Whose finger is on the nuclear trigger is a matter of grave concern to all of us. The very real and frightening possibility that fanatical zealots are so close to realizing their deluded dream of hastening the Last Days through an armed insurrection or even a nuclear holocaust should keep us all up at night, trembling under the covers."

Again Weinstein pauses, taking a deep breath to gather his thoughts. "The purpose of this book is not to just to protect the lives and safety of those who have directly experienced the horrors perpetrated by these en-emies of civilization. It's to protect the lives of all of us who are imperiled by those who work day and night to gain control of the most powerful military and deadliest arsenal in existence. America has built the most lethal fight-ing machine in human history. Control of that machine is the ultimate goal of this fundamentalist Christian cabal.

"When I first began this battle, it wasn't with some noble aspiration to save the world from religious extremism in its most lethal manifesta-tion, within our military. I simply wanted to stop the shit I was seeing, the blatant infringements of constitutionally guaranteed rights, and to point out the threat to good order and discipline posed by such activities. And I certainly didn't see myself as the champion of oppressed soldiers and sailors, be they Protestants, Catholics or Jews, Wiccans or Zoroastrians or straight up pagans. But then I began meeting some of these people, in their tens and hundreds and ultimately thousands. I was confronted with the human dimension of what otherwise might seem to be an abstract argument of constitutional principles and procedures. There's human faces to this ongo-ing tragedy in our nation, and those faces are literally crying out for justice."

Weinstein doesn't hesitate to call out Christian fundamentalist en-croachment in the military for exactly what it is. "Sedition," he flatly asserts. "It's treason, pure and simple. This is an ongoing attempt at a de facto coup by radical fundamentalist Christians to seize the levers of military power and enforce their maniacal doctrines on the country and, eventually, the world. Their egregious, ongoing violation of strict prohibitions against pros-elytizing, such as that laid out in General Order 1B, is only the tiniest tip of an enormous submerged iceberg. They see the War on Terror as a historic opportunity to advance their agenda of eradicating, either through coer-cive conversion, brute force, or even death, any religion that competes with their deliberately misconstrued Biblical claims of divine right. No clearer indication of their true intentions can be found than in their systematic persecution of other spiritual traditions within the ranks of the military. I know because I have heard firsthand from their victims, men and women who stepped forward to tell their stories to me in hopes that I would help to stop this conspiracy before it's too late."

Is it too late? Weinstein stubbornly refuses to entertain that possibility. "In 2006, I wrote the book *With God On Our Side* in part to explain how I took up this fight. It's now five years later. It's time for another book, one that describes the true enormity of what is happening and what still needs to be done—every day in every military installation, office building and forward operating base, across the country and around the world—to stop the fucking madness. Maybe the fact that this book needs to be written at all means we're losing the battle. Or maybe it means that we've reached another, more intense and protracted, phase of the war. Either way, the lines are drawn and the conflict will continue until the last person is standing. With the help of the Military Religious Freedom Foundation, its staff and its supporters, its learned attorneys, my family and friends, my colleagues, associates and concerned citizens from every walk of American life, I intend to be that person."

PART ONE

CHAPTER ONE

FATHER'S DAY 2008

The slight sliver of a crescent moon hung over the high desert landscape of Sandia Heights, an upscale bedroom community nestled against the arid foothills of the Sandia Mountains in the northern reaches of Albuquerque, New Mexico. The wan glow cast deep shadows over the well-tended yards in the Southwestern-themed subdivision, a profusion of cactus gardens, rock-strewn yards and festively tiled patios. The steep ascent of the mountain was bisected by a tramway, built to carry sightseers up to a dazzling panorama of the vast undulating plain stretching uninterrupted to the west. The warm June night of the 15th—Father's Day, 2008—was still and quiet, punctuated only by the persistent barking of dogs emanating from a low slung adobe-and-wood beam residence set on its own promontory overlooking the pristine primordial setting from a row of expansive picture windows.

The din of the dogs, agitated and angry, echoed through the neighborhood, a place where residents kept largely to themselves, their wide-spaced homes a testament to the hardscrabble individualism that had served to settle this serene, severe region. No one peered out their back door or ventured into their driveway to see what the ruckus was about. Folks minded their own business in Sandia Heights, adhering to the rugged Western virtue of live-and let-live. But it must have been hard to ignore the alarm set up by the anxious animals. Something was happening at the house on the hill, something furtive and hidden, even from the encompassing view of its wood framed windows.

20

Inside the home, nestled on a bend along Laurel Loop and impeccably appointed in a richly detailed Southwestern motif, a young woman named Amber Stearns had no notion of the dogs' barking just down the hallway from the closed door of her bedroom. In that perpetually dry atmosphere, most residences in the area employed swamp coolers to keep the desert heat at bay; big, noisy appliances that kept up a dull rumble throughout the night. The cooler installed in the hall roof outside Amber's door was no exception and the drone of its motor muffled any other sound, including the warnings of the two German Shepherds whose fanciful and affectionate names, Ginger Honey-Bear and Crystal-Baby Blue-Bear, belied their fierce protective nature and single-minded dedication to guarding the premises against any and all intruders.

Amber, an attractive, blonde twenty-year-old, whose dark eyes reflected a serious mien beyond her years, was deeply immersed in her college studies, She felt safe in the confines of her room, secure in the house that had, two years previously, become her home, welcomed there by a family she had come to call her own.

Perhaps more than others at her age, Amber put a premium on safety and security. They had, after all, been conspicuous in their absence for more than a few years during her younger life. Born and raised in Pecos, a picturesque community some fifty miles north of Albuquerque up Interstate 25, Amber's idyllic childhood was shattered at age thirteen when her parents divorced. It was only then that she learned that the man who she had been told was her biological father had assumed that role after the identity of her real father could not be determined. The man she thought was her father was subsequently forced to move away because of a family illness. He encouraged Amber to accompany him, but she chose to stay in New Mexico where she had come of age. Her mother would later take up with an alcoholic boyfriend. At age sixteen, to escape her deteriorating domestic situation, Amber left home, dropped out of high school and moved into a small apartment, supporting herself as a salesgirl in a clothing store in nearby Santa Fe.

Of course, the ravages of divorce and a broken home are, sadly, not all that uncommon, but for Amber, a sensitive young woman with a yearning for a stable, safe environment, the effects were devastating. The course her life had taken was a source of deep shame for the struggling adolescent. She never told anyone of her plight and even her closest friends weren't exactly sure where she was living and why she wasn't in school anymore. As is the case with so many children of divorce, Amber doubtlessly blamed herself for the troubles that had befallen her. "My mother's boyfriend made it uncomfortable to live with her anymore," she recalls. "I had no choice but to try and make it on my own. But I didn't want anyone to know the truth and that was a very lonely way to live."

That loneliness was alleviated, at least for a time, when she met a confident and caring young cadet attending the United States Air Force Academy in Colorado Springs. His name was Curtis Weinstein and the two dated for about a six-month period. But Amber had been keeping what she considered her shameful secret to herself. It was only after meeting Curtis's parents, Mikey and Bonnie Weinstein, that she found a way to reveal her painful past.

Immediately attracted by their warmth and compassion, she saw in them the kind of parents, and the kind of family, she needed in her life at that particular time. As she puts it, "I just knew I could trust them." It was that trust that finally broke down the barriers that Amber had erected between herself and the world. Without quite realizing how much she needed to tell someone what had happened to her and the track that her life had taken, she instinctively understood that she could no longer cover up the truth. She finally summoned the courage to reveal her secrets to Mikey and Bonnie. "Once I started," she recounts, "I couldn't stop. It all just spilled out."

The Weinsteins' response to Amber's tearful confession might have come as a surprise to anyone who hadn't encountered the encompassing empathy and intense personal interaction that defines the Weinstein family. It was these qualities that immediately prompted Mikey and Bonnie to invite Amber to move in with them, assuming without a second thought the responsibility for her well-being and providing that essential sense of safety and security that she had for so long done without. It was, by any measure, a remarkable offer and one for which, as Amber remembers, they refused to take no for an answer.

Yet even after she moved in, she still couldn't quite face up to telling them everything about her past. More than anything she was embarrassed about not finishing high school, instead pretending that she was enrolled in college. What she hadn't counted on was not just the Weinsteins' generosity but also the attendant scrutiny that came with their invitation to open their hearts and home to her.

It took Mikey and Bonnie one day to find out the truth. For his part, Mikey was saddened and disturbed by the deception and wondered aloud to his wife if they hadn't made a mistake taking Amber in. Bonnie, for her part, counseled patience and understanding. She realized immediately what their young charge had gone through and why she was trying to cover it up. After a heart-to-heart with her husband, they just made arrangements for Amber to earn her General Education Diploma, after which they assisted her in applying to college. "They both believed in me," she says, "even when I didn't believe in myself."

In the process of regaining that confidence in herself, with the help of her loving and supportive new family, Amber began to come to grips with her own potential, even as she took her place in the Weinsteins' tight domestic circle. Realizing she had an untapped aptitude for math opened up a wide vista of new possibilities for her future, even as Casey and his younger brother Curtis became her de facto siblings. More than a few friends and acquaintances found it strange that Amber was formerly dating someone who, for all intents and purpose, she now considered to be her brother. "But it's just because they don't really understand the family dynamic between us," she explains.

After Casey met and married Amanda, another Air Force Academy graduate, the two young women became fast friends. "We talk a dozen times a day at least," Amber reveals. "I know that I've been given a sister, too."

Quickly assimilated into the Weinstein clan, Amber had come to think of the Laurel Loop home as a sanctuary, a secure haven against the vicissitudes of life she had been forced to face on her own. Up against the steep flank of the mountain, where an aura of splendid isolation held sway, it seemed as if nothing could intrude into the safe perimeter the Weinsteins' had provided for her. In time, she would take Weinstein as her legal last name, eventually completing the process of full and legal adoption. It was a heartfelt tribute to the family that had done so much for her.

Deeply into her textbooks, Amber was oblivious to the alarm, still muffled by the swamp cooler's rumble that Ginger and Crystal had raised and which had steadily risen to frantic pitch. What would at last catch her startled attention was the sudden appearance of Mikey Weinstein, as he slammed open her bedroom door with a look in his wide eyes that signaled something deadly serious. The two were alone in the house, Bonnie having left town a few days before to visit friends on the east coast.

"Didn't you hear the dogs?" he demanded, a sharp edge in his voice that sent a shiver of sudden fear down Amber's spine. The question rose above the drone of the cooler and it was only then that she became aware of the aggressive baying of the two animals from the front entryway down the hall. She leapt from her desk, suddenly breathless with apprehension. She had never seen her father like this before, tense and preemptory, his eyes darting around the room as he assessed the situation.

If anything, Mikey Weinstein consistently projected an air of quiet competence and almost preternatural calm, offset by a voluble streak and intense, often passionate nature, compacted into his fireplug frame and shaved head. He carried his compact frame nimbly, exuding the kind of effortless grace of a man comfortable in his own skin and fully cognizant of his capabilities. But in that moment, bursting into her room, Amber saw in him a whole other kind of focus, a man suddenly facing down a clear and present danger, confronting a dangerous threat to the place she had come to know as home.

"What is it?" she cried, jumping to her feet and feeling her own quickening fight-or-flight response to the formless threat that had intruded on the warm summer night.

"Someone's outside," Mikey replied tersely, even then moving back down the hallway after determining that Amber was, at the moment, safe. "Stay here. Don't move."

She ignored him, following Mikey from the rear of the house into the living room, where the pump of a large indoor koi pond—a 40th birthday gift from Bonnie to Mikey—bubbled placidly in sharp contrast to the electric tension that now filled the house. It was hard to imagine how she hadn't heard the racket set up by the dogs. Their barking was now deafening as they crowded at the front door, peering unblinking into the darkness beyond.

"What is it?" Amber repeated, her voice now in a hoarse whisper. Mikey had moved to the screen door at the front entrance and, like his guard dogs, was staring into the dark night.

"Someone's out there," he replied, as much to himself as to her. "I saw a car in the driveway. They knocked out some of our security lights. "

"Is it still there?" she asked, trying hard to keep the tremor from her voice.

Mikey shook his head. "It pulled away when I came outside," he responded tersely. "I think they're gone."

"Who?" The word sounded a sharp piercing note.

Mikey turned to look at her. "Go back to your room," he said. "Wait there until I come for you."

She ignored him. Whatever was happening, she needed to be close to the man who represented a strong and steady presence in her life. It was Father's Day and the place she needed to be more than anywhere was with the man she considered to be her father.

A long moment passed as the barking of the dogs subsided into worried whines. Mikey slowly opened the screen door, with a faint squeak of its hinges. He flicked on the porch light and stepped out beneath unfinished log beams of the overhang. Amber followed close behind.

The heat of the encroaching summer warmed the still night air and the familiar bulk of the Sandia Mountains loomed in the distance like stoic sentinels. The two stood stock still, listening to the silence and staring into the dim light casting shadows across the driveway. The neighborhood streets were empty. It was late. Most of the windows of the adjacent homes were dark and shuttered. In any other circumstance, the scene would have seemed placid and tranquil. But this wasn't any other circumstance. Something had been violated. The all-but sacrosanct perimeter of hearth and home had been breached. Amber couldn't shake the feeling that things were never going to be quite the same again.

It was then that they saw it, almost simultaneously, as if drawn to the evidence of intrusion and trespass by some inaudible signal. There, by the front door, crudely scrawled on the yellow-toned abode of the exterior wall were two symbols: a cross and a swastika. They had been rendered in a hurry, a furtive act of defilement all the more shocking for their rudimentary rendering: hateful graffiti left behind as a taunt, a warning, a grim harbinger of an implacable and irrational enemy.

Amber let out a strangled gasp. Tears welled in her eyes. She felt an overpowering surge of emotion: fear and anger and something else, almost unnamable, like the sudden crushing realization that the world, with all its threats and dangers, would always be lurking in the darkness beyond.

For Amber everything changed in that one moment of time. It was as if all the good things that had happened to her since she met the Weinsteins were suddenly at risk and she felt almost as if she had fooled herself into thinking that, after all she had been through, she wasn't going to have to go through any more. It was naïve, perhaps, but she wanted so badly to believe that the worst was behind her. Now, without warning, something worse had happened. And she couldn't shake the feeling that it would keep happening.

It was a feeling underscored in no uncertain terms in the days that followed the fateful Father's Day incident. A security detachment regularly patrolled that bucolic stretch of Laurel Loop, and every member of the household was trained in the use of firearms, including Amber, who was equipped with a gun to keep next to her in the house at all time. "I cried the first time I fired it," she reveals. "It was like I was getting one more confirmation that my life wasn't going to be the same."

Yet, at the same time, Amber, like the rest of the Weinsteins, evinced remarkable fortitude in the face of the ominous, anonymous threat to their well-being. Even as she began the training necessary to obtain a carry-and-conceal weapons permit, she continued with her college studies. She went to the movies, hung out with her friends and tried to take in stride the presence of a bodyguard assigned to her for special, high profile events.

The trauma of the events of that night would linger. Amber perhaps expressed it best in a subsequent article that had been written about the event in the *Albuquerque Journal*. "I am living my own horror story," she asserted. "I am filled with anger...why would someone do this? People filled with enmity exist; they always will. I wish I could look at whoever did this straight in the eye and let them feel my internal pain and my family's internal pain...I want them to understand the enormity of what they did. I will never be able to remove this picture from my memory....I won't forget the person who did this to our home. The person engorged with such hate."

At the same time, Amber was not about to let fear rule her life. Fully realizing now that, by becoming a Weinstein, she had stepped into the eye of a brewing storm, she also acknowledged that it was a condition that came with the territory. Mikey and Bonnie's commitment to Amber had engendered the same in her, a devotion to the family and to the cause they had embraced, regardless of the cost.

"I knew my father had enemies," she observes, shrugging with a kind of philosophical resignation. "I just didn't know how far they were prepared to go. Now I know."

CHAPTER TWO

WEINSTEIN'S WAR

There is something strangely fitting in the juxtaposition of symbols that defaced the Weinstein home that June night in 2008. A timeless sign of an enduring faith and the infamous standard of the most evil regime in human history: was there some correlation between the two that the intruders were emphasizing by their act? Or had they been left as twisted calling cards, a way for the perpetrators to identify themselves by the ideologies to which they adhered? Whatever else they might have signified, the cross and the swastika etched deep into the stucco wall spoke as eloquently as Amber had about the enemies that Mikey Weinstein had made in his long and lonely fight for a singular principle of surpassing importance. They were, it seemed, prepared to go to any length to express their hatred of the man and his mission.

It was, of course, also highly personal, a targeted attack on the sanctuary of a family that has been long familiar to so many of those who share Mikey Weinstein's heritage. Too often, for Jews throughout history, the butchery that has been perpetrated in the name of either or both of those symbols equates to the same indistinguishable genocidal impulse, as well as the means and determination to carry it out. Bringing them together evoked that history in the most violent and visceral way possible. The message and the warning were clear: by the nature of their birthright, the Weinsteins were in the crosshairs.

But anti-Semitism was only the initial and most bluntly obvious factor in the tangled web of social, religious and political fanaticism that Mikey

27

and his family had dedicated themselves to opposing. It wasn't just the fact that Mikey was Jewish that had put him and his loved ones in direct danger. It was the fact that he was an outspoken, persistent and resourceful Jew, a vocal opponent of the cherished ideals and hidden agendas of a confederation of very formidable foes. The reality of the peril into which the Weinsteins' had been plunged may have been made explicit on Father's Day, 2008, but it hardly came as a surprise to this battle hardened veteran in his war against those forces of intolerance that had marched before the cross and the swastika, in all their various guises.

He was a muckraker, a troublemaker, and the fact that he had raked a lot of muck and made a lot of trouble to great effect in the three years that led up to the attack, was exactly what had brought on the shocking act of reprisal. In the process of carrying out what he saw as his constitutional duty, Mikey had put himself and his family on the frontlines of a long and protracted conflict. It was inevitable that sooner or later, the formidable forces arrayed against him would act out their anger and hatred.

In point of fact, the Weinstein family had grown only too accustomed to the howls of outrage and hatred that erupted against Mikey with clockwork regularity. Simply put, he had been called every variation of every vile name in every book imaginable, excoriated in terms that evoke the primitive loathing and rabid fear mongering that has always infected the extreme elements of the American body politic.

A quick sampling of the volumes of hate mail he receives suffices to vividly illustrate the point. "Rejoice, Spawn of Satan!" read one typical email rant. "Your day is at hand!" While the logic of the statement may have been convoluted, the sentiment was all too clear, as it was in the thousands of other messages that regularly clog Mikey's inbox. "My money's on we gas you fucks first," read another, "and this time get it right." "We will not be safe," a third maintained, "until…people like you are eradicated like cockroaches from the land of the USA." More often than not, sentence structure, punctuation, spelling and even coherence were dispensed with entirely as the screed directed at the Weinstein family was given full vent: "You fucking piece of shit jew and your stinking jew woman and inbred jew children and jew-lover traitor daughter-in-law deserve to torture die you filth jew liberal america hating jesus hating basterd (sic)."

Others essayed an even wider range of slurs, insults, sputtering tirades and dire prophecies. "It is in your low nature to oppose God," claimed one correspondent, while another simply promised, "you WILL be punished and held accountable!!" "Kill any Christian babies lately?" asked a third, while yet another urged him to "Do the right thing," and "commit mass suicide." One even presented his point of view in the form of a particularly odious resume:

Education Background: I learned how to fuck at your mom's house.

Current Job: Plotting the death of Mikey Weinstein

Areas of Interest: Killing gays, killing liberals, killing fags, killing in general

Religious Preference: I believe God will curse you to die.

Mike the Kike; commie cunt; terrorist loving communist; Field General of the Godless Armies of Satan…the vitriolic litany against Mikey Weinstein takes on a kind of numbing cadence that would be all too easy to dismiss as the ravings of the most bigoted, ignorant and rabidly foaming homegrown fanatics were it not for the very real threats that came with them, sometimes in the form of heavy breathing phone calls in the dead of night or, as on more than one occasion, shots fired at the inviting target of the Laurel Loop home's large picture windows.

Yet another form of attack comes from deliberate distortion and a concerted campaign of disinformation. Recently, for example, a Wikipedia page describing Mikey's activities was hacked and inserted with a blatant attempt at smearing both his reputation and the motivations of his mission, erroneously describing him as "an atheist who uses the norms of Christianity and the laws of the United States in a dedicated program of attack and smear against all things Christian. For example, he believes Christians want to hasten the destruction of Israel in order to 'bring about the second coming.' Mr. Weinstein holds himself and his front out to be fighters of racism and bigotry but by his very actions proves himself to be the worst kind of racist there is—a religious racist."

Suffice it to say, if success is measured by the hostility of one's opponents, Mikey had achieved an extraordinary and lasting level of success.

But it was an accomplishment measured in infinitely more gratifying terms by the equally extraordinary outpouring of solidarity, encouragement and appreciation that, over the years, have far outweighed the bulk of hate mail and evil tidings with which the Weinsteins have been forced to contend. Aside from spurring Mikey's efforts by letting him know, in no uncertain terms, that there are many who understand and actively support his work—often expressed in the form of donations large and small—these expressions of esteem and admiration also point to the fact he is far from alone in the war he wages. It is a point underscored by his busy schedule of personal appearances and the raft of local, state and national awards he has received on behalf of his work. But, more often than not, these encouraging expressions are of a touchingly personal nature, reflecting the manner in which the cause to which Mikey has given his life directly affects the lives of others.

It is a sentiment summed up in one heartfelt letter that reads in part, "Thank you for the personal inspiration that helped shape my future and thank you for all the work you are doing which touches so many." Another referred to Weinstein as "a source of encouragement to all Americans, especially for those of us who are on the receiving end of...hateful behavior. You deserve our respect, admiration and above all our support." Still another conveyed the fervent hope shared by many for "continued success in this epic battle for America's values and ideals." But it is perhaps in one of the most poignant statements found in Mikey's correspondence files that the true impact of his mission is made most clear: "*You are the voice I wasn't allowed to use.*"

The saga of how Mikey Weinstein became that voice is inextricably bound up in the personal and professional life of the man himself. Both his most inflexible enemies and most ardent admirers might well be surprised at the fascinating mix of enigmas that define him, a counterintuitive combination of quirks, convictions and contradictions. There is, for starters, the incongruity of his nickname, a boyish handle for a man with such a formidable bearing, appended to him in his later teenage years thanks to the same quirkiness about food displayed by the obstinate toddler in the *Life* cereal TV commercials. Even as he outgrew the initial reasons for his nickname, the stubbornness remained a defining characteristic. Now, at age fifty-six, it has morphed into a pit bull deportment accentuated by his bullet head and sturdy frame, toned by a workout regimen that at one time had stretched unbroken across multiple thousands of days. Chronologically on the trailing edge of the Baby Boom generation, Weinstein nevertheless favors the hardcore heavy metal and punk of such head banging bands as Metallica and Slayer. His idea of an enjoyable evening out would often include a trash-and-thrash session in a local mosh pit.

But the paradoxes reach even deeper. For a man regularly accused of being a godless pagan, a Christ-hating atheist and worse, Mikey retains a healthy respect for the concept of a Creator, even as he freely expresses his doubts over the actual existence of God and an even more abiding skepticism about the claims of organized religion. Yet he is scrupulous in delineating his own self-imposed rituals of belief and even the lack thereof. Over the headboard of his bedroom is a framed picture of a rabbi lighting a Hannukah menorah to which Mikey pays his own form of nightly devotion, a silent petition uttered in Hebrew as much to honor his heritage as to acknowledge the precepts of monotheism. He also regularly recites the Lord's Prayer, particularly before his strenuous exercise sessions, a practice that says as much about his gratitude for the blessings in his life as it does his adherence to any doctrine or dogma.

So, too, do Mikey's complex incongruities reflect themselves in his attitude toward duty and discipline. The son of a distinguished graduate from Annapolis who became a career U.S. Air Force Officer, Mikey's father maintained strict discipline in a spit-and-polish household, and the hammered-home habits of military life. Mikey was, in short, raised on the rock solid precepts of honor, obedience and service to his country. Yet there also exists within him a streak of rebellious pride, an insistence on questioning authority and a mistrust of all hierarchies and the abuse of privilege that too often accompany them.

It was that aspect of his volatile personality that, out of necessity, he suppressed and sublimated when he followed his father's footsteps into military service. But his inclination toward principled dissent never dissipated, even under the rigors of an active service career. "I realized early on that being an American meant we had the right, the responsibility, to express ourselves freely," he asserts, "even if it is in opposition to authority." He pauses before adding, "Especially in opposition to authority. As the great historian Howard Zinn said, 'dissent is the highest form of patriotism.'"

There wasn't much opportunity to exercise that right in the Air Force, the military branch into which Weinstein became a commissioned officer, a career decision based primarily on its reputation for excellence and its high standard of achievement. Mikey would meet and exceed those standards during his tenure in the air forces of the U.S. military. It was a natural step for a young man who had already distinguished himself in any and every field of endeavor to which he turned his attention. Senior Class President in high school, a varsity athlete who played tennis, baseball and football, and upon graduation had secured three prestigious Presidential Nominations, which opened the door for subsequent Presidential Appointments to the Air Force Academy, Annapolis and West Point, each of which had recruited him as a Division 1 intercollegiate athlete.

But for Weinstein, the choice was a foregone conclusion. The Air Force was considered by many to be the leading branch of the armed forces, an elite outfit attracting the best and brightest with a tradition that melded smart, motivated young men and women with cutting edge technology, putting their fingers, in the process, on the triggers of some of the most lethal weapons on the face of the earth.

But even there, Mikey took a decidedly different path from his fellow Air Force Academy cadets, realizing early on that he had no interest in flying the aircraft on which so much of America's armed might, and its ability to project it, depended. "I knew after my initial flight training that I wasn't going to be satisfied being a pilot," he recounts. "Frankly, it bored the shit out of me. I found myself being drawn instead into the law. I was good at writing and even better at arguing. And I understood instinctively that it was the law that actually protected us and kept us free."

There was only one problem. Despite the fact that Weinstein graduated from the Air Force Academy with honors in 1977, there was no clear career path of operational command for an aspiring attorney within the service, which had no law school of its own where he could earn a degree. Weinstein didn't let that stop him. He applied on his own to several respected institutions, including McGeorge School of Law at the University of the Pacific, near Sacramento. Under an obscure Air Force provision known as Excess Leave, he was able to continue active duty at McClellan Air Force Base while at the same time attending classes. After a year of study, he was accepted into the Air Force's Funded Legal Education Program, and went on to earn his juris doctorate degree. From there, he became a judge advocate general at Holloman Air Force Base in southern New Mexico. He became what he called a "jack-of-all-trades," taking on an array of both prosecution and defense cases and handling everything from union negotiations to walk-in divorce counseling. Weinstein showed an immediate aptitude for his catchall role as a JAG, with an emphasis on discerning the intersection between the letter and spirit of the law, as well as developing well-honed interpersonal skills, abilities that would serve him well in the challenging years to come.

Aside from his legal training, Weinstein had also gone through combat communications school upon graduation from the Air Force Academy and it was that aspect of his resume, as well as his proven skills at organizing information and executing strategy, that put him on the fast track to a plum assignment for the Air Force. The military was looking to upgrade its communications capabilities, especially as it applied to the legal ramifications arising from the close linkage between the service branches and AT&T, which was about to be broken up by regulators. His new job entailed moving to Scott Air Force Base near St. Louis, bringing along with him his pregnant wife Bonnie and infant son Casey, a German Shepherd named Sandy and a cat called Louie, short for Lieutenant. Once the burgeoning family had settled into their new quarters—a duplex constructed on what used to be a cornfield—Weinstein began an extensive round of traveling around the country, briefing the military brass and private sector senior executives about the impending divesture and its implications for the new communications environment in the military.

His outstanding performance in anticipating and explaining that environment brought him to the attention of influential movers and shakers within the government. Most notable was David Stockman, the much-celebrated White House Budget Director for the Reagan Administration, who in 1983 poached Weinstein directly from the Air Force and hired him to oversee many of the same communications issues with which he was already dealing, this time at the White House level.

Mikey would remain at the White House for the next three years on a steadily ascending career arc. From the White House Office of Budget and Management, he became Assistant General Counsel to the White House Office of Administration, Executive Office of the President of the United States, where he proved his public relations and legal management mettle by helping the beleaguered administration coordinate its response to the Iran-Contra investigation. "I had an up close and personal education in stonewalling, plausible deniability and slow rolling," he recounts with a grin. It was another skill set that would later help him in spotting the delaying and deflecting talents of his adversaries. "But at the same time I was becoming accustomed to operating in significant spheres of power and influence, which gave me a lot of confidence, as well as connections, moving forward."

As if in recognition of his own growing influence, and the assistance he had rendered in helping to manage the scandal, Weinstein was subsequently offered an even more prestigious job at the White House Office of Administration. "But by that time I had a family to think about and I needed to make some money," he recounts. "Working in the White House is sometimes referred to as a "trampoline job": you bounce from there into something more lucrative in the private sector. I wanted to make that bounce." But the Air Force had a prior claim, announcing that, after ten years of active duty, he was still obliged to serve because of the time he had put in at the Academy and, subsequently, law school. Only after threatened lawsuits and countersuits, was Weinstein free to work in the private sector in Washington, an early example of his readiness to take on entrenched power structures.

The family Mikey needed to support had begun with his wife Bonnie whom he had met at a cadet mixer while he was still at Air Force Academy. The poised and statuesque daughter of a decorated Air Force pilot, possessing a compelling personality mix of blunt candor and abiding compassion, Bonnie had been raised in the typically transient tradition of most military offspring, as her father, who had flown over two hundred combat missions in the Korean War, was stationed variously in posts ranging from Athens, Greece to Los Angeles, California before finally retiring in Colorado Springs, Colorado. Every bit as passionate and principled as the voluble young cadet, Bonnie and Mikey embarked on a courtship lasting over two and a half years, due to the Academy's strict rule against its cadets marrying before graduation.

Raised as a nominal Presbyterian, the contrast between Bonnie's Christian background and Mikey's Jewish heritage was an early hurdle for the young couple. "Our family pastor told me that unless I was careful, Mikey would swallow me up," she recalls, a bit of advice that might well have seemed prescient given her young husband's ambition.

But Bonnie proved every bit his equal, expressing her own individuality in some surprising ways, especially when it came to religious convictions. As a preteen, the perspicacious young woman realized that she couldn't swallow some of the most basic precepts of the Christian faith that she was being asked to accept. "From that point on," she recalls, "church became a place I went with my family, to be together."

It was initially in the interest of togetherness that Bonnie began exploring the spiritual heritage that came with marriage to a Jewish spouse, even one as avowedly secular as Mikey. "Judaism answered a very deep need that I didn't even realize I had until I began my inquiry," she reveals. "It was a way to understand both the blessings and trials of life that made a lot of sense to me." Bonnie would subsequently convert to the faith of her husband and take an active part in the Jewish community in Albuquerque, where the couple moved in 1994. It was there that Bonnie and Mikey buckled down to the business of raising their two sons, Curtis and Casey. Bright, engaged and possessed of a special self-confidence that was the gift of both their parents, the boys accounted in large part for the blessings Bonnie counted in her life. The trial came in early spring of 1998 when she became paralyzed over the course of two days, as a numbness that started in her right foot spread to her left and then traveled upward to her mid-chest. Treatments were given for diseases she didn't have, but eventually the drugs helped to diminish the symptoms. By the late fall of that same year, Bonnie was officially diagnosed with multiple sclerosis. It was, she recalls, "a major fork in the road. It gave us a new appreciation of what we all mean to each other as people, as family. It's made us stronger by testing us in every way imaginable. But it's never been an excuse for not doing the best we can with what we've been given. Like everything else in the life we've shared, we've been required to call on reserves of strength that I don't think we even knew existed before we needed them. That's as true of the MS as it is of the work that Mikey has taken on. In the end it's about family, the ties that bind and the unequivocal loyalty we share. Without that, we simply couldn't have survived."

CHAPTER THREE

PISSED OFF PARENTS

Considering Weinstein's nearly uninterrupted career climb, beginning with his halcyon days in the Air Force, as well as the loving and close knit family over which he and Bonnie presided, it would be hard to imagine any circumstance that might threaten his sense of well-being and the settled assumptions on which he had built their life. That threat, when it came, struck at the very heart of the Weinstein's identity and individuality, a blow from an entirely unexpected quarter that called into question a lifetime of hard won virtues and values.

Resolute about the goal of maximizing every advantage of the "bounce" that his stint in the White House provided, Mikey briefly served as a senior attorney for prestigious law firms in both Washington, DC and New York City. At that point, opportunity knocked with particular forcefulness in the form of a short, feisty and famously outspoken billionaire named H. Ross Perot. The Texas born technology entrepreneur and one time independent presidential candidate, Perot was a close friend and fellow Annapolis classmate of Weinstein's father. He tapped Mikey for the key post of general counsel to his newly created Perot Systems Corporation. It was a tenure that would test the mettle of both men. "Let's just say that Ross was a very demanding and rewarding man to work for," Mikey remarks with uncharacteristic brevity.

Following up on the demands and rewards of that high profile position, Weinstein spent the next few years at a series of private and public sector high-technology businesses, both start-ups and established firms, before eventually returning to the communications services sector as director of business development for a number of Department of Energy programs, once again for his old employer and family friend, Ross Perot. To that point he had managed to leverage his own energy and expertise to create an impressive resume. The future looked bright and promising for a man who had not only racked up a sterling service record and achieved conspicuous success in the legal field, but had been firmly at the forefront of the information technology revolution that was in the process of reshaping the world. Simply put, Mikey Weinstein's professional life was as diverse and richly variegated as his own counterintuitive character traits.

But there was, without a doubt, a point of identification that outweighed every other aspect of his history, both personal and professional. The Air Force, and specifically the time he spent as a cadet at the Air Force Academy, was the measure of accomplishment, pride and fulfillment, against which all else was measured. The school had been a backdrop to most of the important events in his life, up to and including his marriage to Bonnie, two days after his graduation, at a ceremony that marked the first ever Jewish nuptials, complete with chuppah, to be held in the Academy's iconic Protestant Cadet Chapel. In keeping with the ecumenical nature of the event, a Protestant USAF chaplain, who was a close friend of Bonnie's family, married the two in a traditional Jewish ceremony.

When asked what constitutes his special bond to the institution, Mikey will more often than not quote from memory the words of author Pat Conroy in his moving tribute to his own days at the legendary Citadel military college in the book *My Losing Season*.

"I carried the Citadel inside me," the passage reads in part, "...It's a civilization and a way of knowledge, a paradox, a bright circus of life, a mirror and bindery of souls...a preparation for the journey, a trailblazer and road map...and an insider's guide to the dilemma of being alive and ready for anything the world might throw your way." It's rare that Weinstein can get through Conroy's words without choking up, but it wasn't only his own experience at the Academy that had earned it a special place in his heart. Both his sons Casey and Curtis would follow their father's footsteps into those hallowed halls. It was also there that Casey, just as his father had before him, would meet his own future wife, another outstanding cadet by the name of Amanda Baranek. A San Diego native, raised in Colorado Springs, attractive, engaging and inquisitive, she had been raised in an evangelical Christian family and had greatly excelled both athletically and academically, earning a prestigious and highly competitive U.S. senatorial appointment to the Academy from the hardest state in which to garner such an honor, Colorado, the home state of the Air Force Academy. As a Cadet Lieutenant Colonel, she outranked Casey when he proposed to her on the eve of their graduation, forging another strong link between the Weinsteins and the Academy in the process. It would, in fact, hardly be an exaggeration to say that, for Mikey and his family, the Academy was a bastion of all that was good and honorable, pure and principled about America in particular even as, in a more general sense, it embodied all the highest ideals to which humanity strives.

It was that bedrock conviction that cracked and crumbled one fateful day in late July of 2004 when Weinstein made the trip from his Albuquerque home to his beloved alma mater, roaring up Interstate 25 in a fiery red Dodge Viper GTS to attend the Air Force Academy's vaunted Graduate Leadership Conference held annually on the Academy grounds. A three-day invitation-only gathering of the cream of the school's elite alumni, the conference brought together 174 distinguished "Zoomies," as the graduates were affectionately dubbed, some of whom had hailed from as far back as the inaugural class of 1959. The confab was hosted by the Academy's Association of Graduates with the stated intent to "record, preserve and enhance" the Academy's heritage and traditions.

Those traditions were built on the pillars of academic, military and athletic achievement, as well as what many considered to be the Academy's most important purpose: the job of building character in its cadets. But that lofty goal had recently come under withering scrutiny with a scandal alleging widespread sexual assault against female cadets that had rocked that foundation to its core. A shameful stain on the institution's own character, the headline-grabbing story had prompted a plethora of internal inquiries that had begun to resemble the stonewalling and slow rolling that Weinstein was familiar with from his White House Iran Contra days. The end result was a series of self-serving reports, accompanied by the usual search for scapegoats, in this case the administrators at the center of the scandal, who would subsequently be absolved for having acted in "good faith."

Such wagon-circling stratagems had largely succeeded in tamping down the scandal by the time the Zoomies had gathered at Doolittle Hall at the commencement of the Graduate Leadership Conference's long weekend.

Opening remarks by Academy administrators took pains to assure the attendees that the unpleasant episode had been dealt with and the reputation of the Academy all but restored.

But, as Weinstein was shortly to discover, there were much more egregious and entrenched injustices that had become tightly woven into the cloistered culture of the Academy. The bearer of those grim tidings was his younger son, Curtis, who had followed his brother's and father's, two uncle's and future sister-in-law's footsteps into the Academy earlier that year. Curtis, an affable and phlegmatic young man, had, in fact, just completed the notorious "Doolie Year," the demanding freshman course, with a heavy academic, military and athletic load specifically designed to weed out the weakest members of an incoming class, while giving the strongest and most resourceful a chance to prove their mettle.

But the harrowing trial of physical and mental endurance was not all that Curtis had been subjected to since his arrival at the Academy. When he rendezvoused with the father at the Graduate Leadership Conference reception that afternoon, Mikey could immediately sense something deeply troubled in his son's normally easygoing demeanor, even before a single word was spoken. Even before he could ask what was wrong, his son asked in a low whisper if they could go someplace to talk, someplace off the Academy installation and Cadet Area.

At a nearby McDonald's, Curtis at least felt safe to reveal to his father the shocking news.

"What is it?" Mikey had prompted, fearing the worst: a pregnant girlfriend, a drug problem, or expulsion from his beloved Academy? "What have you done?"

"It's not what I've done," Curtis replied, staring straight into his father's eyes. "It's what I'm going to do."

"Tell me," Mikey urged.

In a tone of voice all the more ominous for its icy certitude, Curtis said, "I'm going to beat the shit out of the next guy who calls me a 'fucking Jew.'" Once loosed, the words poured out. "I'm going to beat the shit out of the next guy who accuses me, or our people, of killing Jesus Christ." He paused and drew a ragged breath. "I just thought that before it happens you and mom should know."

***

For Weinstein, his son's stunning words would effectively close out one chapter of his life and initiate—precipitously and in a sudden rush of highly charged emotions—another. In the process, Mikey would discover the mission to which he has dedicated every waking hour since that fateful summer afternoon. A date with destiny, a divine appointment...whatever else it might have been, his meeting with Curtis resounded to the depths of Weinstein's being, stirring both cold, hard rage and a steely, implacable resolve.

His response, as he brooded late into that evening, alone in his motel room behind shuttered blinds where he nursed a fifth of rum, was hardly surprising considering the sense of betrayal with which he was grappling at multiple layers. First, and most obvious, was his immeasurable anger at the Academy and the blind eye it had apparently turned toward virulent religious intolerance within its ranks. Of course, anti-Semitism within the U.S. military was hardly a stop-the-presses revelation. As a hothouse microcosm of American attitudes and assumptions, intolerance in all its forms had infected the ranks of the armed services virtually since its inception.

But hadn't the Academy always been, somehow, different, a shining beacon of egalitarian principles embodying the belief that excellence should be nurtured and rewarded, regardless of race, creed or color? It was another of the elements in the churning anger with which Weinstein wrestled: a deeply wounding sense of embarrassment, even shame, for the institution that had meant so much to he and his family, the institution that defined them all.

But the consuming fury and crushing disappointment drew down on something even more traumatic, an event from Mikey's own early days as cadet that he had done his best to put behind him. It was in 1973, during his first semester at the Academy, when, in response to the Yom Kippur war, he made a request up the chain of command to be allowed to set aside some of his meager cadet pay to donate to the United Jewish Appeal. The request was granted, but shortly thereafter, he began receiving threatening messages, scrawled on notepaper and slipped under the door of his quarters. "You can run, Jew, but you can't hide," read one, the words written beneath a crudely drawn swastika. It wouldn't be the last time he would be confronted directly with the symbol of genocidal intent.

More notes followed, culminating in two savage beatings, one in the Fairchild Hall academic building stairwell and another a week later in one of the same building's bathrooms. It was the latter that sent him to the hospital. When he was released, Weinstein was confronted by the officer charged with investigating the incident, who tried to coerce the eighteen-year-old cadet into signing a confession, admitting that he had sent the notes to himself and, by implication, beat himself up, twice. Frightened and explosively angry, in shock at what was happening, he attacked the investigator, a superior officer, laying him out with a single blow to the jaw. He fled back across the Terrazzo-tiled Cadet Area to his dorm room, convinced that at any moment he would be converged upon and summarily dragged to the Academy's jail facility.

A blatant offense in any military organization, the act was especially serious within the confines of the Academy, where the chain of command is given utmost deference. If the incident had been reported, Weinstein's expulsion would have been automatic, but that same chain of command instead chose to first ignore, and then bury, the whole affair. Mikey continued his study schedule in the days that followed. The hateful notes stopped. There were no further assaults. It was as if nothing had changed, as the whole nightmarish episode had never happened and all its horrendous implications had vanished in a puff of smoke.

"I think that was the worst of it," Weinstein would subsequently reflect. "No matter how hard I tried, years later, to get at the truth by talking to my old roommates, seeking out Academy graduates from that era, and filing comprehensive Freedom of Information Act requests for official records, I could never find out what had actually happened. All I was left with was this enormous dead feeling."

It was that same feeling that was suddenly resurrected with the story Curtis related of his own harassment at the Academy, now compounded for Weinstein by his accentuated awareness of the historic Jewish struggle for survival. "I had come to realize," he recounts, "that two of the most important figures in my life were Adolph Hitler and Jesus Christ. Hitler because of the Holocaust and Christ because in his name it could all fucking happen again." To underscore the point, in both his personal life and in the responsibility he feels toward his people, he had the inside band of his cherished Air Force Academy ring inscribed with the words, "Never Again." "I wanted to remind myself of what I had gone through as a cadet," he explains. "But of course, it's really about what my people have gone through."

Now Curtis was going through it too, and as the neon sign outside his shuttered motel window grew brighter and the evening deepened, Mikey struggled with his own sense of impotence, pitted against his determination to face down an old enemy. It was that determination which, before the night was over, had prevailed.

In the days that followed, Weinstein would take the first steps in what would eventually become a wide ranging, fierce one-man assault against religious intolerance and unconstitutional coercion at the Academy. One of his most informative early sources revealing the depth and degree of the problem was his older son Casey who, due to his longer tenure at the military school at the time, had a more comprehensive grasp of the actual extent of the crisis than Curtis.

Affable and charismatic, with his mother's fair complexion and something of Mikey's fiery spark in his eyes, Casey had, like his father, entertained a wide variety of higher educational offers, including attendance at Annapolis and West Point, with an invitation from the Coast Guard Academy thrown in for good measure. He had opted for the Air Force Academy because, in his words, "I could see how good it had been for my dad."

It was a decision he would soon have ample cause to question, beginning soon after he became a fourth-class cadet. Looking back, as he subsequently related to his father, he had come to realize how something as seemingly innocuous as a scheduling conflict reflected a hidden agenda within the Academy power structure. "Every Friday night we had mandatory physical training," he explains, "which interfered directly with Shabbat services. We were forced to make a choice. Maybe that doesn't seem like such a big deal in itself, until you consider that unit cohesion is one of the most important building blocks in Academy life. Separating yourself from your squad sent a message that you had other priorities and I regularly caught hell from classmates for going to Friday night services. The bottom line was that you had to choose training or faith. Of course, if you were a Christian worshipping on a Sunday, that choice didn't apply."

But that was, as Weinstein soon found out, only the tip of the iceberg. When Casey went on to detail the mandatory inspirational speaking events that cadets were required to attend, more often than not with a blatant Christian message, an alarming picture of religious strong-arm tactics began to emerge. Encountering one-on-one evangelizing attempts from fellow cadets, to use another example, represented an egregious abuse of the institution's emphasis on cadet cooperation, camaraderie and common purpose. "If you are in the outside world," Casey explains, "you can just tell a person to mind his own business. But in the Academy, your business is everyone else's. You're together all the time, being told to trust and depend on each other. If someone is determined for you to meet Jesus, what does it say that when you refuse to accept what is so important to them?"

Eventually, Casey would seek counsel from other cadets as well as a trusted superior officer. "They basically told me that I had to learn to put up with it," he recounts. "They told me that the reason they were doing it was because they wanted me to be in heaven with them."

But the methods used to induce conversion were far from benign. During basic training, for instance, there were often up to three church services a week. "Attendance wasn't mandatory," Casey explains, "but they had a very persuasive way of convincing you to go. During meals, when announcements of the services were broadcast on the mess hall PA, all those who chose not to attend were compelled to line up in formation and march back to their quarters. The degrading ritual had come to be known as the 'Heathen Flight,' a pagan perp walk that clearly indentified those who didn't adhere to the Academy's none-too-hidden agenda, forcing them to continue with the duties while the sanctioned cadets sat around and drank soda."

What both Casey and Curtis described as a suffocating atmosphere of extreme religious intimidation, countenanced and increasingly instigated by Academy brass, reached critical mass in the early spring of 2004, shortly before Mikey's fateful rendezvous with Curtis during the Leadership Conference. "The Academy was like a room filling up with gas," is how Casey describes the explosive tipping point. "*The Passion* was just the spark."

The incitement to unbridled zealotry to which he refers is *The Passion of The Christ*, Mel Gibson's blood drenched cinematic retelling of the crucifixion of Jesus Christ, a box office smash that had come in for withering criticism for its unabashed anti-Semitic tone. Within days of its release in February of that year, the movie had become a Christian cause célèbre and a proselytizing tool par excellence. Churches across the country and around the world organized screenings, many triumphantly reporting spontaneous conversions by the third reel.

The ruling fundamentalist Christian cabal within the Academy was not about to pass up this prime opportunity to push their agenda. A frenzied promotional campaign was duly launched on the prestigious Academy's campus, with posters of the film splashed on every available bulletin board, posting site and empty wall. Trailers for the film were being continuously shown on a loop to the point of saturation all over the Academy and mass emails, exhorting attendance at upcoming screenings, were posted with the approval of Academy's most senior ranking cadets and officers. In a direct violation of constitutional prohibitions against promulgating sectarian, proselytizing religious messages on government property via government communication media channels, the entire Cadet Wing, numbering over 4,000, would arrive for meals in the cavernous Mitchell Hall dining area, only to find flyers for *The Passion* waiting for them on their plates.

"When I heard the stories from Curtis and Casey about what was happening in the Academy," Mikey recounts, "I immediately sat down and talked it over with Bonnie. At that point we were just a pair of pissed-off parents, angry and appalled that our sons and Amanda had been subjected to these fucking unwarranted and illegal attempts at religious bullying. But we both knew that there was a lot more to it than just a personal affront. This issue struck at the very heart of the whole concept of a command structure on which any military organization lives or dies. It was one thing when Casey or Curtis were buttonholed by fellow cadets, Academy staff and invited lecturers and hectored to give their lives to Jesus. Proselytizing happens every day in the civilian world, in malls and street corners, in living rooms, and around kitchen tables. But what was going on at the Academy was of an exponential order of magnitude more dangerous and damaging. The way *The Passion* was promoted was a good example. What message were the Academy's commanding officers and senior cadet commanders sending by praising and universally approving the film? Was it simply a 'suggestion' that the entire Cadet Wing take in the movie if they were so inclined? Or was it something more direct, a de facto order to attend a manifestly sectarian religious event? Bedrock constitutional lines were being blurred and, in the confusion, any cadet could be forgiven for erring on the side of caution, regardless of personal conviction. His or her standing at the Academy, not to mention any career prospects in the Air Force itself, might well depend on how they responded to this officially-sanctioned proselytizing 'invitation.'

"There is a reason why we have the Establishment Clause front and center in the First Amendment of the Constitution. Any legal scholar, any informed citizen for that matter, will tell you that it prohibits any preference by the U.S. government of one religion over another, or even religion as a whole over no religion at all. The last time I looked, the Air Force was an arm of the U.S. government. Which made this a constitutional issue of the first magnitude."

That issue, and the furious war Weinstein was about to wage, would become the defining event of his life, and a crucible in which he and his family would be severely tested. The battle was about to be joined.

PART TWO

CHAPTER FOUR

THE BELLY OF THE BEAST

In the immediate aftermath of the Air Force Academy Graduate Leadership Conference, the cognitive dissonance endured by Mikey Weinstein reached deafening proportions. It was impossible for him to square his abiding love for an institution that had been central to both his life and that of his family with the horrendous constitutional abuses laid out in shocking detail by the sons who had so proudly followed in his footsteps. His own harrowing encounter with anti-Semitism at the Academy in 1973 added another layer of anguish to his conflicted emotions. As a result, he couldn't help but wonder if things might have been different had he not allowed, albeit tacitly, the Academy administration to sweep the incident under the rug, effectively burying what would have been an ugly blot, and a blatant civil rights infraction, on the institution's sterling reputation.

But, in another significant way, the threats and physical violence Mikey suffered as a cadet had paradoxically served to prepare him for the epic struggle on which he was about to embark. "I'm not a big believer in fate, or destiny or whatever you want to call it," Weinstein reflects, "but sometimes I can't help thinking that the shit I went through back then put me on a path that eventually defined who I am and what I was somehow meant to do. It's true that I had no interest in becoming a pilot and that I found what I considered to be my true calling in the law. But that decision was based, in part at least, on the growing conviction that I had been horrifically railroaded as a young and vulnerable cadet. Of course, I was all of eighteen years old. I had hit a superior officer and fully expected that my career was over and perhaps even my freedom as well. I had no idea what my rights were and as a result of that ignorance, I let them perpetrate what amounted to a massive cover up. If I walked away from that experience knowing anything, it was that I never wanted to be in a position again where I didn't know my civil rights. The law is the ultimate guarantor of our individual liberties and responsibilities. If I knew the law, especially the United States Constitution, I would then know what my rights were and could make sure they would never be trampled underfoot again. The choice I made to become a lawyer was based on my own predilections, but it was also a choice predicated on an excruciating experience that changed my life. When I look back on it, despite the very real pain and anguish, it seemed to me that that change was for the better."

Suffice it to say, by early 2004 there was perhaps no one more qualified than Mikey Weinstein to forcefully confront the Air Force Academy and, by extension, the Air Force itself, as well as the entire Department of Defense, over the issue of religious intolerance and Constitutionally-breaching, fundamentalist evangelical overreach. But in the days and weeks that followed Curtis' shocking revelations, Mikey had no notion of the scope and magnitude of what he was facing. As far as he knew, the issue was confined to the Academy alone, and it was to the Academy brass that he went first, seeking resolution.

A meeting was arranged with General John Rosa, the superintendent of the Air Force Academy, along with Colonel Michael Whittington, the Academy's head chaplain. The fact that they responded to Weinstein's insistent demand for a face-to-face explanation of what had gone so wrong at his beloved alma mater, had less to do with Rosa and Whittington's concern over allegations of anti-Semitism than with the clout Mikey wielded as a highly distinguished Academy alumni.

If their intent was to calm down a distraught and fractious father, the general and the chaplain were in for a jolting surprise. Mikey was not about to be lulled by sympathetic murmurs and vague promises to look into the matter. There was more at stake here than ruffled feathers. A lot more. "I have a low tolerance for any breach in the firewalls of power," Weinstein explains, "especially when it comes to constitutional mandates for the separation of church and state. My own knowledge of history has demonstrated beyond a doubt the horrors that ensue when those institutions become entangled. Something in my own constitution has made me exquisitely sensitive to those violations and it always has."

As proof, Weinstein points back to an incident that occurred in the late seventies when, as a mere second lieutenant, he lodged a complaint with his superiors over the use of taxpayer dollars for the funding of a quixotic quest to establish the authenticity of the controversial Shroud of Turin, utilizing an Air Force Academy laboratory and its scientific equipment for the project. "They ignored me, of course," he continues with a rueful smile, "but that's not the point. Someone has to stand in the breech and since no one else was stepping forward..." He leaves the sentence unfinished, the implications clear.

Clear also were the implications of the egregious proselytizing proclivities that, as Mikey was becoming increasingly aware, were becoming standard operating procedure at the Academy. Constitutional rights were being deliberately and systematically ignored, abused and circumvented for the sole purpose of attempted fundamentalist Christian conversion by means of blatant pressure tactics, countenanced and often initiated by superior officers and cadets, using their rank to browbeat and intimidate those who were otherwise helpless under their command.

What was less clear were the tactics and strategy needed to put an end to the dangerous precedents that were being set at the Academy. Weinstein was only one man, regardless of his standing as a distinguished graduate. It seemed unlikely, to say the least, that he would be able to singlehandedly take on the entrenched powers that were behind this assault on the constitution. "Look," he points out, "I'm not fucking naïve. It's obvious to anyone who's spent any time there that an absolutely clear religious sectarian 'consensus' exists at the Academy. It's part of the most intrinsic culture of the place, aided and abetted by the fact that its located smack in the middle of Colorado Springs, which is probably exceeded only by the Vatican or maybe Mecca as a center of religious activity. There are more churches, missionary organizations, Bible schools and evangelical outreaches on behalf of fundamentalist Christianity in that city than anywhere else in the world. Some of the fundamentalist Christian premises and preconceptions that inundate the town have certainly seeped, if not flooded, into the Academy. But by the same token, I knew that my sons and I were hardly the only ones who had refused to drink the goddamn Kool-Aid. We might not have represented a large proportion of the Academy population over the years, but the fact was that many of its most notable and respected graduates have been either Jewish or of some persuasion other than full-on fundamentalist

Christians, intent on dragging every one with them into heaven, whether they liked it or not."

It was to this small but crucial constituency that Mikey first turned. "I put the word out," he explains, "contacting some of my old classmates and a few friends and colleagues that were on the Academy staff." The response he got was both dismaying and a further indication of precisely how deeply rooted the culture of fear and trepidation had become at the institution. "Although a few professors compiled a list of grievances and forwarded them to me, most of them refused to talk on anything other than an anonymous basis," he reveals. "That, all by itself, was a severe wake-up call."

Considering their reluctance to be indentified with the inquiry Weinstein was launching, it is perhaps not surprising that most of the individuals he contacted early on also counseled Mikey to be cautious. "I tried to encourage him to be patient," one recalls, "to work up the chain of command. But the problem was, of course, that the chain of command was broken. I mean, how can you make something right if you don't believe it's wrong in the first place? The great French philosopher and writer Voltaire observed that, 'It is dangerous to be right in matters on which the established authorities are wrong.'" I can't think of a more appropriate application of his prophetic words.

Despite that only too obvious impediment to his quest for a redress of grievances, Weinstein did indeed attempt to work within the Academy's entrenched structure, at least until it became clear that such a reasoned approach was a decided dead-end. "I honestly believed that, once these abuses were brought to their attention, the powers that be would do something about it. I had a kind of vestigial confidence in military lines of authority, combined with what I considered to be a crystal clear constitutional case. It was difficult for me, at that stage, to understand how anyone in a position to right these wrongs wouldn't do so once they'd been apprised of the terrible severity of the situation."

In the meantime, Weinstein set about assembling evidence to bolster his already-damning argument. There was, it quickly became clear, no shortage of outrageous examples amply demonstrating the overweening influence of rampant Christian fundamentalism in virtually every aspect of the Academy's policies and practices. In one such example, a Christmas issue of the *Academy Spirit*, the school's official military installation publication, was festooned with New Testament sectarian citations, boldly announcing that the "only hope for mankind is Jesus Christ." The magazine featured a full page ad announcing in a boldfaced headline, *Jesus Is The Reason For The Season*, and adding the entreaty "If you would like to discuss Jesus, feel free to contact one of us." Over two hundred senior Academy officers and their spouses had signed it. Another glaring case in point involved an Academy sponsored lecture in coordination with the Christian Leadership Ministries that was titled "Why We Cannot Let You Have Your God While We Have Ours." Meanwhile, the New Life Church, headed by the soon-to-be disgraced pastor Ted Haggard, was allowed to dispatch vans onto Academy grounds to transport cadets to its cavernous sanctuary in downtown Colorado Springs. "Do all in the name of the Lord Jesus," read one message on the Academy's official email service, "pray as if it all depends on God."

As flagrant and appalling as these instances might have been, they were no more than the tip of a large and deliberately submerged iceberg. By the spring of 2004, Weinstein had assembled a thick file detailing the worst offenses and dispatched it to the office of General Rosa, the Academy's Superintendant, who also wears the dual hats of both the Commander and university president of the Air Force Academy. "As much as anything," he asserts, "it was a function of my confidence that the Academy would handle the problem. I'd done my duty by bringing it to their attention."

As it turned out, Mikey's confidence was misplaced. So too, it seems, was the dossier he had forwarded to Rosa. When he inquired as to the status of the file he was met with shrugs and mystified looks from Academy administration officials. Once again, those whose business it was to ensure the smooth operation and unblemished reputation of the Academy had made seemingly unpleasant realities vanish into thin air.

Yet, despite the best efforts of the school's top brass to obfuscate and obscure the flagrant constitutional violations, Mikey had chronicled in such stark detail, it was becoming increasingly difficult to hide what was, to all intents and purposes, plainly evident in virtually every aspect of the Academy's operations. And Weinstein, whose mounting determination was only inflamed by the stubborn resistance he was encountering, would soon come to discover that he was not alone in trying to sound the alarm. He had allies, despite the conspicuous lack of other Academy staff and alumni willing to come to his aid.

Weinstein would find an unlikely supporter in a most unexpected place:

the virtual belly of the beast. A Distinguished Graduate of the Air Force's Basic Chaplain Course, Captain MeLinda Morton, a rangy soft-spoken, highly intellectual Lutheran with Cherokee blood, had been one of four group chaplains assigned to the Academy, a post she had held since 2002. Shortly after her arrival, the sexual assault scandal erupted into national headlines and promptly put the chaplaincy office front and center in the attempt to deal with the emotional and psychological fallout from the assaults themselves. "I was overwhelmed with young cadets who had actually been assaulted," Morton recounts. "Along with a few of the other chaplains, we were the only ones they could turn to."

Morton was able to observe firsthand the desperate attempts of Academy officials to contain the damage both inside and outside the school's cloistered confines. In an especially ominous development, fundamentalist Christian voices at the institution used the conflicted and confusing circumstances in which many cadets found themselves to further promulgate their religious message. According to Morton, "The scandal, they claimed, was the result of a lack of sexual purity and the lack of moral authority from the administration and teaching staff. The cadets were there because God had chosen them for a special purpose and the enemy was doing his best to tempt them away from that purpose. The problem was spiritual and the solution was a stern spiritual program."

In an effort to refute this odious presumption, while at the same time provide the best pastoral care she could, Morton enlisted the aid of Dr. Kristen Leslie, a professor of pastoral counseling at Yale University Divinity School and an ordained United Methodist Minister. Morton invited Leslie to the Academy on several occasions, under what was termed an Assess and Improve protocol, to witness first hand the escalating crisis. In the process Leslie was provided with up close and personal contact among the cadets, unprecedented access that included direct observation of the grueling Basic Training Course, appropriately nicknamed "Beast" and held in Spartan camping sites on the rugged terrain of nearby Jack's Valley, a wilderness alpine vale that had been set apart for just such survival rigors. It was during that intense period of mental, emotional and physical testing and conditioning that the professor noted some of the most horrendous incidents of nakedly sectarian pressure tactics employed by the staff. In her subsequent report, the name of Major Warren "Chappie" Watties appeared again and again. Honored as Air Force Chaplain of the Year in 2004, Watties had served a stint in Baghdad during the Iraq War, where he earned his status for unbridled fundamentalist zealotry by baptizing soldiers in one of Saddam Hussein's swimming pools.

Watties fire breathing reputation followed him to the Air Force Academy. It was front and center when Leslie and her Yale team members watched as the chaplain brandished a bullhorn to berate Christian cadets. Watties' amplified exhortation encouraged the cadets to actively and aggressively attempt to convert their unsaved tent mates, in the process sparing them, according to Watties from "burning in the fire of hell."

It was only one example of the literally inflammatory language that Leslie's report cited as challenging "the necessarily pluralistic environment of training." Watties' "overwhelmingly evangelical, fundamentalist tone encouraged religious division and fostered vile disrespect rather than promoting spiritual understanding."

That was putting it mildly, which was the deliberate intent of the evenhanded "after action" account. In dispassionate academic terminology Leslie managed to depict with harrowing accuracy the hothouse environment of fundamentalist Christian fervor let loose during the basic training period so critical to determining which cadets were suited to the Academy's demanding rigors. She described "consistent specific articulations of evangelical Christian themes," that included cadets being encouraged to chant in unison, "This is our chapel and the Lord is our God," and to pray for the salvation of those in basic training who did not share the prevailing sectarian consensus. Submitted to Colonel Whittington in July of that year, the Yale report was all the more damning for being so studiously unbiased.

But it would take more than scholarly composure to stir the Academy administration into addressing the rampant religiosity that had infected the institution. Paying lip service to the findings of Leslie and her team, the Academy's senior leadership instituted what was fancifully dubbed the RSVP program, an acronym for Respecting the Spiritual Values of all People. The primary intent of this effort, it soon became evident, was to trivialize the matter by attempting to place the blame for religious intolerance and its attendant strong-arm conversion tactics squarely on the shoulders of a few overzealous cadets. It was, of course, a time honored scapegoat strategy that not only provided convenient cover for those who were actually responsible for the illegal actions, but allowed them to carry on their insidious activities with impunity by attempting to pillory a handful of hapless cadets. It was also an obvious and infuriating stalling tactic, a way for the Academy's fundamentalist Christian cabal to play for time in hopes that the controversy would burn itself out on its own accord. Before it was finally put out of its misery, the RSVP program, described by MeLinda Morton as nothing more than "a dog and pony show," and which Mikey had taken to calling the "Really Stupid Values Program," would go through seventeen separate iterations, each more confused and compromised than the last.

Predictably, Weinstein's increasingly unbridled outrage was in no way assuaged by this transparent and palpable ploy. It had been seven months since he had forwarded his hefty packet of incriminating evidence to General Rosa. While he had initially been willing to allow the Academy the opportunity to clean up its act, he found himself struggling more and more with "the feeling you have just before you realize the comprehensive enormity of the problem you're facing." Even given the snail's pace of most attempted remedies within any military bureaucracy, time had clearly run out. The moment had arrived to take action. Decisive action.

CHAPTER FIVE

CONTAGION

The RSVP program might have provided, at least for the time being, a flimsy fig leaf behind which the Academy's hardcore fundamentalists could hide. But there was no disguising the continued and escalating atmosphere of sectarian chauvinism that was strangling the constitutionally protected liberties of the cadets, as well as any staff member who dared to dissent against the prevailing militancy of the institution's spiritual elite. A kind of Orwellian doublespeak prevailed: an outward endorsement of religious plurality, as personified by the RSVP's transparent charade, hiding a noxious and deeply rooted intolerance for any opposition to the established orthodoxy, inviting instead a triumphant Jesus Christ to lead a vengeful army of the righteous in the total war against the heathen in their midst.

It was hardly surprising that, given the hostile and volatile environment being actively fostered at the Academy, the number of nakedly anti-Semitic incidents to which Weinstein was often anonymously alerted increased with alarming frequency. The slurs hurled at Curtis were echoed and amplified as the summer of 2004 wore on and Mikey conscientiously chronicled each occurrence of insults, ranging from "fucking Jew" to "filthy Jew" to the all purpose "Christ killer" that came to his attention.

But Weinstein had long since passed the point of believing that dutifully recording such outrages and passing them along to the proper authorities would suffice. His faith in military due process was in tatters and he had come to the sober realization of the enemy he was facing, and the resources they commanded. "Fundamentalist Christians had spent a lot of time and energy establishing a stronghold at the Academy," he asserts. "They were not about to give up without a fierce fight."

It was in late September of 2004 that Mikey would bring his own fight directly to the doorstep of the Air Force Academy. "I needed a way to circumvent the normal channels of command and control," he explains. "Clearly, there were forces within the administration that would do whatever they could to deflect attention from the constitutional violations that they were deliberately perpetrating. The only choice I had was to make an end run around the whole fucking authority structure. I needed to go public and this time I wasn't going to give them the benefit of a heads up."

Weinstein's plan was simple: to take the damning information he had initially provided to General Rosa, distill it, contextualize its constitutional implications, and shout it from the rooftops. Accordingly, and with the able assistance of a fellow attorney and close friend named Steve Aguilar, he prepared a cogent, nineteen page summary titled *The Religious Climate of the United States Air Force Academy*. In case anyone should miss the point, the subhead of the brief read, "A Clear Violation of the U.S. Constitution." And, as if that were not enough to sound a clarion call, Weinstein and Aguilar stated up front and in the clearest possible language what they intended to accomplish with the paper. "...To impel the command structure of the United States Air Force Academy to vigorously enforce the First Amendment in all aspects of Academy life." They sought nothing less that an Academy that "never promotes or favors any single religious belief."

As a founding document for the epic struggle on which the Weinsteins' were about to embark, *The Religious Climate of the United States Air Force Academy* served to crystallize and clarify the essential principles from which Mikey and his family would stubbornly refuse to back down. But it was only the first step in what would quickly become a ferocious and unforgiving campaign waged in the glaring light of public scrutiny. Girded by this unequivocal statement of intent, buttressed by the unassailable constitutional tenets it embodied, Weinstein was emboldened to embark on an intensive media effort that would, in time, reap a whirlwind.

But before Mikey could unleash his public relations blitz, there were consequences to consider. "Both of my sons and my daughter-in-law were in the Air Force," he explains. "The shit I had a hand in uncovering shook their confidence in the institution to be sure, but they still had their careers in the military to consider. Casey and Amanda had just graduated a few months before from the Academy and were, thus, just beginning their active duty Air Force careers. The last thing I wanted to do was to jeopardize their futures. I was especially concerned about Curtis, who would still be at the Academy for another two and a half years, and could well be left open to retaliation."

"We talked it over as a family," Bonnie remembers. "It was a unanimous decision. Considering how we all felt about the legacy of the Academy in our lives and how that legacy was being viciously and savagely torn apart, there was really no fucking choice. Somewhere along the way we had collectively reached a point of no return. We had no idea at the time what we were getting ourselves into, there. But even when it became clear what the costs were going to be, there was never a question of backing down. We would face the consequences together or not at all." Considering the travails that the Weinstein family would all-too-soon come to endure, her words had the ring of dire prophesy indeed.

With the full support of his tight knit family behind him, Mikey was free to make the opening gambit of what he calls a "crawl, walk, run strategy." It was an approach that began by making contact with Pam Zubeck, a canny, well-connected and boundlessly tenacious investigative reporter for the *Colorado Springs Gazette*. "What better place to throw down the gauntlet," he remarks wryly, "than in the pages of the newspaper delivered to every true believer in Colorado Springs?"

On November 18, 2004, the paper published an article titled "Air Force Academy Faces Faith Bias Allegations," under Zubeck's byline. It would be the first in a string of stinging exposés into the school's glaring disregard for established First Amendment law, each increasingly damning and impeccably well-sourced, thanks in part to Weinstein's assiduous efforts to arm the respected reporter with the welter of details he had complied over the previous months. The resources Mikey provided to the irrepressible Zubeck, a sharp, experienced and tenacious investigative journalist, proved to be in sharp contrast to the Academy's obfuscating response to the mushrooming controversy.

"We didn't get a lot of help from the Academy," the journalist recalls with characteristic understatement. "One might get the impression they were scrambling. They kept asking us why we were bothering to cover it, that the problem had already been dealt with."

The Academy administration's increasingly strident attempts at a concerted cover-up only served to add fuel to what quickly became a media firestorm. As Weinstein recounts, "we all knew that sooner or later this was going to show up on the national radar. That was part of the plan from the inception."

It was a plan that kicked into high gear in early 2005. "We were at a wedding in Las Cruces, New Mexico for one of Casey's friends," he continues. "I got a call from ABC's *Good Morning America*. They wanted me on the show." Immediately after that, the floodgates were opened wide. *The New York Times* picked up the story, followed in quick succession by *Oprah*, *Maury Povich*, *NBC's Dateline* and *Time Magazine*, which ran a scathing article titled "Whose God Is Their Co-Pilot?"

Once the Academy had belatedly realized that it couldn't wish away the storm of negative press Weinstein was generating, it responded in the time honored manner of every hidebound bureaucracy by announcing the formation of a blue ribbon task force, charged with issuing, in due time, a report that would put the matter to rest once and for all.

The gambit was itself a bit of wishful thinking. The blatant whitewash was headed by Lieutenant General Roger Brady, deputy chief of staff, manpower and personnel, for the Air Force in the Pentagon. It was an assignment that, above all else, needed the imprimatur of total impartiality, a requirement the Air Force completely ignored by the appointment of Brady, a bonafide evangelical. "They put a born again Christian in charge of investigating the degree to which born again Christians were systematically violating the Constitution at the Academy," Mikey says, shaking his head in mock bewilderment. "Didn't anyone pick up on at least the fucking *appearance* of impropriety?"

Apparently not. The resulting report excused the inexcusable with, in Mikey's words, "A combination of 'boys will be boys' and 'kids say the darnedest things.'" The actual intent of Brady's exercise in furious tap dancing was made clear twenty-four hours before its release when none other than General Rosa, Superintendent of the Air Force Academy, along with an obsequious aide, showed up at Weinstein's front door with a freshly printed copy of the report.

"It was pretty awkward," Mikey recounts. "I think he expected me to sit down and read the whole thing there and then while he waited. So I kind of glanced through it out of politeness until I came to a passage that jumped out at me like a tarantula on a wedding cake."

The hairy arachnid in question occurred on page eleven of the document and concerned the grandstanding of Chaplain Watties during basic training exercises, as described in the Yale report of Kristin Leslie. It referenced directly his command for the cadets to chant, "This is our chapel and the Lord is our God," and his dire warnings that unsaved classmates would burn in hell's everlasting lakes of fire. Then came the kicker. "While these comments, if they were made," the report blithely asserted, "may be considered offensive or unnecessarily strident by some, they are not uncommon expressions of Foursquare Gospel doctrine."

"I took it as the first clue that the report wasn't going to be all they advertised," Weinstein recounts with palpable scorn. "'What is this shit?' I asked Rosa. Since when does any branch of the government, much less the military, countenance clearly unconstitutional behavior as 'not uncommon expressions' of one religious belief or another? As an excuse for Watties' behavior it was just lame. But as a justification for the Academy's lack of action it bordered on the criminal."

"There was no lack of precedent for such ignorance of the basic principles of the Constitution," interjects Bonnie. "There was a time when it was mandatory for every cadet to study, in great depth the Constitution, in a course that stretched over an entire semester. Since then, the instruction that focuses on the First Amendment has been reduced to one class hour and, even then, it is optional."

In the end it was Bonnie who delivered the most telling summary judgment of the Brady Report fiasco. She had been listening attentively to the whole conversation from the kitchen and as Rosa, clearly rattled by Weinstein's angry response, was preparing to leave, she pulled him aside at the front porch. "He was a big man, very tall and formidable," she recalls, before adding with characteristic irony, "but I'm no shrinking violet myself. Since no one was stating the obvious, I told him myself that, in my humble opinion, the entire situation was his fault. He had a total of six stars on his shoulders. The whole thing could have been cleared up with a direct order from him. But he never gave that order and that was, purely and simply, a glaring failure of leadership."

"His aide was clearly shocked that anyone would have the fucking audacity to talk to his boss that way," she continues. "I could literally see the blood draining from his face." She smiles. "I have to say, it was very gratifying."

The Academy's weak-kneed response over what amounted to a fundamentalist Christian conspiracy at the highest levels of its command may have been laughable had the implications not carried with them such deadly serious weight. "The ability to withstand the privations of military service and face the prospects of death," Brady maintained in the closing pages of his report, "...requires strength of character that is founded upon religious faith. It is a source of strength in time of trial."

"That's just bullshit," is Weinstein's blunt rebuttal. "And if that's really the conviction of those who send our young men and women off to fight and die, then I guess the next step is mandatory religious conversion." He pauses, letting the words sink in. "Think about it. Suicide bombers. Jihadists. A martyr's death. Aren't those the methods and motivations of our enemies? We are not about creating a holy army, consecrated to do God's will by smiting the heathen. Our warriors are not supposed to be Crusaders. Our warriors are supposed to be patriots. There *are* atheists in foxholes, I've met them, and they are every bit as dedicated to protecting this country and its founding principles as the most fervent fundamentalist Christian. There is certainly nothing wrong with drawing on one's faith in a time of trial. But it's the first step down a very slippery slope straight into the swamp of religious tyranny when your superior officers mandate what that faith should be. That's not what this country is about. In fact, the right to believe whatever you want, or to believe nothing at all, is one of the reasons we've fought wars so often and so tenaciously in the first place. It's the reason I went to war against those sinister forces that would deny that right to any of my fellow citizens. It's the single goddamned reason I keep fighting."

That fight would rage on during the long, hot summer of 2005. Prompted by the avalanche of publicity Weinstein was generating, the House Arms Service Committee held a hearing, purporting to examine the religious climate at the Academy, held in Washington in late July. In the event, it proved little more than an opportunity for politicians to do what they do best: grandstand and posture. Much of the day was taken up with bellows of outrage from those who objected to the whole purpose of any hearing to determine what exactly might be the extent of extremist religious infiltration at the Academy. "Democrats can't help themselves when it comes to denigrating and demonizing Christians," fumed Indiana Republican and hard shell Baptist John Hostettler, while Texas Republican Kay Granger railed against "the long-term impact this excessively negative impact will have on…those who are dedicating themselves to the service of our nation. The Academy is a national jewel…it deserves our support and praise, not our criticism." "I'm a Christian," Granger's Texas GOP colleague, Michael Conaway, proclaimed to no one's particular surprise. "And Jesus Christ is my personal savior." Hostettler, apparently fearful of being left off the bandwagon, hurriedly chimed in with his own profession of faith during the committee's questioning of Dr. Kristen Leslie, who had been summoned to Capital Hill to shed light on the only too obvious conclusions of the Yale report. "I'm a believer in Jesus Christ," Hostettler thundered at the witness, before adding with a contemptuous sniff, "I'm sorry if that offends you." The whole circus wound down with a toothless plea by the committee for the Academy to "further define appropriate religious behaviors."

Weinstein, a registered Republican himself, might well have been disappointed in the ludicrous outcome of the proceedings if he had had any expectation of effective action from legislators in the first place. "I gave up on both fucking parties pretty early on," he reveals with a sigh. "My personal mantra had always been to keep Democrats out of the boardroom and Republicans out of the bedroom, but we were light years beyond that now. It was simply more trouble than it was worth to try and actually get something done in Washington."

Instead, Mikey redoubled his efforts to stoke the media flames, hoping to turn up the heat under the influential rear ends at the Academy, where sonorous expressions of congressional concern had conspicuously, if predictably, fallen short. Predictable also was the media's continued and intense scrutiny of the ongoing and unfolding story which, after all, had constitutional ramifications that only the most obtuse—which apparently included members of the House of Representatives—could have missed. A scathing editorial in *The New York Times* titled "Obfuscating Intolerance" delivered a well-aimed deathblow to the Brady Report, charging it with "throwing up a fog of implausible excuses" in the face of "obvious and overt religious bias." The newspaper promptly followed its opinion page shellacking with an extensive and hard nosed investigative piece by national-desk reporter Laurie Goodstein headlined, "Evangelicals Are a Growing Force in the Military Chaplain Corps."

Front and center in Goldstein's exhaustive reportage was a statement by Brigadier General Cecil Richardson, deputy chief of Chaplains for the

Air Force, who in a moment of unguarded candor told the journalist that, "We reserve the right to evangelize the unchurched." It was, as Weinstein would later characterize the comment, "an absolutely astonishing statement on the face of it." It was also the pivot on which he would launch a blistering new assault on the entrenched fundamentalist Christian elements who, through Richardson's bald faced assertion, had broadcast their intentions to the whole world and in no uncertain terms. As news of the declaration resounded across the country and around the globe, Mikey used the ensuing furor to call directly for the resignation of Bush Administration Secretary of Defense, Donald Rumsfeld. "To make this astonishingly shameful statement," he wrote, utilizing a practiced rhetorical flair in precise proportion to the magnitude of Richardson's remarks, "constitutes a despicable blood libel on our nation's revered Constitutional Bill of Rights."

The gloves had come off, and in case anyone doubted the sanguine nature of the escalating conflict, Weinstein underscored his David-versus-Goliath determination by loudly and publicly calling for an immediate retraction of what essentially amounted to the verbal line in the sand drawn by Brigadier General Richardson. He took his demand straight to the top, communicating directly with the newly appointed Secretary of the Air Force, Pete Geren. A former four-term Texas congressman, Geren joined the Defense Department in 2001, as Special Assistant to the Defense Secretary with responsibilities that included inter-agency initiatives, legislative affairs and special projects. One of the "special projects" Geren would later be involved in was the notorious "Christian Embassy" promotional video, which featured Geren as well as a number of military officers, including four generals, appearing on camera in military uniforms to extol the virtues of the Christian Embassy evangelical outreach.

"I told him to take it back," says Mikey, recalling his blunt ultimatum to Geren regarding the Richardson bombshell. "I just couldn't believe it. To me, it was a litmus test, plain and simple. If the Air Force conceded that it did *not* have the right to evangelize the unchurched, then maybe there was a basis for moving forward."

But instead of acknowledging the seriousness of the situation and initiating any momentum to correct the egregious excess, Geren instead simply kicked Weinstein's demand over to Mary Walker, the general counsel for the Air Force. It was the Brady syndrome all over again. "I was contacted by Walker," Mikey relates. "I quickly found out that she was not exactly interested in resolving the situation. In fact, just like General Brady, and Air Force Secretary Pete Geren himself, she was a born again Christian. Walker had co-founded a group innocuously titled the Professional Women's Fellowship, which turned out to be an offshoot of Campus Crusade for Christ. I was truly beginning to wonder if there was anyone left in the Air Force who *hadn't* given their lives to Jesus in that elite, exclusionist way that was the hallmark of fundamentalist Christianity."

Conspicuous in both the Bush Administration's repellent attempt to circumvent the Geneva Conventions in the run up to the Iraq War, as well as its subsequent efforts to justify the torture policy that had led to the abuses of Abu Ghraib, Walker asked Weinstein for a week to respond to his demand for a retraction of Richardson's statement. The seven days passed without a word, as did the next seven days. "I had absolutely zero fucking confidence that anything substantive would come of this," Weinstein recounts. "But I held back as long as I could."

In point of fact, from the moment he read it, he had immediately recognized that Richardson's statement, laid out in the nation's paper of record, was exactly the wedge he needed to pry up the rock under which fundamentalists at the Academy carried out the clandestine Christian agenda. "I had them dead to rights," he asserts. "The legal side of my brain saw a slam dunk, but I wanted to see how things would play out. I knew this was the opportunity I had been waiting for and I wanted to maximize its impact."

It didn't take long. Walker's utter and offensive lack of response provided the trigger for Weinstein's nuclear option: A Complaint for Violation of Constitutional Rights, filed on October 6, 2005 in the U.S. District Court for New Mexico in downtown Albuquerque. Named as defendants were both the United States Air Force and acting Air Force secretary, Pete Geren. The lawsuit had in fact been in the works for some time, thanks in large part to Weinstein's well-founded anticipation of obfuscating inaction on the part of his adversaries. The extensive preparation of the historic six-page document, a collaborative effort between Mikey and a close friend, the colorful, talented litigator, Sam Bregman, was reflected in the choice of targets that had been selected. "Even given the fact that the abuses I had focused on were centered at the Academy," Mikey explains, "I wanted to emphasize the reality, and the responsibility, of the Air Force command structure as it was constituted. Ultimately the blame rested squarely with the Air Force. That was the seat of real power and it was also the one institution that could, if it so chose, make the essential changes so desperately needed. So it made sense to go directly after the source with as much legal clout as we could muster."

Which is exactly what Mikey's incisive, razor-edged action served to accomplish. "Over the course of the last decade," the suit stated, "a pattern and practice has developed at the Academy where senior officers and cadets have attempted to impose evangelical Christianity…" It was, Weinstein and Bregman maintained, a flagrant violation of the Establishment Clause, fostering rampant "discrimination and harassment." There could be, the action confidently asserted, absolutely no question of the constitutional principles at stake, but in case anyone missed the point, the complaint sought as injunctive relief to the effect that "no member of the USAF is permitted to evangelize, proselytize…involuntarily convert, pressure, exhort or persuade a fellow member of the USAF to accept their own religious beliefs while on duty." By the same token, "The USAF is not permitted to establish or advance any one religion over another religion or one religion over no religion." It was language borrowed directly from the ruling made by Supreme Court Justice David Souter in the just-concluded Kentucky case regarding the display of the Ten Commandments on a courthouse lawn. Geren was named specifically in the complaint for the simple and compelling reason that he had failed to respond to Mikey's repeated requests that the Air Force categorically refute General Richardson's contention that he and his cohort had that right to evangelize anyone and everyone that came across their fundamentalist Christian radar. Geren's refusal to do so, alleged the suit, was a de facto ratification of that policy.

What person-to-person appeals to the top level of command at the Air Force had failed to achieve, the lawsuit accomplished in a matter of hours. Six and a half hours to be exact, which was exactly how long it took for Mary Walker to respond to the filing. Her written reply, forwarded to Bregman, was for Weinstein a remarkable admission of the responsibility and culpability he had long maintained rested squarely with the Air Force brass. "There is no existing Air Force policy," Walker staunchly maintained, "endorsing 'proselytizing' or 'evangelizing.' An earlier Chaplain Service document that might have been understood to represent such a policy statement has been withdrawn."

That seemed to be a direct reference to Richardson's incendiary remark in *The New York Times* and, there, just beneath the surface of Walker's seemingly innocuous blandishments, was the proof of a widespread Christian conspiracy that Weinstein had for so long suspected. "The assumption," he explains, "had always been that Richardson had been speaking off the cuff. Now, suddenly, here was a tacit admission confirming that evangelizing the unchurched *was*, in fact, policy and had been all along. There had been, according to Walker herself, a document to that effect generated by the Chaplain service. I was determined to get my hands on that smoking gun."

With the help of MeLinda Morton, Mikey quickly uncovered what he was looking for in the 2002 handbook for the Basic Chaplain Course. There, buried among all the bland bromides and warm and fuzzy spiritual terminology, was a single statement that, with one stroke, conclusively proved what Weinstein had long suspected, that there had been a well-established precedent to exercise exactly what Richardson asserted had been his right. "I will not proselytize from other religious bodies," the manual read, "but I retain the right to evangelize those who are non-affiliated."

"It was chapter and verse what Richardson had claimed," Mikey continues. "He was essentially quoting from sanctioned Air Force procedures. It was all part of the unspoken assumption that fundamentalist Christianity had an exclusive claim to the truth and that everyone else was wrong. I wondered what the Air Force would do if some imam or rabbi insisted that they reserved the right to Islamize the unmosqued to Judaize the unsynagogued."

The answer to that question was left to dangle provocatively in the wind that whipped up Weinstein's suit when, just eight days after the initial filing, Mikey offered the Air Force a settlement. Simply put, if a "Stipulated Order" was issued banning any form of proselytizing or evangelizing by any member of the USAF while on duty, he would consider the matter resolved. "It was the bottom line of what I had been after all along," he recounts. "If they went for it I could fucking declare victory, pack up my tent and go home."

This time Walker and the Air Force legal team were again quick to respond with an obtuse, thirty page "Memorandum of Points And Authority," the twisted language of which boiled down to a single dubious premise. "Any sermon or religious message," the document maintained, "delivered by Air Force chaplains cannot be attributed to the Air Force as government speech."

"Who's paying their salary," was Mikey's withering rejoinder. "What emblems are they wearing on their epaulets? Who are they appealing to when they make religious pronouncements, on Air Force time, on Air Force property and on the Air Force payroll? The argument was fucking absurd on its face."

Absurdity, however, has never shown itself a detriment to any legal strategy with the benefit of time, money and personnel to drag any case to its post-logical extreme. It was that same time-honored tactic that the Air Force employed to refute the compelling claims made in Weinstein's lawsuit. Although the case was ultimately dismissed in federal court, a clear and significant victory was achieved when the Air Force unilaterally agreed to withdraw any reference in its chaplain's training material that could be construed to grant chaplains the right to view their Air Force turf as a "mission field" to evangelize the unchurched.

But by that time, Mikey had moved on, far beyond the specific con-stitutional contraventions that he had initially exposed at the Academy. "Filing that lawsuit taught me a lot," he explains. "The first lesson I learned was that I was just one person, trying to take on a behemoth that com-manded vast resources and was ready to use them to protect its image and its interests against any threat to the status quo. I wasn't going to be able to prevail against that kind of entrenched power by myself." He pauses, as if seeking words to describe the deeper meaning of his protracted struggle with the Air Force. "But what was ultimately an even more important re-alization," he continues at last, "was that this deadly disease had spread far beyond simply the Air Force Academy. As we took on this fight and gained national and international attention in the process, men and women from every branch of the armed services began to step forward; first by the tens and twenties, then by the hundreds and eventually by the thousands. Most of them were afraid," he pauses, weighing his words. "Make that utterly scared shitless," he continues. "They had everything to lose by telling me their stories of persecution, harassment and discrimination in the name of religion. It took courage, a lot of courage, to reveal to me the breathtaking magnitude of subversion to authority and the abuse of military command and control that they had experienced first hand. It didn't take me very long to realize that there was an unconstitutional, fundamentalist Chris-tian contagion that had spread throughout the armed services, one that had to be stopped. These brave individuals had done everything they could to sound the alarm, even when it potentially exposed them to great risk, both personally and professionally. How could I not answer the call? This was a huge fucking fight, bigger and more brutal than my family or I could ever have imagined. We had to step back, take a deep breath, and count the real world consequences, the actual cost to our well-being and peace of mind. As a family we counted and weighed and assessed and tried to measure the risk on every level possible. But the truth was we really had no way of knowing the magnitude of what we were up against.

"There were more than a few moments when I told myself that I hadn't signed on for this," Bonnie reveals. "When Mikey and I got married, I knew that I was going to be an Air Force wife, with an Air Force life, and all the continuity and security that came with it. I hadn't bargained for taking on an army of fucking religious extremists that would seemingly stop at nothing to advance their agenda. But life is full of surprises. You never know what you're able to cope with until you're face to face with it. I'd be lying if I said that I had no second thoughts about what Mikey was doing. I was struggling with MS, trying to be the best wife and mother I could be under the circumstances." She pauses searching for the words to describe the life changing decisions at which she at last arrived. "But in the final analysis none of that mattered," she continues at last. "What we were about to undertake, as a couple and as a family, outweighed any personal consideration. It was too important to let my expectations of a normal, uneventful life and marriage get in the way. Sometimes you're called upon to forego what you want, or even need, in the service of something more important. This was one of those times and together we gave each other the courage, the nurturing, it took to move forward."

Mikey adds, "There have only been a few moments, a few crossroads, in life like that one. When I was a kid I remember hearing about the murder of Kitty Genovese," he continues, referring to the 1964 stabbing of a young woman in Queens, New York, carried out in full view of her unresponsive neighbors and subsequently the premise for a psychological condition known as the 'Bystander Syndrome.' "It really had an effect on me," Weinstein reveals. "I told myself that I would never fucking let that happen: that I would refuse to stand by while someone was threatened or in danger and there was something I could do about it. The memory of that childhood commitment came back and helped to bring about what I call a 'magic moment' of clarity. And from that exact moment on, my family and I shared the same, unshakable certainty to fight on with every resource we had and even some we didn't: there was going to be absolutely no turning back."

CHAPTER SIX

THE FOUNDATION

It had been in the summer of 2004 when Weinstein had first learned of the poisonous atmosphere at the Air Force Academy directly from his son Curtis. Almost two years later, by the early months of 2006, it had become clear that his adversaries were resisting the lawsuit he had filed against the Air Force, detailing the unconstitutional outrages at the Academy, with every available means. It was a period of time marked by a tumultuous, often wrenching reevaluation for Mikey and his whole family. The most significant cornerstone on which they had based their shared values—unbounded admiration and unquestioned loyalty to the United States Air Force Academy and everything for which it stood—had been cruelly and completely compromised. In its place was the inescapable realization that the school, its proud traditions and its heritage of high ideals, was being hijacked by a cabal of fundamentalist fanatics bent on imposing what amounted to an American fundamentalist Christian version of Sharia law. Weinstein had thrown everything he had into fighting for the restoration of the Academy and its egalitarian constitutional principles. And, while he had scored some significant victories, not the least of which had been in the court of public opinion, it was also true that he had come to realize the true, exponential extent of the problem.

The monstrous outlines of religious extremism, not just in the Air Force, but in all branches of the United States armed services, first began to emerge in the weeks and months after filing the lawsuit in the fall of 2005. There was a completely unexpected snowballing effect as news of

Weinstein's battle began to avalanche. Anticipating that the Air Force's strategy would be to contend that he lacked the requisite legal standing to support the suit, he had immediately amended the complaint to include his son Casey, and three of his fellow Academy students, as plaintiffs.

One of them, a classmate of Casey and Amanda's, and an avowed atheist named Patrick Kucrea, had previously filed a complaint directly with the Pentagon, citing, among other grievances, the systematic ostracizing he had suffered for his perceived godlessness while attending the Academy. The other two plaintiffs, Ari Kayne and Jason Spindler, were cadets in the class of 2004 with a proud sense of their Jewish heritage. Spindler in particular had been raised in a conservative Jewish family in upstate New York and early on had run into the same deliberate scheduling conflicts for sporting, military and academic events that Casey had encountered, when Academy activities that were meant to foster team spirit achieved the opposite by impinging on Jewish observances of high holy days. It was part of an insidious strategy on the part of fundamentalist Christians in the Academy administration to force the issue of religious convictions by insisting that cadets either participated in all the activities of their chosen faith...or none at all. That was hardly an option for those who wanted to be part of both their religious traditions *and* life at the Academy. In fact, Spindler's entire time at the Academy was, he recounts, marked by "constant reminders that, no matter how I might have excelled as a cadet, I was still considered an outsider. For someone like me, whose beliefs shape who they are, there was a pervasive sense of exclusion." Like Curtis, Spindler was subjected to a concerted campaign of anti-Semitic slurs, including one particularly popular Academy joke to the effect that Jews were the best magicians because they could come in the door of a building and go out the chimney in a puff of smoke. When confronting the senior staff cadet who had made the shockingly insensitive remark, Spindler observed that "he was genuinely surprised that I would take exception to it. To me, it was symptomatic of a broken system."

It was a sentiment shared as well by yet another plaintiff who quickly reached out to Weinstein's unprecedented lawsuit as an additional potential plaintiff, an active duty United States Air Force NCO (non-commissioned officer.) Hardly a neophyte cadet, this individual was a senior ranking enlisted Air Force veteran, who had worked as a recruiter at a large USAF military installation in the continental United States. Hardnosed, outspoken and constitutionally confrontational, the airman had taken strong exception to what he called "regular and persistent proselytizing by superior officers." As part of a blistering addendum to the pending lawsuit, the NCO recounted meetings of Air Force enlistment personnel that featured exhortations to "use faith in Jesus Christ while recruiting." Ultimately, by mutual agreement, the NCO did not join the lawsuit. Weinstein and his lawyers felt that the very real fear of retaliation from the Air Force played a key role in this decision.

It was as if the lawsuit instituted by Weinstein had given a powerful voice to those who had for too long been forced into silence and almost immediately another officer outside the confines of the Academy stepped forward. Stationed at Bolling Air Force Base in Washington, DC, his name was Bryce Batchman and his hair-raising account of religious extremism within the facility included a first sergeant who regularly evoked the name of Jesus at squadron staff meetings and freely expressed his anger that prayer was not more actively encouraged on the base.

"Batchman and the NCO might have been the first outside the Academy to call attention to what was happening within the entire armed forces command structure," Mikey recounts, adding with heavily weighted understatement, "but they certainly weren't the last. In retrospect, it made perfect sense. Christian fundamentalists were hardly going to be content with exerting their influence at the Academy alone, regardless of how esteemed and influential an institution it might have been. The further we went in exposing their agenda, the clearer it became that the Academy was a bridgehead that had been established with the aim of infiltrating the entire military culture of the nation. Their activities in Colorado Springs were just the opening salvos. This war—which is exactly what it had become—was going to be fought on multiple fronts."

But the forces of religious extremism were, it seemed, intent on pushing the frontlines even beyond the realm of the armed forces. Shortly after Weinstein's lawsuit was filed, a revealing mass email surfaced that shed a glaring light on just how far this fundamentalist Christian cabal hoped to extend their reach. The missive in question came from an Air Force Major General by the name of Jack J. Catton Jr. (United States Air Force Academy class of 1976), who at the time was Director of Requirements, Headquarters Air Combat Command at Langley Air Force Base in Virginia. As a fellow cadet, Mikey recalls that Catton was higher in the pecking order, thanks largely to his strict observances of the rules and regulations. The fact that his father had been a four-star Air Force general didn't hurt either.

In the late spring of 2006, Catton sent a fundraising appeal on his official email account to over two hundred fellow Academy graduates soliciting contributions to the congressional campaign of another Air Force general and Academy graduate, the recently retired Bentley Rayburn, an avowed fundamentalist. "We are certainly in need of Christian men with integrity and military experience in Congress," Catton's message read in part.

"You didn't have to read between the lines," Mikey remarks dryly. "It might as well have been written in bold face. For all the money and manpower vested in the armed forces, the military was itself just another stepping stone, leading to the placement of likeminded coreligionists in the halls of Congress and from there, to the policy making circles at the highest levels of government. There was a concerted effort underway, a fundamentalist Christian coup in the making. It was clear that one individual, even one willing to shout fire in a crowded theater, was not going to be able to stir the kind of outrage and indignation that would wake up the country. It was also clear that even the handful of courageous individuals willing to step forward, often at great risk to the future, to tell their stories of religious persecution, was not even going to be enough to do the job."

He pauses, reaching back to reconstruct the impetus for the historic events he was about to put in play. "I'm a military man," he continues at last. "I thrive on structure, organization, a chain of command. In order to attack this insidious enemy, to contain this fascistic contagion of fundamentalist Christian exceptionalism and triumphalism, I was going to need an army. I had to find a way to first identify and then motivate the men and women who would understand what was at stake—our precious constitutional liberties—and be willing to do what it takes to keep them safe. It was time to mobilize."

It was against this unremitting drumbeat of calculated constitutional encroachment that Mikey began having intense discussions and strategy sessions with Bonnie. "We had a lot of very earnest pillow talk," she reveals. "We knew we had to do something, but the necessitated degree of our dedication and the requisite extent of our commitment was more than we could ever have anticipated. We just held our breath, took each other's hand and made the plunge."

In the last month of 2005, Mikey and Bonnie Weinstein announced the formation of the Military Religious Freedom Foundation. It would be an aggressive, confrontational civil rights organization to which he would, in time, devote the full measure of his dedication to enshrined First Amendments principles, meeting the crisis at the heart of the armed services establishment with every last resource at his command: endless hours, family financial assets and, not least, the formidable reserves of energy that embodied his intense commitment to the cause.

"Whatever shit we had faced before was just a prelude to what was coming," remarks Bonnie with characteristic candor. "The formation of the foundation was the inevitable next step, but there was no way that we could have been prepared for what it would mean to take that step. We really didn't have a clear idea at that point of the deeply entrenched forces we were facing and their determination to take us down. We were on a steep learning curve and the enormity of the job we were taking on would only reveal itself over time, one fateful step after another."

There were costly requirements. Lots of them. The mission of the Military Religious Freedom Foundation would inevitably overlap with the Weinstein family dynamic in such a way as to test the essential bonds that held them together and kept them focused on a cause that was greater than themselves. To describe Mikey's engagement in establishing the fledgling foundation as one bordering on complete obsession would not be to overstate the case. "From the very beginning it was a twenty-four-seven proposition," Bonnie continues. "As the dimensions of the problem came into sharper relief, any concept of spare time—a moment when the phone wasn't ringing, reporters weren't knocking on the door, or a new and urgent brush fire didn't need to be put out—simply ceased to exist. The Foundation literally became our life and vice versa."

Any family faced with the daunting magnitude of the task of protecting constitutional freedom within the sprawling complex of the American military would have felt the stresses and strains that came with the territory. The Weinsteins' were no exception. "Was there a time when I wished it would all go away?" Bonnie asks rhetorically. "Of course. The fucking hate mail, the threats, the pressure put on us from those we had stood up against, the terrible silence of some of our immediate and extended family and those we thought were close friends...there were more than a few moments when I fervently wished it would all go away. I wanted my husband back. I wanted a normal, tranquil life, out of the media fishbowl, away from all the massive public and private attention that the Foundation generated as a matter of course. I had very real concerns for the safety of my children and my hopes for a secure future." She sighs, a heartfelt expression of the trials and travails she has endured. But at the same time there is nothing helpless or self-pitying in her description of the cost that comes with fighting the good fight. "I wouldn't change any of it," she adds with a smile. It's an expression which mixes the inevitable resignation that comes from being married to a force of nature with the realization that there are some things worth any cost to preserve, protect and pass down. "This is a high calling," she continues. "Above all else we were standing up for the Constitution. Of course it's going to require a great sacrifice. Anything worth doing does. I'm proud of what Mikey has accomplished, of what our family together has accomplished. Other wives and husbands, other children, may never face the challenges, the setbacks, sometimes even the heartbreak that we've faced. But we're not those people. What we've gone through has made us stronger, closer, more resilient, with a wisdom had comes from hard won experience. We're a source of aid and assistance to thousands and thousands of honorable people and their families. U.S. military personnel, who are genuinely and seriously suffering and really need someone in their corner because there is absolutely no one else willing and able to fight this fight for them. As a measure of the meaning of our lives together, there's nothing to compare with that."

The certitude that Bonnie reflects after nearly three quarters of a decade in the trenches of the First Amendment frontlines was by no means a given when they initially put the wheels in motion to create the Military Religious Freedom Foundation. "At first it was just Bonnie, the kids, and me," he recounts. "We had no budget, no staff, no offices." He grins ruefully, glancing around the Laurel Loop home that is still the Foundation's central command. "Not that much has changed. We still run a tight ship, operate on a shoestring budget and stay close to the ground. Bonnie and I were never interested in building an institution for its own sake. In many ways, despite our high profile, this is a guerilla operation. We grew slowly as devoted volunteers stepped forward to help, but even then we tried to stay under the radar as far possible. Of course, that's not always possible. By the very nature of our work, we have a high public profile." He shrugs, a gesture that neatly sums up the risk assessment he and his family have long since factored into their daily lives.

But as much as the Military Religious Freedom Foundation still reflects its ad hoc origins, there was also courageous and conspicuous support for the organization almost from the beginning: a coterie of concerned citizens willing to put the reputations and resources on the line to support the Weinsteins' historic undertaking. It's an endeavor aptly summed up in the Foundation's articles of incorporation, presented as part of its application for non-profit status. "The sole mission of the Military Religious Freedom Foundation," the document unequivocally states, "is to protect the constitutionally guaranteed civil rights of United States armed forces personnel and veterans. In this regard, the Foundation focuses exclusively on protecting its clients' religious freedom civil rights as specified in both the 'Free Exercise' and 'No Establishment' clauses of the United States Constitution and, additionally, Article VI, Clause 3's guarantee of 'no religious test.'"

"My son Casey put it in a nutshell," Mikey recounts, "when he said that we are dedicated to protecting our service men and women so that they can protect us. But in case anyone's still wondering what we are fighting for, let me quote the relevant constitutional clause directly: *'The Senators and Representatives before mentioned, and the Members of the several State Legislatures, and all executive and judicial Officers, both of the United States and of the several States, shall be bound by Oath or Affirmation, to support this Constitution; but no religious Test shall ever be required as a Qualification to any Office or public Trust under the United States.'*

"To my mind and, I might add, the minds of the best constitutional scholars our country has ever produced, there's no room for interpretation in those words. But that hasn't stopped a lot of the theologically obsessed fundamentalist Christian fringe from giving it their best shot. They try to twist those crystal clear words to suit their own agenda. So let's be clear: there is to be no—none, zero, nada—religious test ever required as a qualification to any office or public trust in this nation. You can finesse or finagle that however you want when it comes to the military, but the last time I looked, the military was part of the public trust. They protect us and we pay their salaries. From an historical perspective, there is a compelling reason why the stipulations in Article VI were so clearly stated. This country was founded in part by religious dissidents seeking to escape the depredations of a state sanctioned belief system. The pilgrims, the Puritans; it's part of what every kid learns in school, as much a part of America as Thanksgiving and the 4th of July. You could even call it our foundation myth, except that there's nothing mythical about it. It's a reality kept alive by an informed citizenry. One might be correct in saying that America was founded as a Christian nation, primarily by religious dissidents who, ironically, were fleeing the persecutions they faced in the Old World. But when it came time to create the United States of America, far different principles were established. It couldn't be any clearer. What does the First Commandment from the Bible say? It says you cannot have any other Gods. But what does the First Amendment of the United States Constitution say? *Oh, yes you can!*'"

Weinstein pauses for a moment, swept up in the magisterial significance of that which he has sworn to protect. "Article VI is a prime example of the genius of the founding fathers," he continues after expelling a deep breath. "But I suppose you could consider it an example of the law of unintended consequences. Thomas Jefferson was a deist who didn't believe for a moment that Jesus Christ was the Son of God or that he healed the sick and revived the dead. Washington, Franklin, Madison, Hamilton: they all had their religious convictions, or lack thereof. But let's not fucking kid ourselves. Their primary intent in so carefully crafting the language Article VI, Clause 3 was to curb the kind of abuses that had been perpetrated by the Church of England. They knew from firsthand experience that religion, regardless of its tenets, had no place in good governance. It was for that reason that the framers of the Constitution made the deliberate decision not to evoke any deity."

He pauses again, marshalling his thoughts. "At the same time I agree in some ways with the fundamentalists who claim that this country was, paradoxically, founded on religious principles. There was Christian consensus, no question about it. God is mentioned by name in the Declaration of Independence. And I'm sure that when they formulated a prohibition against any sort of religious test in government, the men who wrote and signed the Constitution weren't thinking about protecting Jews or Buddhists or atheists or whatever gods were worshipped by the slaves that some of them owned. But that's the way it turned out. That's the way it's been interpreted and passed down as people of many faiths, including no faith at all, we were drawn to this nation by the same promise they had set down on parchment with a quill pen. Religious freedom, as defined by the men who created this country, applies to citizens whose beliefs they could never have imagined and of which they might well have disapproved. A Wiccan has as much right as any hard shell, Bible believing, washed-in-the blood Baptist to serve his or her country in the armed forces without being subjected to humiliating harassment or destructive discrimination. Any citizen's personal rights as a Christian to practice their fundamentalist faith can never, and should never, trump a fellow American's civil rights.

"The scope of the Constitution, as revealed in the sweep of America's historical destiny, may well have been grander and more inclusive that its framers had intended or could have imagined. That's what makes it such a singularly astonishing document." He smiles. "As I've said many times, I don't consider myself a particularly religious person. But I have to admit there's something almost inspired about the way the Constitution was constructed to durably insure life, liberty and the pursuit of happiness down to this present day. It's stood the test of time, and no more so than by its enshrined protection against any and all religious tests."

Weinstein's concise and clear-eyed assessment of the Foundation's historic mandate hinged on the high calling that the Constitution has bequeathed to a modern civil society. It's not surprising that, as a result, the MRFF has attracted a stellar roster of conspicuous supporters. Many of those who offered their services on the Foundation's initial advisory board had already stepped up to join Mikey in his first forays against the Air Force Academy. They included former Air Force chaplain MeLinda Morton and Dr. Kristen Leslie, then a professor, and an ordained Protestant minister, at Yale Divinity School. Also lending his name and prestige to the board was David Antoon, a retired Air Force Colonel and 1970 graduate of the Academy who had first been alerted to what was happening at his beloved alma mater in much the same way as Mikey. Just as Casey, his wife, Amanda, and Curtis had revealed virulent anti-Semitism that had been allowed to fester there, so too did Antoon's cadet candidate son Ryan report back to his father about the excess of evangelical zealotry on display during a summer introductory program and an Air Force Academy orientation for the newly appointed, incoming "doolies" (freshman) in the spring of 2004.

Antoon's dedication to the school had matched Mikey's in every respect. Yet he was so disturbed by what he discovered after investigating Ryan's observations, that he eventually advised his son not to attend the Academy. "It wasn't the same place it was when I had gone," Antoon recounts, as much in sorrow as in anger and echoing the same grim evaluation of Jason Splindler. "Something was broken."

Yet his genuine grief over the harrowing effects of fundamentalist encroachment did not stop him from taking definite and decisive action when the time came. "Having David come aboard as part of the Foundation was a tremendous boost," Weinstein reveals. "This was a man who had flown two tours of duty in Vietnam and went on to oversee the test flight program of some of the most advanced aircraft in our country's arsenal. He was widely respected, not just in Air Force circles, but also throughout the armed forces. He gave us a critical aura of legitimacy just at the point when we needed it the most."

So, too, did the addition of Vice Admiral Bernard Marvin Kauderer to the Foundation's nascent board of advisors. An Annapolis classmate of Mikey's father, Kauderer had an exemplary thirty-three year career in the Navy, setting an historical precedent by being the first officer ever to command the U.S. submarine forces of both the Atlantic and Pacific fleets and subsequently being put in charge of the entire NATO submarine force. Kauderer cut directly to the chase in his unequivocal support of the Military Religious Freedom Foundation. "It's a basic principle," he asserted. "Young men and women in the military should be secure in their own beliefs, whatever they might be. Harassment and intimidation impinge directly on the good order and discipline that is essential for any military organization to carry out its mission. This is simply good policy." Kauderer would eventually resign from the Foundation's advisory board, but his early endorsement as well as active and very public service on its behalf served the fledgling organization in good stead.

It was the kind of cut and dry logic that appealed to the no-nonsense military pragmatism for which Weinstein has such innate and abiding respect. "The spiritual aura that surrounds this issue only serves to obscure the simple facts," he explains. "The reality is that religious coercion in any form only serves to undermine the fundamental precepts by which any military organization stands and falls. There are well-established firewalls that protect not just the expectations of superior officers that their commands will be obeyed, but also ensues the rank and file that their basic rights will be respected and observed. Anything that undercuts those structures undercuts the effectiveness and cohesion of a fighting force. By the same token, any officer worth his or her stars and bars, or an enlisted trooper worth his or her stripes, knows that their authority is based on the trust and confidence inspired in his or her subordinates, not the religious convictions or the exploitation of their superior rank to promulgate their faith. Sectarian divisions destroy armies. What follows from that fact is not the imposition of religious conformity but the institutionalized tolerance, strictly enforced, of religious plurality." Leaning forward with his trademark intensity, he drives the point home. "It's generally acknowledged that solders in foxholes don't fight and die for god or country. They do it for their buddies fighting and dying next to them. What does it say about that selfless instinct if they are taught that the trooper next to them is a godless sinner, condemned to burn eternally in the flames of hell? Religious intolerance is dehumanizing and, whatever else it might require, a military depends on some of the most ennobling aspects of human character—bravery, sacrifice, loyalty, character, integrity, honor, obedience—to achieve its mission.

"Of course," he adds, "it could be argued that an effective military also depends on some of the basest of human traits, such as a willing to kill your fellow man. I would only respond by saying that the most savage, brutal and merciless soldiers throughout human history are most often the ones who believe they are on a mission from God and that their reward is a paradise, whether that be harps and angel wings or the proverbial seventy-two virgins."

Mikey's incisive presentation of the essential dividing line between the military duties and religious sensibilities of fighting men and women was a powerful motivation for Richard Klass, another key addition to the Military Religious Freedom Foundation. An Academy graduate and Rhodes Scholar, former Air Force Colonel and lifelong Catholic, Klass was also a genuine war hero, having flown over two hundred missions in Vietnam, including sorties during the storied battle of Khe Sanh. His honors include, among others, a Silver Star, Legion of Merit, Distinguished Flying Cross and a Purple Heart. A one-time flight instructor at the Academy, Klass became aware of its rampant fundamentalist Christian encroachment at a graduate leadership conference in the summer of 2005 when he met Weinstein for the first time. As with Vice Admiral Kauderer, Klass eventually stepped down from the board but continues to be active, and to have a direct impact, with his personal and financial support.

It was an unforgettable encounter. "We were in a restaurant after the conference," he recalls. "It was there that I first heard Mikey defending his position. He asked one of the fundamentalist alumni in attendance if he believed that Catholics were Christians. Not only did the guy insist that we weren't, because we didn't have a 'personal relationship with Jesus Christ', but he went on to draw what I considered to be a repugnant distinction between born again Christians and jihadist Muslims. The first, he said, were compelled to go out and save people. The second was compelled to go out and kill people. I was shocked and I remember asking myself, 'what's going on here?'"

It was Weinstein who helped answer that question. "The abuses Mikey uncovered go far beyond the Academy," Klass contends, "It's not hard to find a correlation between them and the ongoing attempt to breach the wall of separation between church and state."

Other influential figures of the highest rank in the U.S. military establishment also gave enormous impetus to the fledgling foundation. Among them was the late four-star general Robert T. Herres, former vice chairman of the Joint Chiefs of Staff and commander of the North American Aerospace Defense Command and the United States Space Command, overseeing the nation's entire nuclear arsenal. His endorsement was direct and unambiguous: "Mikey Weinstein has taken on a tough and unpopular issue that goes to the very heart of one of our nation's most important and long cherished principles."

It was the staunch defense of those principles, as exemplified in the charter of the Foundation, which prompted so many thoughtful and passionately patriotic individuals to add their names for the growing roster of early advocates. In the case of John J. Michels Jr., another significant early member of the Foundation's advisory committee, the constitutional crimes Weinstein was exposing underscored his own trenchant analysis of the parlous condition of that crumbling wall of separation. As part of that analysis, Michels, an Academy classmate of Weinstein's and a renowned attorney with a degree from Duke Law School, has given careful thought to some of the same existential issues Mikey has raised.

"The armed forces are comprised of people who, of necessity, deal with death and the taking of life," he explains. "Naturally that raises big questions that religion helps to answer. Belief in a higher power is a remarkable moral tool. For evangelicals part of that belief is the command to actively spread the message. That is their right, to practice their religion as they so choose, and that right is guaranteed by the Constitution. But that must stop at the gates of any military institution, especially considering the fact that evangelical Christians are providing free access to their coreligionists to armed forces facilities in direct contravention of the Constitution."

Yet, despite the obvious interest that active and retired military men and women evinced in the pioneering work of the Foundation, Weinstein's supporters were hardly confined to the ranks of the armed forces. Among the more notable non-uniformed members of the advisory board was former ambassador Joseph C. Wilson IV, whose wife, CIA agent Valerie Plame, was outed by the Bush Administration after Wilson revealed false claims regarding the Iraqi nuclear arms program. With wide-ranging experience in the Foreign Service and a take-no-prisoners attitude toward political hypocrisy in all its forms, Wilson also has had direct connection with the military establishment. He served from 1995 to 1997 as Political Advisor to the Commander in Chief of U.S. Armed Forces, Europe in Stuttgart. His tenure in the post gave him invaluable insight into the battle Mikey and the Foundation were waging. Additionally, in the years since they first lent their vocal and enthusiastic support, Valerie and Joe Wilson have become the closest of personal friends with Mikey and Bonnie Weinstein.

Prominent Republican Party consultant and former GOP gubernatorial candidate Doug Turner also lent his support as did former *Los Angeles Times* and *Denver Post* publisher and CEO Richard Schlosberg. Added to the early roster was a highly celebrated, articulate and engaged constitutional attorney with the memorable name of Pedro Luis Irigonegaray.

"The notion that God is on our side has been entwined throughout our military history," asserts the outspoken Cuban-born lawyer who first came to national prominence in his fight against the teaching of creationism in the Ground Zero of America's Bible Belt: the Kansas school system. "It comes with the territory. But shouldn't each individual have the freedom to decide what God they are fighting for and praying to?" It's a variation of Weinstein's insights into the rationale of soldiers in foxholes, and Irigonegaray's overarching conclusions are strikingly similar. "It's the right to worship, or even not worship, as we please that has been one of the abiding reasons we send our sons and daughter to fight and die. We need to preserve that right at all costs."

It was the highly charged interface between conflict and religious confession that prompted another significant early ally to voice his unequivocal support for the Foundation. Reza Aslan is an internationally respected author, print and television journalist, and a respected global voice on Islamic and Middle Eastern issues and former President of the Harvard University chapter of the World Conference on Religion and Peace. Aslan immediately saw the international significance of the work Mikey was doing, as it applied to the post 9/11 international climate. As the scholar succinctly states it: "The idea, promulgated among religious extremists on both sides, that we are in the midst of a cosmic battle between Islam and Christianity, will become a self-fulfilling prophecy. This is not a clash of civilizations, and if we insist on framing it that way, we will reap the whirlwind. Using the military as an instrument of sectarian subjugation will be an unmitigated disaster for the West. By keeping religion out of the armed forces we can take the first step in stripping radical ideology from an enormously complex and volatile conflict. I can't think of a more important task."

With a stellar line-up of high profile officers, scholars and concerned citizens lending their name and prestige to the Foundation, it was time to tackle that important task head on. The question was how to go about raising awareness of fundamentalist Christian incursion in the military and stepping in to stop its spread.

"It was a target rich environment," Mikey recounts. "Once we started turning over rocks, fundamentalist Christian fringe elements and zealots of every description began scurrying out. But exposing their unconstitutional activities to the light of day was just the beginning. We knew we had to take a multi-pronged approach, in the courts, in the press, wherever we could get the most attention and apply the most leverage. But I had learned something from the lawsuit against the Air Force and Pete Garen. These people had the time and resources to tangle you up in court for years. We'd be tied down filing briefs and appeals while they were out steadily advancing their agenda. Of course, the legal remedy was essential for us to pursue at every opportunity. After all, this was a constitutional issue of the highest magnitude. We needed to apply the full force of the law in order to address this grotesque injustice. But it hardly stopped there, as we discovered with each new revelation."

Again he pauses and again he leans forward, unmistakably signaling the significance of his next words. "The unavoidable fact was that there were real human lives at stake here," he says, his voice dropping to a low register. "Young men and women were getting chewed up and spit out by a system that fucking refused to realize the peril they were in. No, far worse than that; the system, itself, *was* 'the peril'". It wasn't just some abstraction, some procedural glitch we were trying to correct. The anger, humiliation, degradation, dehuminization and grief and profound disillusionment were only too real. Fundamentalist Christian extremism, vile religious coercion, and bitter sectarian bigotry were destroying lives. If we didn't acknowledge that reality and do everything we could to put a stop to it, then we might as well have packed it in before we began. If the Foundation couldn't expeditiously provide real help to real people, then there was no reason for us to exist in the first place."

CHAPTER SEVEN

VOICES IN THE WILDERNESS

Well before Weinstein had gathered together the exemplary assembly of committed colleagues that would comprise the advisory core of the Military Religious Freedom Foundation, he had had the kind of direct experience with the very real human dimension of the crisis that formed the Foundation's overriding *raison d'etre*. It was an experience that cut close to home and underlined for him in no uncertain terms, the implacable nature of the opposition he and his family faced.

The ordeal endured by his beloved daughter-in-law Amanda had provided that unsettling object lesson. Bright, beautiful, articulate and immensely gifted, Amanda had met Mikey's oldest son Casey in the summer of 2003 when they were both First Class cadets (seniors) at the Air Force Academy. One and a half years later they were married in a picturesque ceremony in New Mexico, after which they began laying out plans for a shared future, bright with promise, both in service to the Air Force and in their long term professional prospects. But before those sunny scenarios could unfold, Amanda, who had achieved a conspicuous leadership position in the Air Force Academy Cadet Corps, had to confront the same extremes of evangelical arm-twisting that Mikey was even then beginning to expose at the Academy.

The far-from-subtle pressure tactics included an encounter with the Commandant of Cadets, Brigadier General Johnny Weida, who exhorted her to invite as "many non-Christian cadets as possible" to an evangelical extravaganza being held in one of the myriad fundamentalist mega-churches in nearby Colorado Springs. "It felt weird," Amanda later recounted. "I remember thinking to myself what business of it was his whom I invited or why, and at the same time I couldn't help but wonder whether it was some kind of a test. If I did invite every non-believer I knew, would I be getting extra credit from the General? And what if I didn't? Would he be disappointed? Or angry?"

It was a glaring glimpse into exactly the kind of violation of the sacrosanct chain of command that Weinstein was trying to address within the Academy. "It's hard to overstate how much authority and respect someone like the Commandant had in our eyes," Amanda explains. "You could really live or die by a kind or critical word from him. There is always that striving to meet with approval, to get noticed and make an impression."

The impression that Weida seemed to require was that Amanda would willingly participate in an attempt to sway the spiritual convictions of her fellow cadets. She resisted the idea. "Sometimes," she says with a trace of regret, "religion seems like nothing more than a way to drive a wedge between people."

The eager, highly articulate, athletic and attractive young cadet would soon come to directly encounter the divisive effects that strident religious convictions too often engender. It proved to have a devastating effect on the bonds that united her family. "My parents were kind of hippies," she recounts. "Then they had a spiritual experience and were 'born again' before they had me. I don't know if I ever truly understood what that experience had been and when they talked about having a personal relationship with Jesus I always felt a bit leery about the terminology. I remember thinking that I had already been born once: why did I need to be born again? I couldn't exactly make the leap of faith my parents had made, but Christianity is the view I had been taught and I accepted that. When it comes to Christianity, I think Lady Gaga puts it best: I was born that way. I think the Buddhists actually explain it best when they talk about an inherent spirituality in everything from a rock to a dog to a person to Jesus. It's just the degree of spirituality that differs and can also change.

"My parents made sure I respected and fairly treated all cultures, genders, and races. But I don't think they quite realized I would extend that tolerance to all religions, too. Christianity is the perspective from which I view spirituality, but I don't think it is any better than any other perspective. Sometimes I like to step out and see things from different angles, too. I don't like labels and I don't need to make a show of my beliefs to make someone else happy."

That tolerance would be tested to its limit in the overheated spiritual atmosphere of the Academy. As official promotions for the Mel Gibson film, *The Passion*, reached a fever pitch, Amanda and Casey attended one of the all-but mandatory screenings. "Casey got very offended by various aspects of the movie," she remembers. "It opened my eyes for the first time as to how a Jewish person may perceive things differently from what I was used to. I think it was a turning point for me, a moment when I saw the world as someone else might see it."

That turning point became even more pronounced as Weinstein's efforts to turn back the fundamentalist Christian tide at the Academy began attracting national media attention. Inevitably, Casey was linked directly to the controversial campaign his father had launched and so, by extension, was his wife, Amanda. "My parents just couldn't understand how I could be a part of something like that," Amanda recounts. "I tried to explain to them, to show them what Mikey was standing for and standing up against, but they just saw it as a betrayal of everything they believed in."

Amanda's father expressed that aggrieved sense of betrayal through the most public forum available to him, in an act that seemed designed to bring the maximum degree of shame and disgrace to his daughter. In a letter to the *Colorado Springs Gazette*, responding to an article that covered Mikey's ongoing struggle with the Academy, Paul Baranek railed, "When will you guys get it that we don't care what Mikey Weinstein thinks, says or does? He is not promoting religious freedom. He is trying to snuff out any expression of Christianity. He is looking for publicity. Do you just take your information from him or do you check out your sources? I happen to know the man. My daughter is married to his son. This man's motives are anything but noble and the more publicity you give him, the more you encourage his crusade against Christianity. Please stop."

If it was Baranek's intent to inflict guilt by association on Amanda, effectively disowning her over what he perceived to be her traitorous apostasy, the attempt backfired badly. A flood of letters followed his tirade, the vast majority expressing shock at his callous disregard for his daughter's feelings and reputation. "I was deeply saddened," read one, "by the hateful comments of Mr. Baranak, who is obviously so full of bile that he is willing to injure his own daughter just to spite a man with whom he disagrees." "It breaks my heart," another ran, "to see a father abandon his children for any reason. Religious bigotry, as a reason, is doubly disturbing. Mr. Baranek sees the world through the prism of narrow and archaic Christian doctrine; doctrine that would be far better suited for the Inquisition or Salem witch trials."

Yet Baranek also had his supporters, hateful and unhinged as they might be. "I have spent many hours on the phone with Paul Baranek," began one such screed. "I truly pray that your heart will quit or your brains will bleed out or your liver will develop cancer. I pray that God will remove you from the earth sooner than later so as to stop the damage you have done and put an end to your insidious plans. I am praying for the death of you, your followers and coconspirators."

But the last word, fittingly, remained Amanda's. "Technically speaking," she wrote in a letter of reply to the Gazette, "Paul Baranek is my father. But it is more accurate to describe Mikey Weinstein as my father. It is not by blood but by heart and choice that makes Mikey my father. He is the one who protects me. He is the one who defends me. He is the one who stands by and speaks for me when no one will listen. He is the one who knows me. And he, Mikey Weinstein, is the one that I call father. Paul Baranak is none of these things to me. He does not know or speak for me and has even less claim to know my father, Mikey."

Amanda's mother, meanwhile, was more accepting of Weinstein and the principles for which he—and his daughter-in-law—steadfastly stood, and maintained an open line of communication with Amanda. Shortly before her graduation from the Academy in May of 2004, her parents were divorced.

The whole experience was devastating for the Weinsteins. "I couldn't help but feel that, in some way, I was personally responsible for the rift between Amanda and her family," Mikey reveals. "I'm sure when she married Casey she had no idea what she'd be signing up for, and I'm sure the experience of rejection by her parents caused her great anguish. How could it not? Of the over three hundred guests attended their wedding, only two were from her family. It was as if she had ceased to exist for them. Amanda is a smart, strong and supremely capable young woman. She has two Masters, one in economics and another in operations research (applied mathematics) and is the later stages of earning for her PhD in applied economics at Ohio State University. But no amount of academic achievement can compensate for the kind of emotional trauma she experienced. It's a testament to her extraordinary character and pristine integrity that she has never looked back. It was certainly excruciatingly painful for her to lose all contact with her biological father, but what seemed to matter more to her—besides, of course, her deep love for Casey—was her understanding of what was at stake in this battle. I'm moved to tears more often than I can say when I think of how she sacrificed to stand up for what she believed. My respect for Mandy is exceeded only by my love for her. She's truly one of the most extraordinary human beings I've ever known. She's not a 'daughter-in-law' to Bonnie and me, nor just a 'sister-in-law' to Curtis and Amber. She's a daughter and sister. Period."

In the months and years that followed the formation of the Military Religious Freedom Foundation, Mikey would have occasion to hear many stories of personal tragedy and heroism in the face of the heartbreak invariably brought about by religious intolerance. And while none may have hit quite as close to home as the rift between his daughter-in-law and her family, each in its own way served to underscore the acutely intense human dramas that were often played out beneath this epic struggle for constitutional principles.

One of the most striking examples of the degradation and humiliation that inevitably accompany spiritual strong-arm tactics is vividly illustrated in the case of U.S. Army Sergeant Dustin Chalker, one of the highest profile soldiers ever to seek assistance from the Foundation.

It would be hard to imagine anyone who had given more to the service of his country then the affable, engaging Chalker. A native of Mobile, Alabama, Chalker served over nine eventful years in the military, joining the Army Reserves in 2002 while still in high school. In 2004, he signed up for active duty as a combat medic and served a year in South Korea. He was subsequently transferred to Fort Riley, Kansas, home of the legendary First Infantry Division: The Big Red One. Within a year of working in the on-post clinic, Chalker volunteered to transfer to a combat unit for a fifteen-month deployment with the 1st Engineering Battalion. As a member of a route clearance team, he survived nine separate Improvised Explosive Devices (IEDs), suffering multiple concussions and being awarded both the Purple Heart and the Combat Medic Badge, a citation reserved for medics who have provided care under direct fire.

But it was upon his return home to America, stationed once again at

Fort Riley, that Chalker's real trial by fire began in earnest. An avowed atheist, Sergeant (then Specialist) Chalker was compelled by his superior officers to attend numerous blatantly religious events where battalion chaplains prayed to the Almighty on behalf of the assembled soldiers. At every such occasion, Chalker requested to be excused from the assemblies and was summarily denied permission each and every time.

"The America I believe in," Chalker would later assert, "the America I would die for—is a secular nation built upon the framework of the world's first godless constitution. I don't use those words lightly. Look at the document for yourself and see if you find the words 'God,' 'Jesus,' 'theocracy' or anything else that would indicate that the Founders had any intention of creating a so-called 'Christian nation'. They just don't exist. The word 'religion' is only used to keep religion out of government, and government out of religion."

"Not only were the incidents Dustin endured clearly illegal," observes Mikey, "but they displayed a shocking insensitivity. This soldier had put his life on the line, not once, but over and over again, in defense of this country and of the freedoms for which it stands. Paramount among those freedoms is the liberty to choose when and how to worship or, as in the case of Dustin, not to worship at all. By forcing him to be present at these transparently sectarian events, the authorities at Fort Riley were making a mockery of his sacrifice.

"Dustin related to me a particularly poignant story during one of our innumerable conversations together," Mikey continues. "He had been told by his command chain that he would be required to attend these mandatory military formations where prayers would be recited. He was informed that he could follow his own theological dictates on his own time. It was then that he decided to stand up to his superiors' demands to attend these illegal formations and told his superiors that 'his own faith' required him to separate himself from people attempting telepathic contact with imaginary beings. That's one of the most amazing retorts any MRFF client has ever made!"

"You can imagine the sense of betrayal I felt," Chalker adds, "when I was involuntarily drafted into these religious gatherings and forced to put on a charade of praying along with Christian clergyman, whose salaries were paid with tax dollars. These ceremonial prayers were not innocent acts of 'free exercise,' but forced exercise that non-Christian soldiers cannot escape."

In a subsequent lawsuit filed on Chalker's behalf by the Military Religious Freedom Foundation, a persistent pattern of unashamed proselytizing throughout the military was detailed. Routine practices included what was dubiously termed a "Spiritual Fitness Program" held for hundreds of personnel at an Air Force base in the United Kingdom. During these fundamentalist indoctrination sessions, the scientifically discredited tenets of creationism were openly espoused, as were Christian-based techniques applied to suicide prevention programs. At Fort Leonard Wood, Missouri, the Foundation called attention to a practice of providing personnel a "Free Day Away," that was actually funded and facilitated by a local Baptist church. They also revealed that the once-suspended practice of dipping the American flag before the altar of a chapel at the U.S. Naval Academy in Annapolis, Maryland had been surreptitiously revived. Subsequently pointed out was the grossly illegal and inappropriate appearance of a U.S. Army Major General in uniform at a concert performance by a fundamentalist evangelical vocalist who went by the single name of Carmen.

"Obviously the unadulterated courage Dustin Chalker displayed in stepping forward served as a lightning rod for us," Weinstein explains. "We were able to file a comprehensive brief against the entire Department of Defense as well as Defense Secretary Robert Gates that included many of these outrageous practices. Our primary purpose was to support Dustin's contention that being a person of no religious belief had in no way caused a diminished performance of his duties or compromised his ability to follow commands. By allowing us to seek, in his name, an injunction against mandatory sectarian prayer sessions we were able to call attention to a number of other clear violations of the Constitution. We owe him a great debt of gratitude, as does the rest of the nation. I might add that his countrymen also owe Dustin a universal and comprehensive apology. After giving so much, to then be subjected to this kind of evil and base harassment is simply beyond the pale. We were determined to establish from the outset that the fundamentalist Christian insistence on the 'will of Jesus' as they, and only they, interpret it, is not and never will be acceptable American military policy."

In the end, Chalker's case was dismissed on the grounds that internal remedies were not sought within military channels. But, Chalker notes, "That's simply not true. The Ft. Riley Inspector General office refused to investigate. My commander denied my first Equal Opportunity complaint. This same commander then lied in his statement to the court, saying that

I never brought my problem to his attention until after filing the lawsuit. The Department of Defense's legal team therefore denied that my initial complaint even occurred. By deliberately deploying these lies and obfuscation the Department of Defense chose to reinforce the cultural dominance of religion over non-religion and deny equal opportunity to non-religious soldiers. Such men and women live and work in an openly hostile environment where every public event begins and ends with a reminder that they are not equals in the eyes of the government. Their duty is to pay these state clergymen their tax tithes, shut their mouths, and bow their heads in respect to the discrimination being perpetrated against them."

In point of fact, as groundbreaking as Specialist Dustin Chalker's lawsuit against the Defense Department had been, it was not the first to be launched, with the help of the Foundation, by an atheist in uniform. In 2007, another unswerving non-believer, also stationed at Fort Riley, had lodged a remarkably similar complaint. He was Private First Class Jeremy Hall and his grievances did much to expose a pattern of harassment at the vast and storied Kansas army installation against those who had rejected all religious belief. According to his landmark lawsuit, again naming Defense Secretary Robert Gates as one of the defendants, Hall had refused to participate in a prayer service held on the base during the Thanksgiving holiday. It was a courageous act by a self-taught young man who had been raised in poverty by his grandmother and had to strive for any advantage in life. But he was not about to let his hard won independence be stripped away.

According to the filing: "Immediately after the plaintiff made it known that he would decline to join hands and pray, he was confronted, in the presence of other military personnel, by a senior ranking staff sergeant who asked the plaintiff why he did not want to pray, whereupon the plaintiff explained that it was because he was an atheist. This response so infuriated the staff sergeant that he told the plaintiff that he would have to sit elsewhere for the Thanksgiving dinner. Nonetheless, the plaintiff sat at the table and finished his meal."

But the ordeal of Pfc. Hall was just beginning. A few months later, after duly receiving permission from the proper authorities, Hall organized a meeting of other combat soldiers in Iraq who shared his atheistic beliefs. In the midst of the gathering, a superior ranking field grade officer barged in and broke up the assembly, threatening to bring Hall up on unspecified charges under the Uniform Code of Military Justice. Even more ominously, the apoplectic Major named in the complaint, a fundamentalist Christian, also vowed that if Hall's atheist group ever dared to meet again, he would block the Private's attempt to reenlist in the Army.

The groundbreaking lawsuit was filed on Constitution Day, September 17th, 2007. Hall had been posted at Combat Operations Base Speicher in Iraq. It was there that the threats against him began to escalate to a new and alarming level. News of his courageous legal action against both Defense Secretary Gates and the Major who had disrupted his meetings with other nonbelievers, apparently had followed him into the war zone. In close touch with Weinstein via email, Hall described relentless goading and clear threats by his fellow soldiers, promising to "beat his ass" and calling him "a faggot" and, more to the point, an "atheist ass pirate."

Hall had good reason to believe that it was more than empty macho posturing. Due to the increased frequency of "fragging" incidents on the front lines, in which renegade soldiers turned on their own under the cover of ongoing combat conditions, Hall, now an outcast in his own squad, had good reason to fear for his safety. An example of the unremittingly hostile attitude of his fellow warriors occurred one day after a fierce firefight when Hall narrowly escaped death after a Plexiglas shield on his armored vehicle deflected a bullet. "Now do you believe in God?" his superior officer smugly asked in the aftermath of the skirmish. "No," Specialist Hall promptly replied. "I believe in Plexiglas."

Mikey wasted no time springing into action. In a statement released to the national press he demanded that "the Secretaries of Defense and the U.S. Army take absolute immediate action to do two things: provide for the comprehensive personal safety of our co-plaintiff Army Specialist Jeremy Hall, and immediately investigate all U.S. Army personnel...threatening the personal safety and indeed the life of Specialist Hall. If one fucking hair on Hall's head is touched, there will be hell to pay."

Weinstein went on to use the occasion to hammer home the mission of the Military Religious Freedom Foundation, directly referencing Hall's bold legal action. "This landmark federal litigation," he declared, "is just the first of a galaxy of new lawsuits that will be expeditiously filed against the Pentagon in a concentrated effort to preserve the precious religious liberties guaranteed by our beautiful United States Constitution. Today, we are boldly stabbing back against an unconstitutional heart of darkness, a contagion of fundamentalist religious supremacy and triumphalism noxiously dominating the command and control of the technologically most lethal organization ever created by humankind: our honorable and noble United States armed forces."

Hall was spared further threats and the distinct possibility of direct physical violence, thanks to Mikey's prompt and concerted action, contacting the Army directly to warn them that the Specialist's situation was being closely monitored. Others who sought help from the Foundation were not so fortunate. The horrifying tribulation of Private Michael Handman had special significance for Weinstein, recalling, as it did, his own descent into the crucible of anti-Semitic violence while a young cadet at the Air Force Academy in the fall of 1973.

Handman's case was not the first incident of rabid hatred of Jews within the military that Weinstein had tackled. The Foundation had previously exposed a pattern of anti-Semitic Biblical teachings by chaplains at Fort Leavenworth and assisted in the defense a former Army Chaplain, Rabbi Jeffrey Goldman, who had been taunted by senior military officers at a prayer breakfast by having Nazi uniforms and swastikas displayed on the wall of the officers' club at Hunter Army Airfield in Savannah, Georgia.

But Handman's ordeal was of a different order of magnitude entirely. It was in mid-2008, when the twenty-year-old Private, who had signed up for an Army stint out of deep patriotism, was in the midst of the grueling Basic Training regimen at Fort Benning, Georgia. Handman's love for America was matched by his commitment to his Jewish faith, which required the wearing of a yarmulke as head covering during his training exercises. This simple sacred act served as an incitement for extreme violence from both his fellow recruits and his commanding officers. Drill sergeants regularly referred to him as a "fucking Jew" and a "Juden," and demanded that he remove the skullcap during meals, an illegal order Handman resisted, but to no avail. Orders were orders, no matter how illegitimate or hateful.

In a letter to his mother, Handman described the noxious taunts and threats that followed him through the training regimen. "I have never been so discriminated against and humiliated about my religion," he wrote. "I just feel like I'm always looking over my shoulder." One of his few friends on the base, Handman related, had told him of overhearing "some guys in the platoon talking about how they wanted to beat the shit out of me tonight when I'm sleeping. The only justification they have is because I'm Jewish."

That, it seemed, was all the justification they needed. One morning in late September of that year, Handman was lured into a base laundry room by a group of soldiers where he was knocked unconscious and brutally attacked while lying prone and utterly unprotected on the floor. Discovered there by other recruits, he was rushed to the base hospital's emergency room where army triage medical staffers treated him for a concussion, facial wounds and what were termed "severe oral injuries." His wounds were serious enough that emergency head and neck CAT scans were required.

Shortly afterwards Michael's father, Jonathan Handman, received an enigmatic phone call from his son's commanding officer, telling him only that his son "was OK and out of the hospital." It was the first that the elder Handman had heard of the savage attack. Probing for more news of his son's condition, he managed to elicit enough information from the stonewalling base officials to realize that Michael was still in grave danger. "I was scared that he might become a victim of friendly fire," the distraught father revealed. "The Army was not doing enough to protect him. They have mentally broken him to the point that he was willing to ruin his life by getting a dishonorable discharge, just to be freed at last from the torment. I feel like this could have been from the movie *A Few Good Men*," he continued, referring to the hit 1992 film about Marines accused of murdering a colleague. "That is what terrifies me. I do not want to bury my only son."

But Jonathan Handman was not about to let that happen. He embarked on a furious letter writing campaign in an attempt to call attention to his son's plight, contacting Georgia Senator, Saxby Chambliss, who, pressured by a determined constituent, demanded that the Pentagon immediately investigate the assault.

With stalling no longer an option, the Department of Defense succumbed to the obvious and reluctantly confirmed that Michael Handman had indeed been a victim of anti-Semitism. "Based on Private Handman's statement and the seriousness of the allegations," the Department of the Army's Deputy Chief wrote in a letter to Chambliss, "the Army found that two non-commissioned officers inadvertently violated the Army Regulation concerning the free exercise of religion by requiring the Soldier to remove his yarmulke and by using inappropriate terms when referencing the Jewish faith. While the actions of the NCOs were not meant to be malicious, and were done out of ignorance for regulations and cultural awareness, this does not excuse their conduct. The command intends to reprimand both NCOs for their conduct; require them to present formal blocks of instruction on what religious soldiers are authorized for wear; and finally, the battalion chaplain will instruct all cadre members on the Army policy concerning religious accommodation."

It was far too little, far too late. With no recourse left to bring the criminal officers to justice, Jonathan Handman contacted the Military Religious Freedom Foundation and, with characteristic alacrity, Weinstein jumped into the fray. "The Army's wretched response to this hate crime is, sadly and typically, to trivialize the entire sordid matter," Weinstein announced in a quickly scheduled mass media interview. "Those found to be responsible need to face a criminal trial by general courts martial. The United States Army needs to learn, and learn fast, that persecuting anyone and marginalizing them by asserting that they lack character, integrity, veracity and courage because of their chosen religious faith, or lack thereof, is exactly the same thing as attacking someone and telling them that they're stupid for the color of their skin or because they happen to be female. Shame, shame on the United States Army."

He next went on to explain the Foundation's rapid response to the outrage at Fort Benning, revealing, in the process, a behind-the-scenes glimpse of the organization's quickly evolving crisis control procedures. "The moment we were contacted by the father, Jonathan Handman," Mikey continued, "MRFF did what it always does in these ever more frequent, tragic matters of unbridled, military-sponsored Christian religious oppression; we moved at light speed to ensure the victim's immediate safety. Next, we demanded that the victim's chain of command comprehensively and fairly investigate and punish those responsible. We know for an absolute fact that our now very public demands precipitated frantic meetings in the Bush White House. The swift result was that the Chief of Staff of the U.S. Army at the time personally called Private Handman at Fort Benning from his office in the E Ring of the Pentagon to profusely apologize for the outrages this young soldier had endured and to ensure his safety from that point on." Mikey pauses, sarcasm dripping from his next words: "As if that was supposed to fix everything."

The notion of forcing a monolithic, fundamentalist Christian worldview on "helpless subordinates" took on a horrific new dimension with the case of Akiva David Miller. A disabled U.S. Navy veteran and Orthodox Jew, Miller had sought medical treatment at the Iowa City V.A. Hospital & Clinic in the late Spring of 2005. What happened to him there stands as a shocking example of precisely how far the forces of fundamentalism will go to enforce their exclusionary doctrines. It was a story of injustice that the Military Religious Freedom Foundation took the lead in both exposing and remedying, using the Navy veteran's own words to describe the abuse he suffered while a patient at the facility.

It began, according to Miller, when he notified the Iowa City V.A. Medical Center that he would now be accessing all of his medical care through their facility. "They directed me to attend the orientation class," recounts Miller. "The class was held in the Chapel, which was decorated with the Stations of the Cross and a large Crucifix, which was brought in for particular services, but had failed to be removed afterwards. When I refused to enter the chapel because it was offensive to me as a Jew, the staff pressured me, telling me I was required to attend the class, that I couldn't receive treatment at the facility unless I did so. When I held my ground, offering to attend the class in another room, the class instructor lost her temper, threw the orientation materials at me and told me that this was the only class I was getting."

From the outset, as both an inpatient and outpatient at the facility—which was funded directly by taxpayer dollars—Miller endured a nearly constant barrage of transparent Christian prejudice. "I experienced volunteer Christian musicians singing and playing hymns and religious Christmas songs in the waiting room of the clinic," he reveals. "More than once I was forced to listen to the music while I sat in the clinic, waiting to see my doctor. In the examination room where a nurse took my vital signs prior to every physical examination, Christian symbols and scriptures were prominently displayed. On nearly every visit I was asked by hospital staff members if it was true that I didn't believe in Jesus, and, if not, why."

"But the most blatant examples of religious discrimination," Miller continues, "revealed themselves during my hospitalizations at the Iowa City V.A. My medical records clearly indicate that I am Jewish. Nevertheless, with each admission I made sure to inform the nursing staff both verbally and in writing that I required kosher food and did not wish to be visited by anyone from the Chaplain's office. Instead, I requested that they contact my Rabbi and provided them with both his name and telephone number. Despite these instructions, during all three of my hospitalizations I was denied kosher food and had to endure each hospitalization without eating. The hospital not only refused to notify my Rabbi as I requested, but they sent a chaplain to see me each time. During the first two visits by the Assembly of God chaplain, he attempted to convert me, trying to convince me that I needed Jesus. Both times the chaplain stood over my bed, refusing to leave despite my protestations, and insisting that I was very ill, that I could die and if I didn't accept Jesus I would go to hell, and finally that Jesus was the Messiah of the Jews too. This happened while I was sedated, confined to my hospital bed, wired to a heart monitor and suffering chest pains. During my third hospitalization, all for the same internal medical problems, a different chaplain visited me. He tried to excuse his visit by explaining that he was there only to find out if I needed a Rabbi. I explained to him that I had informed the nursing staff both verbally and in writing that I wanted them to contact my own Rabbi and provided them with both his name and number, but he said that would be impossible and then deposited a Christian tract from the chaplains' office on my bedside table before he left."

In an effort to curtail the pervasive religious discrimination, harassment and predatory proselytizing, Miller arranged a meeting with representatives from the chaplains' office and a patient advocate. The head chaplain initially agreed to attend but, just prior to the meeting, backed out. The Assembly of God chaplain who did show up insisted that there was nothing wrong with what he had done. He asserted that he had visited many Jewish and other non-Christian patients over the years and none had complained to the patient advocate or hospital administration. The patient advocate, for his part, blamed Miller for what had happened, insisting, incredibly, that he had failed to protest vigorously enough.

Following the meeting, the campaign of intimidation against Miller took a particularly sinister turn. Diagnosed with multiple kidney stones, he was given a prescription for pain medication and told to follow up with his primary care physician. At this appointment he was informed that the Medical Center would be discontinuing the treatment for his kidney stones, including any palliative treatment. When Miller asked why, his physician's only response was, "You're a religious Jew; why don't you try prayer or meditation?"

Refused any further treatment, bedridden and in agony, Miller contacted the Military Religious Freedom Foundation. It was at that moment that the situation began to change. MRFF quickly helped Miller to see a private physician, who immediately prescribed pain medication and arranged for follow up care. Meanwhile, Mikey and the Foundation's legal team set about exposing and putting a stop to the religious discrimination, intimidation and predatory proselytizing at the Iowa City V.A. Medical Center.

With the support of the Jewish Federation, MRFF raised the funds to fly Miller to Dallas to receive medical treatment at the Dallas V.A. Medical Center. Mikey also called a press conference in Des Moines and put legal pressure on both the Iowa City V.A. Medical Center and the Department of Veterans Affairs to enact changes at the facility. Responding to the increasing outcry, the Department of Veterans Affairs appointed Lowell Kronick—Jewish Chaplain, Associate Director of Education for the Department of Veterans Affairs, and renowned medical ethicist—to carry out an investigation.

As a result, significant changes were initiated at the Iowa City V.A. Medical Center, including critical additional training for the staff, adding Jewish chaplains and altering the chapel to make it more religiously neutral, as it was intended to be. The Iowa City V.A. was also made to pay Miller's private medical care for his service-connected disabilities.

"It was no doubt a victory for us and for all veterans," Weinstein allows, "but there was something very sobering about the ordeal of Akiva David Miller, who, in time, would become the Foundation's volunteer director of veteran's affairs. We realized that the forces we were fighting weren't simply trampling on the legal and constitutional rights of military men and women; they were willing to deprive them of even the most basic *human* rights. These doctors and nurses had a responsibility to their patient; to relieve his suffering, to heal his body, to make him whole to the best of their ability. Instead, it seemed they were willing to sacrifice his body to save his soul. I can't think of a more chilling paradigm to illustrate the extreme measures they were prepared to take to accomplish that goal. It was scary as shit, but it also gave us a whole new determination."

PART THREE

CHAPTER EIGHT

THE TEAM

While it is undeniable that Weinstein and the MRFF have found itself increasingly in the crosshairs of its sworn enemies, it is also true that, as word of the Foundation and its vital work began to spread, friends and allies from every quarter have stepped forward with support, encouragement and endorsement.

This often takes the form of financial contributions from supporters across a broad spectrum of society. Within a few years of its founding, the MRFF has been the recipient of underwriting funds that allows it to carry on its mission, even as it expands its efforts to free the military from fundamentalist encroachment.

But it's almost always been touch and go. "We've never been what anyone would call flush," Mikey allows. "We operate on a shoestring budget and finding resources for the Foundation has been a constant challenge. For that reason, a significant aspect of what we do is to simply try and educate the general public to the threat this country and its Constitution faces. We find that once people understand what's really at stake they are almost invariably very generous. But it isn't easy. We face a formidable, well-financed, foe whose ability and willingness to manipulate the media to spin their story should never be underestimated."

What should also never be underestimated is the toll the unrelenting work of the MRFF has had on the Weinstein family. "We had endured more than our share of stress and anxiety," Bonnie reveals with characteristic understatement. "From the constant threats to the steady depletion of our funds, the strain and uncertainty are an inescapable part of our lives. Some-times all we have to fall back on is the sense of humor that we share, the way we have to laugh to keep from crying." She pauses before adding with a smile, "We also like to swear. There's nothing like a string of profanity to relieve the tension. You better fucking believe it."

Meanwhile, the work goes on. A large part of MRFF's educational effort involves maintaining an exhaustive internet archive chronicling in depth the Foundation's numerous activities and posted at www.militaryre-ligiousfreedom.org. In addition to keeping the public up to date on MRFF's work, the website also provides a remarkable research data base that delves deeply into the legal, political and moral issues that are at the heart of the client caseload the Foundation maintains.

Keeping tabs on the welter of interlocking data is Chris Rodda, Senior Research Director for the Military Religious Freedom Foundation and an accomplished scholar and author in her own right. A frequent contribu-tor to such key news media outlets as the *Huffington Post*, *OpEd News*, and Talk2Action.org, Rodda has also penned *Liars For Jesus: The Religious Right's Alternate Version of American History*, a well-regarded exposé of prevailing fundamentalist myths about the founding of this country as written into textbooks and teaching curriculums, legislation, and court opinions. Ad-ditionally, her essay *Against All Enemies, Foreign and Domestic* appears in the book *Attitudes Aren't Free: Thinking Deeply About Diversity in the U.S. Armed Forces* edited by James Parco and David Levy, and published by Air Univer-sity Press, the publishing arm of the U.S. Air Force's Air University at Max-well Air Force Base. It has been acclaimed as one of the most trenchant and damning examinations of the military's dangerous policies toward the Islamic world written since the wars in Iraq and Afghanistan began.

"In early 2007, I had written an article about the Christian national-ist historical revisionism found in the core curriculum American history textbook of the Junior ROTC, which contained a lesson about the 'myth' of separation of church and state," Rodda explains. "That brought me to the attention of Mikey, and after a single phone conversation with him I suddenly found myself caught up in investigating the heavy fundamentalist outreach at an Air Force Memorial Day celebration held at Stone Mountain, Georgia. The event featured a flyover by an Air Force B-2 stealth bomber during a Sunday worship service that featured a very public 'personal testi-mony' by an Air Force Major in full uniform. It was an appalling violation of the separation of church and state, but for me it was just the beginning. The more I learned about Mikey's work at the Foundation, the more I realized that there was a profound overlap with the Christian American history revisionism in education and legislation that I had been investigating and writing about. I saw that MRFF was addressing these issues as they related to the military in a targeted and extremely effective way. From that point on I knew I had found a place where I could make a difference. Within a month, I was working fulltime for MRFF."

For Rodda, that work has been a combination of conspicuous rewards and occasional frustration. "I like to think of us as the 'Little Foundation That Could,'" she quips. "We attempt to do things that other, much larger and better funded organizations wouldn't dare to try. That's primarily a result of the intense focus we put on the military. There are all kinds of constitutional issues being addressed by all kinds of concerned groups. We have the benefit of zeroing in on this one area of fundamentalist overreach. But by the same token, every time some abuse is brought to our attention, it seems like there are a dozen more just like it that we don't have the resources to address. The sheer magnitude of what we're facing requires us to pick our battles very carefully. I think we all look forward to the time when we can better handle the sheer volume of cases and clients that come our way."

As part of her multi-tasking role at MRFF, Rodda helps to evaluate the calls and emails that flood in on a daily basis. Additionally, as MRFF's Senior Research Director, she oversees a phalanx of foundation volunteers who regularly supply her with raw data on the most current fundamentalist abuses within the armed services. One of these is Mark Freedman, who has singlehandedly undertaken the monitoring of scores of military installation websites, newsletters and email traffic in search of the unconstitutional use of government resources to promote sectarian religious views. A quick sampling of his most recent finds suffices to sum up the prevalence of such abuses. Blatant proselytizing, on-line sermons, exhortations to prayer and excoriations of heathens have been discovered in official communications from such far flung locales as Moody, Keesler and Dover Air Force bases; the U.S. Air Force YouTube Channel; U.S Marine headquarters at Quantico, Virginia; Fort Hood, Texas, where anti-Muslim sentiment runs high; and even the naval base on the tiny Indian Ocean island of Diego Garcia. In early spring of 2011, the installation's electronic newspaper ran an article titled, "Our True Home" by Chaplain Robert Spencer, which asked its active duty readers, "So what about you? Will you accept your true home in heaven? Do you have questions or concerns about this? The chaplains at Diego Garcia will help you with these choices that all of us will eventually have to make."

"Compiling and collating the kind of information that Mark and others provide on a consistent basis is essential," maintains Mikey. "There may never be a war crimes trial to prosecute these acts that by any definition must be considered treasonous, but if there is, we'll be ready, with a mountain of evidence."

Aside from Rodda, the other staffers on the MRFF payroll include an Administrative Director. "We run lean and mean," Weinstein explains. "We have to. We receive anywhere from a hundred to several hundred calls and emails from potential clients on any given week. We can have as many as a half dozen legal proceedings underway simultaneously. I travel extensively around the country, giving talks to any number of organizations and groups of concerned citizens. We have to watch every dime and, when we don't have a dime, then we reach into our own pockets."

It's a contention borne out by the Weinstein's own, sometimes tenuous, financial circumstances. "I don't have the benefit of a pension or retirement pay," Mikey reveals. "Along with everything else imaginable, I've often been accused of operating the Foundation for personal gain." He laughs. "It's fucking absurd. There have been many months when I've forgone a salary or any sort of compensation in order to keep this operation moving forward. I can think of a lot easier ways to get rich then to run a non-profit organization dedicated to exposing well-funded Christian fundamentalists. As much as money is needed to fight this war, it's never been about getting rich, or even making a living wage. We do what we do because we have to. Fortunately, there are a lot of dedicated volunteers and individuals who donate on a regular basis."

And without question, the Foundation's most dedicated volunteer is Bonnie Weinstein. While technically on the Foundation staff, Bonnie receives no pay whatsoever for the extraordinary contributions she tirelessly makes to the cause. "I saw the need," she says, with simple clarity, "and stepped in."

Those steps included everything from lending her practiced artistic eye to the MRFF's state-of-the-art website design to initiating and overseeing the Foundation's extensive network of community volunteers. "The military is one enormous society made up of thousands of smaller communities," she explains. "They are scattered across the world in bases and installations, forts and frontlines everywhere. While each is hopefully connected to the larger mission of the entire armed services, they also each have their own special circumstances and conditions to deal with. As the Foundation began to grow, I saw the need to have volunteer representative in place, to give us a clearer idea of what was happening on a local level. They have become our eyes and ears on the ground and it's hard to imagine how we could do our work without them."

But even as Bonnie took on the enormous responsibility of creating this community volunteer network, she was also alert to the smaller, and more nuanced, touches that would serve to personalize the Foundation's work. "Mikey deals day in and day out with hurt, angry, abused and confused people," she explains. "Sometimes the best he can do in the moment is to provide a comforting voice on the phone or offer advice and counsel in an email or a text message. I wanted to find a way to make our care and concern tangible. That's how I came up with the challenge coins."

The concept of challenge coins is a venerable one in military history and the most common tale told of their origin reaches back to the Army Air Corps, the precursor to the Air Force. According to the legend, a World War I fighter ace had a small medallion struck to hand out to his fellow pilots as a memento of their service together in the squadron. One of these airmen was subsequently shot down and captured by the Germans. He escaped, only to fall into the hands of French partisans who mistook him for an enemy saboteur. The only means he had to prove his identity was the small coin he carried with him.

From there a proud tradition grew that any member of any military unit could challenge a fellow soldier to prove membership in his or her own unit by producing a coin emblazoned with the appropriate insignia or emblem. Most often, the challenge is initiated when a challenger pulls out his or her coin and slaps it down, usually on a barroom table. Anyone being challenged must immediately produce the coin for their organization and if they fail to do so, they must buy a round of drinks for the challenger and everyone else who has shown their challenge coin. Should everyone challenged be able to produce their coin, then it's the challenger who must pick up the tab on the next round of drinks.

"It's an old and very cherished custom within every branch of the armed forces," Bonnie explains. "It carries a great deal of symbolic weight. For instance, President Obama placed challenge coins on the memorials of the soldiers slain in the Fort Hood shooting. This is a time-honored way to identify your friends and allies. My simple idea was to take that tradition and extend it to the friends and allies of the Foundation."

To that end, Bonnie created and had manufactured a stunning penta-gon-shaped cloisonné challenge coin decorated with the stars and stripes motif of the MRFF, with the reverse side displaying a stylized silver Ameri-can eagle. "As a result of what is happening in the military, with all the abuses we're fighting against," she continues, "sometimes it's hard to know who your friends are, even when they're in uniform. The MRFF challenge coin is a way for us to identify each other, to acknowledge and affirm what we believe in and the common love for the Constitution we share. In the grand scheme of things, it may be a small gesture, but to the thousands of service men and women who carry them close to their heart, it can mean a lot. There's a sense of solidarity that comes from fighting the good fight. We express it any way we can."

That expression took on powerful and poignant significance when an MRFF client, known only by his call sign, Marine Wolf Redjack 25 was grievously wounded in an Afghan firefight. Flown back to a Department of Defense facility stateside, he lingered between life and death for several months before finally succumbing to his wounds. One of his last acts was to hand his grieving parents his MRFF challenge coin, around which Marine Wolf Redjack 25 had wrapped a copy of his oath of enlistment.

As the reach and reputation of the Military Religious Freedom continued to expand, a remarkable roster of committed individuals from all walks of life stepped forward to lend their support to the Foundation's fierce struggle against fundamentalist encroachment in the armed services.

Along with such instrumental founding members of the MRFF Board of Directors and advisory team as Ambassador Joseph C. Wilson IV; author and Middle East expert Resa Aslan; attorney Pedro L. Irigonegaray; Yale Professor Kristen J. Leslie; and retired U.S. Air Force Captain Reverend MeLinda Morton, a crop of new and uniformly distinguished partners have joined the fray. Notable among them are many current and former military officers, dismayed at the de facto coup that is underway in their beloved respective branches of the armed services. The list reads like a Who's Who of decorated, esteemed and influential officers.

Included are United States Air Force PhD Lieutenant Colonel Edith A. Disler, former ICBM crewmember, arms control inspector, Associate Professor of English at the Air Force Academy and author of *Language & Gender in the Military*; retired Senior NCO Glen Doherty, former Navy SEAL and one time security and intelligence specialist for U.S. Government agencies in high threat regions including Iraq, Pakistan, and Afghanistan; retired Air Force Brigadier General Robert S. Dotson, veteran of one hundred and twenty-eight combat missions and author of *The Light on the Star*; retired Marine Corps First Lieutenant Bobby Muller, President of Veterans for America, cofounder of the International Campaign to Ban Landmines which was the recipient of the 1997 Nobel Peace Prize; retired U.S. Army Colonel George Reed, former Director of Command and Leadership Studies at the U.S. Army War College; retired U.S. Air Force Major General David J. Scott, former Director of Operational Capability Requirements and one time Deputy Chief of Staff, Operations, Plans, & Requirements and thirty-eight year Air Force veteran, retired Brigadier General Tony Verrengia.

Another conspicuous addition to the MRFF military advisory line-up is retired Lieutenant Colonel John Whiteside, who flew F-4 Phantom and A-4 Skyhawk aircraft for the Marines until he stepped down from active duty. In 1990, he was recalled to the Air National Guard, completed fifty-two missions with Operation Desert Storm, and was awarded the Distinguished Flying Cross for heroism in combat.

"It's an honor to be working with all the men and women," Weinstein remarks. "Airmen like John Whiteside are what the MRFF is all about. For many years he served his country with honor and distinction, only to see its cherished principles disgraced by fundamentalists hiding behind the uniform he so proudly wore. His determination to put a stop to this fucking outrage, which he shares with all the rest of these distinguished colleagues, is the fuel that keeps the Foundation running."

For every military man and woman who has courageously stepped forward, there were others who work anonymously behind the scene with quiet determination and focused attention to detail, to help win the Foundation's fight for constitutional protections. "I call them my moles," Mikey explains. "Many of them are of the highest rank, right there in the seat of fundamentalist Christian power, the Pentagon, trying to effect change when and where they can. We've mutually agreed to keep their identities a secret, not only to protect them, but to better enable the actions they take on behalf of MRFF clients."

One such "mole" is an Air Force officer who was a classmate of Weinstein's at the Air Force Academy and who has remained in close contact with him over the intervening three decades. "I stay under the radar as much as possible," this top commander reveals. "That way, when Mikey comes to me with the concerns of his clients, I can formulate a swift response without running into a lot of interference from those who are resisting the reforms he and the Foundation are trying to bring about."

According to this unnamed ally, much of the problem of fundamentalist Christian incursion, both within the Pentagon and elsewhere in the armed service's sprawling structure, springs from a deplorable lack of leadership. "No one in the military has the right to push any one religious brand over another," he affirms. "That's a no-brainer. The problem comes when commanders delegate the responsibility of fostering and maintaining religious plurality to chaplains and others who are supposedly delegated to oversee the spiritual well-being of the troops. That creates a lot of confusion and cross-purpose and allows for those who have no business making those decisions to move into what is essentially an authority vacuum. If clear and unambiguous orders were issued from the top there would be no room for such ambiguities. Everyone would know where they stood and, if they weren't standing there, it would tantamount to disobeying a direct order."

Over several years, this MRFF mole has had wide experience in quietly and effectively dealing with the abuses and excesses Weinstein brings to his attention. "I know it's in the best interest of the Foundation's work for Mikey to shout loudly from the rooftops about this breakdown in authority," he continues. "But in the midst of all the controversy generated, he and I can also work together to quietly bring about resolution for the individual client who has had his or her rights violated. Of necessity Mikey has to employ the heavy artillery. I'm more of a sniper, taking my shots carefully, one at a time. Both approaches have their advantages in getting the job done, but I'm also certain that neither one of us would be as effective as we might be without the other's efforts."

But the clarion call sounded by the Military Religious Freedom Foundation echoes far beyond the realms of America's armed services community.

A truly encyclopedic array of civilians from across the cultural spectrum also freely gives their time, energy and resources to the burgeoning, but often beleaguered, organization.

One such is Leah Burton, a multi-generational Alaskan and author of the highly anticipated new book, *God, Guns & Greed: A Dangerous Path for America.* Burton worked for many years as a lobbyist, fighting for the interests of families and children before becoming one of the country's foremost experts on Christian dominionism in American politics. Burton has focused particularly on what is known as Dominionism, a crypto-theological political and social agenda that's working to put Christians in control by scaling what they call the Seven Mountains of culture. They seek to take over the seven elements that shape and control our culture: business, government, media, arts and entertainment, education, family and religion.

"You can add to that list, of course, the military," says the engaging and articulate Burton in a voice that betrays just a hint of her rough-hewn wilderness heritage. "In a way that's the most pivotal 'mountain' of them all which is why I felt it was so important, and such an honor, to serve on the Board of Directors for the Military Religious Freedom Foundation. When I agreed to take on the position, I had to ask myself what I could contribute to the work Mikey and his colleagues were already doing so well."

The answer came in Burton's own abiding interest and expertise in Christian fundamentalism as it is expressed in a wider social and political spectrum. "To the degree that I've proven useful to the Foundation," she continues, "it's been in my ability to link dominionist activity within the military to the entire spectrum of American cultural life. The reality is that what Mikey has accomplished in uncovering their influence in the armed services needs to be applied to the rest of the country. The forces of fundamentalism and dominionism have crept into every corner of our society and, if I've learned anything during my tenure with the Foundation, it's that we have to attack them with the same resolve that Mikey has shown, anywhere and everywhere that we find them."

By the same token, it is Leah Burton's role as a consultant to the California Council of Churches, representing the interests of nearly two million mainline Christians, that serves to underscore the MRFF's close and abiding affiliation with legitimate and responsible Christians of every stripe.

"The simple fact," Burton asserts, "is that the overwhelming majority—ninety-six percent at last count—of the Foundation's clients are professing

Christians of one denomination or another. This directly refutes the tired claim by Mikey's opponents that he is nothing but a godless atheist intent on destroying Christianity wherever he finds it."

It's a point underscored by the active support of such significant MRFF partners as Joan Slish, formerly an ordained Assistant Minister for the hard-core fundamentalist Assemblies of God denomination. Like Burton, Slish has conducted extensive research into Christian dominionism, as manifest in its infestation of mainline churches in America. She collaborates closely with a nationwide network of experts, working to expose the fundamentally unchristian practices perpetrated by this sect and providing firsthand eyewitness insights as one of the rare "walkaways" from the secretive sect.

The investigative work of Burton and Slish is amplified by the impassioned advocacy of Elizabeth Sholes, an executive for IMPACT, the legislative advocacy sister organization of the California Council of Churches. "The abuses that Mikey Weinstein and the Military Religious Freedom Foundation have uncovered and documented are nothing short of appalling," she asserts with a tone of quietly controlled indignation. "Freedom of conscience in this country is absolute and non-negotiable. The extent to which it is being actively undermined in the military and elsewhere is deeply disturbing. Mikey's call to action is one that every citizen should respond to."

Those responding, according to Sholes, include virtually the entire membership of the California Council of Churches IMPACT. "When IMPACT announced our active support of MRFF," she recounts, "we had the overwhelming support of the organization and its member churches." She smiles before adding, "Well, there might have been one cranky person, but out of a million and half strong, that's not too bad."

Christians committed to reclaiming their faith from the extremist fringe comprise a powerful segment of both MRFF's board and advisory board members. But it doesn't stop there. An expansive array of partners from a dizzying span of professions and disciplines lends the Foundation enormous credibility and in-depth expertise. Among the notable figures who have added their names to this remarkable roster are former Publisher & CEO of *Los Angeles Times*, Richard T. Schlosberg III; former Colorado Governor, Richard Douglas Lamm; Chairman of the Board of the Institute on Religion & Public Policy, Joseph K. Grieboski; Associate Professor of Political Science at the New School, Mala Htun; and renowned actor and progressive powerhouse, Mike Farrell, whose other responsibilities include Chairmanship of the Board for Death Penalty Focus, Co-Chair Emeritus for the California Committee of Human Rights Watch and Good Will Ambassador for the United Nations High Commissioner for Refugees.

Another key participant in the MRFF's network of support is William B. Wiener, Jr., former Chairman of the Secretary of Interior's Advisory Board on National Parks & Monuments under both president Reagan & Carter. An authentic renaissance man, Wiener studied both physics and architecture at Cornell University. After graduating with honors, he joined an underwater archeological dig off the coast of Turkey co-sponsored by the University of Pennsylvania and *National Geographic*. It was a multicultural experience that reinforced his belief of diversity and respect for other cultures, which, in turn, sparked an abiding interest in and support of organizations dedicated to the separation of church and state. It was a commitment that would eventually garner him a Freedom Award from the Louisiana American Civil Liberties Union.

But Bill Wiener's passion for human rights reaches even further back, to the searing childhood experience of seeing a friend of his grandmother's with Nazi concentration camp numbers tattooed on her arm. He asked his grandmother what that was and she revealed to him the horrific story of the Nazi atrocities. At that moment, he determined that he would work to see that history would not repeat itself. He has been good to his word ever since.

A large part of fulfilling that fervent childhood promise has been realized though his support of MRFF. "My connection with the Foundation goes back to its early days," explains Wiener, whose soft-spoken demeanor belies a steely conviction. "I read about its work online and gave Mikey a call. He didn't know me and was, rightfully I think, a bit wary of a stranger calling from out of the blue with an offer of support. So we both did a bit of due diligence, checking each other out, and discovered that we cared deeply about the same thing. It was the beginning of a long and close association.

"I think the single most important distinction between the MRFF and other organizations dealing with the civil liberties issues is results," Wiener continues. "There are a lot of good mission statements out there but not enough happens after that. Mikey has a long list of concrete achievements that speak for themselves. He has been able to bring so many constitutional and ethical violations within the military to widespread public attention and the reason he can do what others can't is because of the legitimacy he brings to this battle. There is simply no one with better credentials. His military record is impeccable; his father and his children have all served their country in uniform; he has worked in the West Wing of the White House and as a Judge Advocate General he knows this world, inside out. And that makes him extremely effective, both in discovering and confronting abuses, as well as putting out the call for others to take a stand."

And there have been many who have responded to the call of conscience from the widest possible range of interests and avocations. Sam Fairchild is the founder of Chiapas Organic Farms, the landmark agricultural organization employing thousands of farmers in Mexico. Hali Jilani is an ethnic Afghan who works with the U.S. Marine Corps, U.S. Army and NATO on counter terrorism, cultural intelligence and international affairs. Smita Singh is a Special Advisor & Director of the Global Development Program at the William & Flora Hewlett Foundation, where she is currently developing new philanthropic programs addressing major global development challenges. Vyckie Garrison is an escapee of the oppressive and surreptitious fundamentalist Christian cult, Quiverfull, and an invaluable resource into the deceptions and dangers of the philosophy and lifestyle Quiverfull and other closely aligned cults.

Naturally, given the Foundation's intense media exposure, the advice and counsel of experienced public relations experts is vital. Standing at the forefront of the media barricades for the MRFF is Haley & Associates, a highly regarded California-based company spearheaded by Charles "Butch" Haley, a close friend of Mikey's since high school.

"There is no way we could do what we do without Butch and his team," Mikey explains. "They are an indispensible combinations of Fort Knox, Grand Central Station and the Library at Alexandria. Their expertise is awe-inspiring and their commitment to our cause is a constant source of inspiration and motivation to us."

Also providing invaluable guidance is former Republican gubernatorial candidate form New Mexico, Douglas Turner, Founder & President of DW Turner, Inc., a strategic communications and public issues management firm headquartered in the Foundation's New Mexico home base. Another advisory board stalwart is Howard Bragman, founder of Fifteen Minutes, another accomplished strategic media and public relations agency.

Given MRFF's necessary emphasis on legal action to protect against unconstitutional encroachment, attorneys, constitutional scholars and experienced litigators also play a key role in the Foundation's ongoing work. Aside from such outstanding advisory board members as John J. Michels, Jr., a senior partner at a respected Chicago-based international law firm, the Foundation's groundbreaking work has served as a magnet for others in the legal professions committed to safeguarding constitutional rights and who have offered their services pro bono. Among them is outstanding attorney Randal Mathis, from the Dallas firm of Mathis, Donheiser & Jeter, who has done pro bono work for the Foundation since 2009. "I've lived in Dallas my whole life," the affable Mathis explains. "It's an area sometimes referred to as the buckle of the Bible Belt. What I've come to learn is that the reality of religious extremism, in all spheres of public life, is a serious concern. For example, my wife Rebekah and I have been involved in mental health causes and fundraising for many years. Now, according to a lot of fundamentalist Christians, there's no such thing as mental illness. Whoever is having a problem just needs to get right with God. That kind of thinking is responsible for a lot of suffering for very vulnerable members of our society. The sort of work that Mikey is doing in the military could serve as a template for other areas where there is undue religious influence. I see him as a trailblazer and whatever legal assistance I can lend is part of my responsibility as an American citizen."

It's a sentiment shared by such respected legal minds as Robert V. Eye, a Topeka, Kansas attorney specializing in constitutional and environmental law, and Caroline Mitchell of the prestigious and internationally renowned San Francisco firm of Jones Day, well known for its prisoners' rights and immigration reform work. "It's our firm belief that the first amendment needs vigorous protection in order to ensure its continued vitality," Mitchell explains. "The Military Religious Freedom Foundation has had a significant impact in this regard, despite the fact that the military establishment hasn't made it easy for MRFF to affect change. The need for aggressive and tenacious legal representation is even greater because military personnel who decide to assert their rights have exhausted every administration remedy available before a courtroom's doors will be open to them. That means MRFF, its lawyers, and its clients have to be in it for the long haul. It's challenging but that's true of any worthwhile effort to protect our constitutional rights."

While Weinstein has brilliantly succeeded in assembling a top-notch roster of allies, supporters and fellow combatants, the fact remains that it is he, and he alone, who remains the face of the Foundation. It is in that role that he has been tested time and again, with a courage and tenacity that has won him the admiration and respect of some of the most significant figures on the American political and cultural landscape.

It has also made him, along with his family, the prime target for enemies of freedom everywhere.

CHAPTER NINE

STRANGERS AMONG US

In late March of 2011, the Senate Committee on the Judiciary convened a hearing under the auspices of the Subcommittee on the Constitution, Civil Rights and Human Rights to examine the issue of "Protecting the Civil Rights of Muslims."

It was a subject that had grown exponentially in importance and urgency in the nearly ten years since the attack by Muslim fanatics on the World Trade Center's twin towers. In the aftermath of the deadliest terrorist assault in American history, the country had gone to war on two fronts, halfway across the world; first in Afghanistan and then in Iraq. The expenditure of blood and treasure had been staggering by any measure, as had the deep divisions that rent the country, as the rationale for the double conflicts came in for increasingly intense and agonized questioning.

What had seemed so obvious and apparent a goal in the follow-up to 9/11—finding and bringing to justice those who had been responsible for the heinous attack—had become progressively more obscured and compromised. An increasingly war-weary citizenry witnessed the descent into what seemed like another Vietnam-style quagmire. Global *realpolitck* and the ineluctable economics of oil seemed to replace righteous indignation over the attacks. As a nation we began to lose sight of the primary motivation for America's stalemated incursions into countries that made no secret of their contempt for our values and principles. Our thirst for vengeance may not have been noble, but it had the virtue of clarity. That clarity drained away as the wars dragged and our brave soldiers increasingly arrived home in body bags.

116

But aside from frustration and cynicism there were other forces at work on the American psyche as well during that dark decade after 9/11. A myriad of voices were raised, some thoughtful, others hysterical, that cast the ruinous wars in the starkest possible terms, as nothing less than an historical clash of civilizations, a battle to the death between opposing cultures for ultimate supremacy in the 21st Century.

What was implied by such assertions was made explicit by those who cast them in terms of an apocalyptic, winner-take-all conflict between Christianity and Islam. The war between these two faiths had, after all, been raging unabated for over a millennium. The enmity between the followers of Jesus and those of Mohammad had, if anything, grown fiercer in the centuries since they first collided. September 11, 2001 was a clear victory for those whose spiritual beliefs were manifestly at odds with the Christian west. According to an increasingly strident segment of the population, it was the duty of America, as the last bastion of Christian virtue, to once again take up the Crusader's banner and strike at the heart of an alien faith.

But much had changed since the era of armored knights rallying the peasant rabble to sally forth and smite the turbaned infidel. The infidel was now in our midst, as Muslims from around the world has flocked to America precisely because of its promise of tolerance for any faith, enshrined by the Constitution and protected by law. Adherents of Islam, arriving hungry for liberty and economic opportunity, laid claim to those protections, just as they earnestly pursued the American Dream. But even as they settled in their adopted home in increasing numbers, demands for cultural exclusion and expulsion grew deafening and naked, sectarian violence increased. Since 9/11 over eight hundred incidents of attacks, threats, and vandalism against Muslims had been reported to law enforcement authorities.

The escalating tension caused by the presence of Muslims among America's predominantly Christian polity called into question the basic tenets of equality, pluralism and tolerance on which the country was founded. The fact that the Senate Judiciary Committee felt the need to take testimony on the topic of "Protecting the Civil Rights of Muslims" only served to underscore the point.

But the hearings, chaired by Illinois Senator Richard Durban, told only part of the story. The other part had been laid out in no uncertain terms only a few weeks earlier, in the same august forums of Capital Hill, when New York Congressman Peter King convened his own hearing, purporting to investigate the prevalence of homegrown terrorists living among us on American soil. Dubbed by *The Washington Post* as "a key moment in one of America's angriest conversations," the King hearing was roundly criticized for adding fuel to the fire of Muslim mistrust and suspicion, which might also well have been one of America's worst kept secrets. The newspaper cited a recent poll in which over 30% of Americans agreed with the statement that mainstream Islam "encourages violence."

But however inflammatory King's grandstanding may have been, the mere fact that he had been able to convene such a hearing pointed to an uncomfortable truth of modern American life: the growing stain of virulent religious hatred directed at a vulnerable minority. It was a hatred that had only become more acute in the wake of widespread public furor at the prospect of a mosque being built near the sight of Ground Zero. The controversy had built on the enmity and anger that had been engendered against Islam in the aftermath of a bloody rampage by Major Nidal Malik Hasan, a deranged Muslim extremist and U.S. Army psychiatrist who gunned down thirteen people and wounded twenty-nine others in Fort Hood, Texas on November 5, 2009.

It was against this highly charged backdrop that the Judiciary Subcommittee hearings took place on March 28, 2011. From the beginning, Senator Durban took pains to distance the proceedings from King's previous media circus.

"Some have even questioned the premise of today's hearing," the Senator remarked in his opening statement, "That we should protect the civil rights of American Muslims. Such inflammatory speech from prominent public figures creates a fertile climate for discrimination. It's not surprising the Anti-Defamation League says we face an 'intensified level of anti-Muslim bigotry.'"

If he was attempting to diffuse the controversy, the effort fell conspicuously short of the mark. The topic was simply too explosive. "I'm a bit perplexed by the focus of today's hearing," sniffed Republican Arizona Senator John Kyl. "If we're concerned about the most egregious religious hate crimes, then I wonder why we're not talking about crimes against Jews and Christians."

It was the quintessential distinction without a difference. The fact was that, regardless of which creed was ostensibly being persecuted, the atmosphere of religious intolerance in America had long since reached toxic levels. Animosity between Christians and Muslims, believers and non-believers, even between denominations within a single confession of faith, spoke to a new inquisitional mentality threatening the nation's essential consensus. To all intents and purposes, the United States was entering its own version of the Dark Ages, a time when men would willingly, even eagerly, condemn, ostracize and even put to death their fellow citizens for praying to the wrong god.

On behalf of the MRFF, Mikey Weinstein had been called to testify in writing before the committee primarily because of his firsthand knowledge of entrenched religious intolerance within all the branches of the armed services. His insight was especially valuable given the steadily increasing numbers of Muslims who had joined the military in recent years. But it was Weinstein's wide-ranging knowledge of the motives and methods of fundamentalist Christian extremists that made him an especially insightful witness.

The Military Religious Freedom Foundation, Weinstein informed the committee members, represented over two hundred and fifty Muslim Americans serving in the armed forces. It was a client caseload, he revealed, that had "dramatically increased immediately after the tragic shootings at Fort Hood."

Weinstein, as was his habit, did not mince words in his testimony to the committee. With a practiced rhetorical flair that matched his outsized personality, he asserted that "the enormity of civil rights abuses against Muslim American U.S. military members can best be described as grievously systemic and perversely and perniciously profound throughout the United States armed forces...anti-Muslim prejudice and discrimination is inextricably intertwined into the very DNA of today's American military." Muslim soldiers, sailors, marines and airmen, he went on, are subject to "abject pain, suffering, degradation, dehumanization and marginalization."

Moving from his blistering overview to harrowing specificity, Weinstein described the "unrestricted and widespread use by military officers and enlisted personnel of the derogatory and racist terms 'towel head,' 'rag head,' 'camel jockey,' or the most universally used term of 'haji' to describe their Muslim American colleagues in uniform." In formal military training exercises, he continued, "Muslim American members are often reminded that 'the enemy' in the War on Terror is Islam as an entire religion and, accordingly, that any of its adherents and followers are seriously suspect...

Muslim American military members have been told repeatedly that they have no place in America's military because of their faith…they cannot and will not be allowed into the otherwise impenetrable brotherhood and sisterhood of trust and loyalty of their respective military organizations."

It was a damning indictment, but Weinstein was just getting warmed up. As the Senators read on with increasing dismay and discomfort, he detailed a litany of criminal and unconstitutional abuses suffered by followers of Islam within the U.S. military. "They have been unjustly denied leave time," he wrote, ticking off the list of well-documented outrages. "They have been unjustly discarded in the military's health care system. They have been unlawfully detained and falsely accused of vile crimes and offenses of moral turpitude. They have been innocent and helpless victims of scurrilous rumors and ruinous innuendo. They have been unjustly ordered to perform odious and remedial military tasks and chores. They and their loving families have been derided as exemplifying 'the enemy among us.' They and their families have been assaulted and abused both stateside and aboard. They and their families have endured hurtful and humiliating taunts and threats, delivered in the middle of the dark night and in the bright sun of daylight, both overt and indirectly nuanced. They and their families have been accused of not being 'real Americans' and told they are not remotely welcomed in America. They and their families have been told to 'go back to your Arab lands.'"

Weinstein then proceeded to drill down on individual cases to give a human face to the evils he was describing. Among the foundation's Muslim clients, he revealed to the committee members, was an honored graduate of one of America's most prestigious military academies who had served multiple combat tours in both Iraq and Afghanistan. For his exemplary courage in battle he had received a Purple Heart as well as both Silver and Bronze stars.

But when it came to the widespread belief that the U.S. was engaged in a crusade against Islam, none of those achievements served to mitigate the persecution suffered by individuals, who remained unnamed to protect him from further harassment. Weinstein went on to tell of the systemic bullying that his client's children were subjected to at the elementary school of the base where he was stationed and where constant attempts at proselytizing were undertaken to "save their soul from the evils of Islam and Allah." In further heartbreaking detail he described how his client's wife was spat on

Mikey Weinstein, 2011 (Mark Garber)

Sandia Mountains, Albuquerque, New Mexico, 2011 (Bonnie Weinstein)

Laurel Loop, Albuquerque, New Mexico, 2011 (Bonnie Weinstein)

Sandia Mountains, Albuquerque, New Mexico, 2011 (Bonnie Weinstein)

Sandia Mountains, Albuquerque, New Mexico, 2011 (Bonnie Weinstein)

The Weinstein Family, 2011: Amanda, Casey, Mikey, Bonnie, Curtis, Amber (Mark Garber)

Mikey and Bonnie Weinstein, 2011 (Mark Garber)

Enabled by Christ's "A Store for the Christian Man," located at the base exchange at Malmstrom Air Force Base in 2007, sending overtly Christian messages to all shoppers via its window displays, such as the large item in the second window, which said, "The Gospel, the power of God for salvation to everyone who believes"

Photo sent to MRFF by a soldier in 2007, showing Ann Coulter's quote, "We should invade their countries, kill their leaders, and convert them to Christianity," hanging on an office door in a Military Police building at Fort Riley.

Mikey standing in front of the FUEL Ministry sign on the side of a chapel at Wright-Patterson Air Force Base, placed where it was unavoidable to any airman going to the commissary, base exchange, credit union, bowling alley, or pharmacy, and sent an inescapable daily message to "Accelerate Your Christian Journey" to the base's enlisted airmen due to its proximity to their barracks and chow hall. Fifty-three airmen and DoD employees, forty-one of whom were Christians, came to MRFF to get the sign removed.

Army basic trainees at Fort Jackson in a Campus Crusade for Christ Military Ministry "God's Basic Training" class, where young soldiers are taught that, according to the Bible, "The Military = 'God's Ministers,'" and that they had a responsibility "to punish those who do evil" as "God's servant, an angel of wrath." Group photos of the basic trainees in uniform, posed holding up their rifles and Bibles, were posted on a Campus Crusade website. MRFF got these photos removed from the internet.

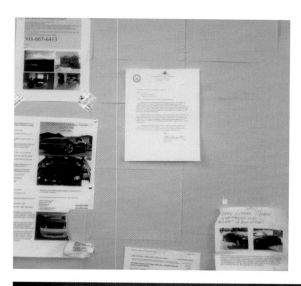

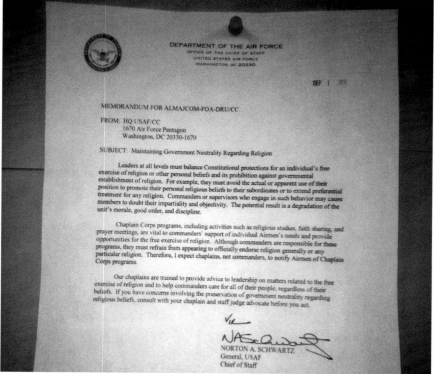

DEPARTMENT OF THE AIR FORCE
OFFICE OF THE CHIEF OF STAFF
UNITED STATES AIR FORCE
WASHINGTON DC 20330

SEP 1 2011

MEMORANDUM FOR ALMAJCOM-FOA-DRU/CC

FROM: HQ USAF/CC
1670 Air Force Pentagon
Washington, DC 20330-1670

SUBJECT: Maintaining Government Neutrality Regarding Religion

Leaders at all levels must balance Constitutional protections for an individual's free exercise of religion or other personal beliefs and its prohibition against governmental establishment of religion. For example, they must avoid the actual or apparent use of their position to promote their personal religious beliefs to their subordinates or to extend preferential treatment for any religion. Commanders or supervisors who engage in such behavior may cause members to doubt their impartiality and objectivity. The potential result is a degradation of the unit's morale, good order, and discipline.

Chaplain Corps programs, including activities such as religious studies, faith sharing, and prayer meetings, are vital to commanders' support of individual Airmen's needs and provide opportunities for the free exercise of religion. Although commanders are responsible for these programs, they must refrain from appearing to officially endorse religion generally or any particular religion. Therefore, I expect chaplains, not commanders, to notify Airmen of Chaplain Corps programs.

Our chaplains are trained to provide advice to leadership on matters related to the free exercise of religion and to help commanders care for all of their people, regardless of their beliefs. If you have concerns involving the preservation of government neutrality regarding religious beliefs, consult with your chaplain and staff judge advocate before you act.

NORTON A. SCHWARTZ
General, USAF
Chief of Staff

Air Force Chief of Staff's September 2011 edict on Religious Neutrality placed on bulletin board at the Air Force Academy. One Academy cadet emailed MRFF that when they asked their cadet chain of command if they could post the Chief of Staff's memorandum on the cadet wing's bulletin board, the response they got was, "Don't go there. Whose side are you on?"

A frequent complaint from service members at numerous military installations is the sale of *The Politically Incorrect Guide to Islam* in PXs, BXs, and other on-post stores, often displayed next to *The Soldier's Bible* and other military Bibles. The author of *The Politically Incorrect Guide to Islam*, Robert Spencer, was the most frequently cited author in the anti-Muslim manifesto of Norwegian mass murderer Anders Behring Breivik. (Photos from PX at Fort Riley.)

while shopping at the base exchange and of the shame and indignation he suffered at being considered the 'go-to guy' to explain and justify any act of terrorism committed by any Muslim anywhere in the world.

The shocking and unconscionable incidents piled up as Weinstein, writing on behalf of his client, made absolutely sure the legislators knew exactly the extent of the inhuman behavior the proud Muslim-American and his family had endured while steadfastly serving their country. Perhaps most egregious was the painful realization that, in innumerable ways, he was being told that he was not "a dependable part of either his own combat unit or the entire United States military because of the fatal flaw of being a 'suspicious Muslim.'" Equally devastating was what Weinstein termed "the ruthless indoctrination…that America's military is a Christian military and that its greatest enemy is Islam." Adding insult to injury were the constant direct and indirect attempts at proselytizing by "fundamentalist Christian military chaplains and equally fundamentalist Christians in the direct chain of military command."

It was at that point, just when the accumulated weight of indictment and incident seemed almost unbearable, that Weinstein bore down on the calamitous implications of his hard-hitting testimony. "Please understand," he urged the Senators, "that the dire consequences of the rampant and universal civil rights abuses against Muslim Americans in the United States military cannot adequately be described as merely a 'problem' or an 'issue' or a 'challenge.' It is nothing less than a full-fledged national security threat. There are three acutely relevant reasons why: (1) its well known existence enrages our Islamic allies both abroad and domestically; (2) it incalculably emboldens our Islamic enemies both aboard and domestically; and (3) it absolutely demoralizes our own troops and, thus, is a fatally divisive and metastasizing malignancy to the necessity and imperative of good order and discipline in the United States armed forces."

In the end, the Senate Committee on the Judiciary's Subcommittee on the Constitution, Civil Rights and Human Rights hearing on Protecting the Civil Rights of Muslims went the way of most government exercises in futility: a studiously even-handed and ultimately innocuous report was duly submitted and filed away in some subbasement of the congressional archives. Mikey Weinstein's impassioned testimony might well have been buried with it, except for the fact that his words have continued to have real world relevance in the conduct of American military policy, both at home and abroad. Simply put, he would not be silenced.

Yet regardless of the ineffectual response to Weinstein's testimony, his words did resonate to those in whose defense he had passionately spoken. "Everything you said is on point," read the email of a Lieutenant Colonel in the U.S. Army Reserves, who had requested anonymity for fear of reprisal. "We Muslims can't seem to be heard or given our day to be understood. It is though we are in a virtual concentration camp and the government has all the controls because we can turn bad in a moment. The laws are against us, people are afraid to go to jail and be lost forever, so they stay silent. We in the military walk on high-tension wires. Thanks for what you do on behalf of the voiceless."

Mikey's voice in the wilderness of religious repression would soon be raised again in defense of Muslims within the military, a vulnerable minority who were increasingly targeted for an especially vicious strain of sectarian persecution.

The victims this time were two soft-spoken and circumspect Moroccan immigrants, Khalid Lyaacoubi and Yassine Bahammou, who had come to America from their impoverished and repressive North African nation seeking freedom and opportunity. In 2009, hoping to serve their adopted homeland, they had both enlisted in the Army, as part of a program dubbed "09 Lima" that sought out Arabic, Dari and Pashto-speaking interpreters. In exchange for their service they were offered such incentives as higher rank, bonuses and an accelerated path to American citizenship.

There was, at the time, a crying need for such linguistic skills within the military. An "09 Lima" promotional video touted the program for its potential to "save both American and local lives," and having Muslims in uniform was seen as a effective means of countering Al Qaeda claims that America was at war with Islam. Army Chief of Staff, General George W. Casey, among others, was a vocal supporter of Muslim troops serving on the frontlines.

Khalid and Yassine were part of a group of five Middle Eastern immigrants who were slated for active duty in Iraq and Afghanistan, considered one of the highest risk assignments in these active war zones. But it was more than just professional and financial considerations that motivated the eager young men. "The United States is known for fighting for other people's freedoms," explained Yassine Bahammou. "I like it and I wanted to help do that."

All of the recruits were similarly determined to integrate themselves into the fabric of their adopted land's customs and traditions. "We wanted to prove to Arabic nations," Khalid Lyaacoubi asserted, "that we were Arabic and that we lived with Americans and socialized with Americans and that we know that they are good."

It didn't work out that way. The group completed basic training at Fort Jackson, South Carolina, an experience they unanimously remembered as a proud step toward fulfilling their goal of service to their new country. The next stage of their instruction entailed a specialized translator's course at the Advanced Individual Training School on the grounds of Fort Jackson. But it wasn't long before the bright promise of their fledgling careers in the armed forces turned into a living nightmare.

The turning point came suddenly and unexpectedly, in the aftermath of the November, 2009 massacre at Fort Hood, Texas, by Major Nidal Malik Hassan. In the outraged aftermath of the attack, the Army's attitude toward the five young immigrants, poised for dangerous deployment on behalf of America's War on Terror, turned suddenly and comprehensively hostile. In an echo of Weinstein's Senate testimony on behalf of his unnamed Muslim client, both Yassine and Khalid recounts numerous incidents of harassment by their fellow soldiers, including being taunted as "terrorists" and "hajis," behind their backs and, eventually, to their faces. The insults escalated. The trainees were regularly referred to as "garbage" and had their bunkrooms savagely ransacked.

But it was about to get worse…unimaginably worse. Within weeks of the Fort Hood tragedy, the Army Criminal Investigation Division summarily arrested Yassine, Khalid and their three colleagues. The absurd charge of conspiring to poison other soldiers at the facility. Yet, as quickly and forcefully as CID swept in to foil this alleged plot, which would grow to include vague insinuations of larceny, mutiny, and conspiracy, they moved with considerably less alacrity when it came to formally charging the Muslim suspects.

For forty-five agonizing days, the five men were confined to their barracks and put under a twenty-four hour armed guard, watched over even when they went to the latrine. As part of this blatantly illegal treatment, they were forbidden from speaking Arabic either to each other or to friends or family members who reached out by telephone in a vain attempt to find out what was happening to the unjustly accused men. Brutal threats and harassment escalated during their long confinement. Their guards told them that they were going to be packed off to Guantanamo and a CID officer threatened to send one of the men back to Morocco "in a box." "'The United States is in a war against Islam and you are a Muslim,'" Kahlid remembers another CID operative telling him. "They were treating us as terrorists."

The treatment continued unabated, despite the fact that the CID had absolutely no evidence to support a case against the five men. As if in belated recognition of that uncomfortable reality, they were, suddenly and without explanation, released. While their nightmarish detention was over, the stigma of the ordeal they had endured would follow them, thanks in large part to irresponsible national coverage of the investigation by the Christian Broadcasting Network, an organization Weinstein characterizes as "known for its opposition to America's foundational principles of religious freedom and the separation of church and state."

Predictably, the entire incident effectively destroyed the men's promising and vitally important careers in the military. As part of a deal offered by the Army, they were sent to Washington, DC where they joined a National Guard unit, but were kept segregated and not allowed to train with their company. The fast track to U.S. citizenship came to a shrieking halt and potential job opportunities vanished once background checks revealed that they had been the subjects of an investigation looking into unwarranted allegations that they wanted to "harm other soldiers." Applying for a job as a security guard, Yassine was denied a concealed-weapons permit because he was the target of the investigation. More ominously still, they began experiencing repeated searches by Washington, DC police after being pulled over for otherwise routine traffic stops. In one outrageous incident in particular, Yassine was kept handcuffed by the side of the road for half an hour while police turned his car inside out, presumably looking for evidence of terrorist plotting.

After fruitless appeals for resolution up the Army chain of command, which even included a letter to the Commander in Chief, President Obama, Khalid Lyaacoubi and Yassine Bahammou at last reached out to the Military Religious Freedom Foundation. "We had no solution," Yassine recounts. "The Army just ignored us. We were desperate. I began looking on the internet for anyone else who might have had the same experience of being treated like criminals for their religion while serving in the military. That's how I found the MRFF. They knew what to do."

"By that time, we'd developed a very proactive approach to directly confronting the dire circumstances our clients so often found themselves in," recounts Mikey. "Yassine, Khalid and the others had already exhausted their options of appealing through established channels for a definitive resolution, not to mention restitution, for what they had suffered. The only approach left was to shame the Army by revealing the extent to which they had systematically denied these men their basic human rights." He smiles knowingly before adding, "We've gotten really expert at using the media to do that job."

Weinstein and his team wasted no time contacting major TV news and print media outlets, breaking major stories on network and cable television and on the front pages of major U.S. and international newspapers and magazines. And, as usual, Mikey was front and center in putting the details of his clients' plight into the larger context of endemic religious intolerance within the military.

"They are reminded every day in every way that they are not as good, they are not as courageous, they are not as trustworthy," he told reporters as the story spread like wildfire. "They are told they have no character, they don't have the integrity necessary to be a member of the military. This is absolutely disgraceful. It's shocking and I wish I could say that I didn't see it all the time."

But, of course, it was becoming only too common in the course of his pioneering work with the MRFF. So, too, for that matter, was the military's obfuscating response. In a feeble attempt to paper over its egregious abuses, the Army announced that it was conducting an internal review. Not surprisingly, it exonerated itself of any suggestion of racism or harassment in its handling of the Muslim soldiers, then went one step further to sweep the controversy under the rug by trying to justify its actions. While grudgingly acknowledging that the CID might have been "overly restrictive" in detaining the men incommunicado, the Army's chief spokesman, Major General Stephen R. Lanza, insisted that it had acted in accordance with the tense situation existing at the time. "To not do so—had these alleged threats turned out to be credible, and in light of the Fort Hood shooting incident that took place mere weeks before these allegations—would have been an unconscionable dereliction of duty and leadership on our part," the general sanctimoniously pronounced. As if to underscore this dubious justification, the CID turned the case over to the FBI, keeping alive the scurrilous suspicions that Yassine, Khalid and the others were, in fact, guilty of something, even if was only their Muslim faith.

"The United States is in a war against Islam and you are a Muslim," Mikey would later write, directly quoting the noxious assertion of the CID officer overseeing the imprisonment of the innocent Muslim soldiers. "These shocking and inflammatory words were addressed to honorable men eager to serve their adopted homeland. These valiant recruits had volunteered to serve as battlefield translators in the most lethal theaters of operation that the United States is contending with. However, these brave men were instead faced with a campaign of anti-Arab and Islamophobic persecution redolent of the worst periods in modern Western civilization, harkening back not only to the days of Joseph McCarthy but to the tribunals of the Spanish Inquisition. Apparently some Americans would like to turn a blind eye towards the unjust jailing of Muslims on flimsy pretexts, promoting or condoning the witch-hunt of entire communities and questioning their patriotism. At the MRFF, it is our duty and responsibility to highlight the unjust treatment of our Muslim brothers and sisters in the U.S. military as well as that of all soldiers, irrespective of religious or non-religious beliefs, shining the spotlight on this hideous campaign for all to see."

It is worth noting that Mikey, in his role as the chief strategist and guiding light of the Military Religious Freedom Foundation, exercises a keen discernment when it comes to accepting clients and selecting cases behind which to put the full weight and prestige of the organization. In late July of 2011, for example, it came to light that a Muslim solider, Jason Naser Abdo, had been charged in a bomb plot targeting the same Fort Hood facility where Nidal Hasan had launched his bloody rampage, setting off waves of anti-Islamic sentiment, two years earlier.

"Abdo had contacted MRFF for help in pressing his case for a discharge as a conscientious objector based on his religion," Mikey recounts. "We turned him down. We just never felt good about him. What we try to do requires a high degree of selectivity. We're not in the business of taking up the cause of anyone and everyone with an ax to grind against the military. There are enough real people being done real harm by religious intolerance to keep us busy for a long time. Of necessity, we've developed a rigorous screening process. From the beginning Abdo utterly failed to meet the criteria."

Despite the Foundation's highly selective criteria, however, it currently represents nearly four hundred and fifty Muslim Americans in uniform, nearly ten percent of all such men and women in the armed services.

Of course, when Weinstein chooses to defend the rights of the genuinely persecuted, he does so with a fiery eloquence and bulldog tenacity that has made him both widely respected and deeply feared. Yet Mikey also knows when to step back and let the voices of those he defends speak for themselves. The power of their words are echoed by the simple poignancy of Khalid Lyaacoubi, when asked by *The New York Times* whether his nightmarish ordeal had killed his hopes and dreams for a better life in the land of the free and the home of the brave. Was he ready now to return to Morocco?

"Why should I leave America?" Khalid replied. "I want to be here, I want to get married here. I want to die here."

His words had the ring of unintended irony. As a victim of a growing intolerance within the military establishment of their adopted country, Khalid, Yassine and the others had indeed come perilously close to perishing. Without the timely intervention of the MRFF, their place in America might well have been an unmarked grave.

CHAPTER TEN

COUNTING THE COST

It was in the nature of the work that Weinstein has undertaken with the Military Religious Freedom Foundation that he would come to grapple with some of the great issues of our time: constitutional law; freedom of expression; the role of government in the lives of citizens; the military's place in a modern secular society. Such was the mission of the MRFF and the mandate provided to it by the tens of thousands of clients that sought its counsel, protection and, often, the simple solace and solidarity that only it could provide.

But it was also the responsibility of the Foundation to treat each and every individual who reached out as, first and foremost, a human being, a real person whose real life had been felt the impact of injustice and intolerance in the context of his or her military service. "Mikey and I wanted to make sure that our clients understood that we didn't just see them as constitutional test cases," Bonnie Weinstein reveals. "These were men and women who, in various ways, had been chewed up and spit out by an institution that, too often, saw them only as defective cogs in a fucking machine. I speak from experience when I say that there is no bureaucracy like a military bureaucracy. If it comes across as a cold and uncaring organization of faceless drones behind steel desks, it's because that's what it is. A big part of what the Foundation does is allow these individual soldiers, sailors, marines and airmen to have a chance to connect with someone one on one; someone who can not only offer actual and concrete help, but just as importantly, a listening ear and even a shoulder to cry on. The last thing we're concerned with is trotting them out under the public spotlight to get headlines or a segment on the evening news, no matter how important the principles at stake in their particular situation may be. Whatever sacrifice they are willing to make to call attention to the wrongs they've endured must be a decision they arrive at on their own. Above all we respect their right to privacy, and honor the personal relationship we strive to establish with each of them. We have an informal credo at the Foundation that goes by the acronym 'AARP.' It's not, of course, the American Association of Retired People," but refers rather to our pledge to provide Anonymity, Action, Results, and Protection to our clients."

Nowhere is that tenet more in evidence than in the unique cases that have been brought to the MRFF by parents and family of those who have all but lost loved ones to the intolerable effects of fundamentalist Christian brainwashing within the armed services. Very early on in Mikey's mission, for example, the distraught parents of an Academy cadet named Alicia Peasley approached him. As detailed in his first book, *With God On Our Side*, Alicia fell prey to one of the many fundamentalist Christian cult cells that operate with impunity both within the Academy and on the fringes of the religiously charged atmosphere in the surrounding town of Colorado Spring. The small, affluent city nestled in the foothills of the Rocky Mountains is home to a vast menagerie of churches and para-church organizations and unaffiliated sects of every description whose primary goal is to recruit new members from among the young and often vulnerable cadets attending the prestigious institution.

Alicia was just such a victim. Alone for the first time in her life and a long way from her bucolic home in rural Michigan, she fell prey to a particularly pernicious fundamentalist faction comprised of a number of satellite cells under the all-purpose heading of the Shepherding Movement. Initiated by a South Florida quartet of fundamentalist preachers in the mid-Seventies, the movement stressed unquestioning obedience to its leaders, which soon came to include an array of unscrupulous charlatans who established a network of shepherding cells across the country. At its height, an estimated 100,000 adherents across the U.S. and around the world had pledged allegiance to the severe tenants of the cult, which consisted in large measure of complete and total submission to a designated 'Shepherd.'

The Shepherding Movement was largely discredited by a variety of evangelical theologians and was judged too extreme even by Pat Robertson, a radical fundamentalist Christian hardly accustomed to moderation in religious matters. But the condemnation of the movement did not come before irreparable harm had been done to many guileless young people as well as their families. The Peasleys suffered greatly as their bright and independent-minded daughter increasingly fell under the sway of a cell group that specialized in luring away Academy cadets. With Weinstein's help, they demanded that the Academy put a stop to the abuses perpetrated by these wolves in shepherd's clothing, but by that time Alicia had effectively been lost to her family.

"It was a sobering experience," Mikey recounts. "It's bad enough when fundamentalists knowingly trample on the long established tenets of separation of church and state as enshrined in the Constitution. But when they insidiously reach into the very hearts and minds of young, impressionable men and women and twist their values into something not even their parents can any longer recognize, then we have entered a fucking Orwellian reality that is extremely difficult to combat."

But combat it he would. "As the foundation began taking a closer look at the shepherding movement," he explain, "we came to realize that there were a myriad of similar cults operating within the military and with the implicit, and often explicit, endorsement of commanders and administrators. We started putting together a dossier, which quickly became ever more comprehensive as we got a handle on just how deeply into the military establishment they reached and just how bold they were in declaring the intentions."

A few examples from the Military Religious Freedom Foundation files suffice to vividly illustrate Mikey's point. The manifesto of a shadowy group called Cadence International, for example, specifically targets those who are "Young, searching, impressionable, moldable, and eager for relationship. Many of those serving in the armed forces," the Cadence International mission statement continues, "are in some of the most strategic moments of their lives—moments of receptivity, of soul-searching, of discovery, and of life transformation. Cadence International exists to be there during these strategic moments sharing the gospel and our lives. It's why we are here—for military people and their families, for these poignant moments of life-change."

Changing lives by disseminating and enforcing doctrinaire fundamentalist Christian dogma is also the stated intent of another key dominionist group operating in the highest circles of the military: the Officer's Christian Fellowship. The goal, as explicitly detailed in their literature, is "To glorify God by uniting Christian officers for biblical fellowship and outreach, equipping and encouraging them to minister effectively in the military society.

"In 2 Corinthians 5:20, the Apostle Paul describes Christians as Christ's ambassadors to a lost world. We believe God calls military believers to be His ambassadors to the Armed Forces. OCF exists to help you become a more effective ambassador, integrating faith and profession with excellence."

Closely aligned with the Officer's Christian Fellowship is the Christian Military Fellowship, which is aimed primarily at enlisted personnel and calls itself "an association of believers who are committed to encouraging men and women in the United States Armed Forces, and their families, to love and serve the Lord Jesus Christ." Christian Military Fellowship, its mission statement continues, "involves all elements of that society including all ranks, family members, and civilian employees. Within the military society, our members, staff and constituents work to introduce people to Jesus Christ and help Christians to grow in faith."

In pursuit of these patently unconstitutional objectives, the Christian Military Fellowship issued what it termed, "guidelines for ministering to one another that are advocated in the operation of the local Fellowship." Among them: "Encourage members to perform their military duties in a professional manner consistent with obedience to God's commands," and "evangelize every segment of the military society by any means which honors Christ."

But such organizations have, at the very least, clearly stated their ambitions, however unwarranted they may be in the incontrovertible light of settled constitutional principles. Other clandestine cell groups operate in an altogether murkier realm, often holding their meetings secretly in the homes of sympathizers well under the radar of those charged with responsibility for the health and welfare of the young men and women under their command. One of the most pernicious of these underground Christian conversion mills is Cadets for Christ. Strategically situated near the Air Force Academy in a suburb of Colorado Springs, Cadets for Christ was hatched by a mysterious couple named Don and Anna Warwick. In what could accurately be described as the shepherding movement on steroids, Cadets for Christ enforces total subservience and submission to the cult leaders in every area of a young cadet's life, including their future careers in the military.

With a technique that calls for a candidate's total isolation from friends and family, relentless immersion in rote fundamentalist Christian teachings and biblical indoctrination, along with other trademark tools of accomplished brainwashers, Cadets for Christ turns bright, articulate and motivated young adults into the equivalent of zombie zealots, marching in lockstep, spouting chapter and verse and willingly estranged from their loved ones. Not even their highest hopes for service in the Air Force is spared this leveling of mental and emotional capacities. In short, Cadets for Christ have drilled into their victims a complete and unquestioning loyalty to a single, monolithic entity: Cadets for Christ.

One of the most tragic examples of the havoc wrecked by the Warwicks in their nihilistic pursuit of shock troops recruits in a new army of Christian crusaders came to the attention of Weinstein and the MRFF in the fall of 2010. The cadet in question was Lauren Baas, a gifted and promising young Gulfport, Mississippi native who had began her studies at the Air Force Academy in 2006 with the lofty goal of becoming a jet pilot.

But four years later, on the eve of her graduation, it was clear to her worried parents, Peter and Jean Baas, that something had gone terribly wrong with their daughter. She had been transformed into a sinister stranger to her family, a smart and appealing young woman who, as a disciple of Don and Anna Warwick, had become a virtual slave to the draconian dictates of Cadets for Christ.

A Catholic family, the Baas' had sent Lauren to Catholic school for twelve years and taught her to respect the tenets of their faith. But all that changed when she became a Cadet for Christ and categorically denounced both her former religion and, along with it, her family. They were, she told them in no uncertain terms, condemned to hell for believing what they believed. But, as sad and shocking as Lauren's outright denunciation of her parents and their values might have been, the invidious influence of the cult cut even deeper than that. Ordered to forego her plans to become a pilot, Lauren was instead instructed to begin training in missile launching, a distinct step down from her previously high flying goals, and a career path with limited opportunities for advancement. "They were clearly targeting leaders," Jean Baas maintains. "My daughter had high aspirations."

As with her professional life, Lauren's personal life was also under the complete control of her Cadets for Christ overlords. The cult arranged for her to marry a cadet two years her junior whom she didn't know prior to becoming involved with the Warwicks. Her intended husband was somebody she had been acquainted with for a total of five months and, in that time, hadn't even been allowed to date. Their only contact was through a Bible study.

The Baas' alarm turned to panic when they happened across a collection of recipes distributed to female members of Cadets for Christ, presumably to equip them for their future roles as compliant cooks, house cleaners, and child bearers. It was entitled the "Baa Baa Sisterhood Cookbook," and a copy had been specifically allotted to "Sheep Lauren."

Not knowing where to turn, Lauren's parents wrote numerous letters to the Academy administrators and spoke at length to a Catholic chaplain. An investigation was promised but the outcome was, purely and simply, an exercise in stonewalling. The Academy did absolutely nothing to address the rampant religious coercion that was going on under its direct auspices, much less take steps to limit the influence of outside groups like Cadets for Christ. The Academy, Jean Baas insisted, took no action "to change the day-in, day-out practices of what goes on with these kids. Taxpayers paid $400,000 for an intelligent person to go to the Academy. What is their ulterior motive: to get the women in their place and the men in their place?"

In desperation, Peter and Jean Baas reached out to the Military Religious Freedom Foundation. One of the first actions Weinstein and his team took was to facilitate the publication of a letter Jean had written in November of 2010 directly to Don and Anna Warwick. It speaks with furious eloquence of a mother's righteous rage and indignation over a beloved child whose heart and mind had been stolen by strangers.

"As the holidays are upon us," she began, "let us give you an update of the Baas family. Lauren will not be coming home. Her presence will be missed enormously as we celebrate our holidays filled with love and rich in family tradition. Words cannot express the heartache you have caused... You have taken Lauren's mind and soul and twisted it to your fundamentalist Christian liking. She was brainwashed to believe she was 'unenlightened' and an 'unsaved fool' in the Catholic faith. She now lives in fear of God and feels 'shameful' if she does not continually stand guard against 'ungodly people.' You have trained your 'soldiers of God' and now cowardly hide behind them. May God truly have mercy on your soul.

"Did you ever have the guts to ask Lauren about her career goals before squelching them? She wanted to graduate from the United States Air Force

Academy and become a USAF pilot. Of course, being a female, you made sure that goal was extinguished. In your words, she is the sheep and her career is to follow the male shepherd. How dare you play God!

"Did you know that we speak for many families that have been destroyed by you? We know you are very aware that many parents do not come forward because they fear irreparably severing a now very fragile relationship with their child. You have taught our children to tolerate us so long as we do not question your 'teachings'. If we do, we are to be cast aside and treated as if we are Satan himself.

"For the above reason, we have joined forces with the only entity willing to selflessly assist us and the only organization that understands the oppressive evil you perpetrate; the civil rights fighters at the Military Religious Freedom Foundation. Together with MRFF we will fight for freedom of religion at the United States Air Force Academy. We will *never* stop fighting against your vile, calculated and cold efforts to subvert the U.S. Constitution and teach our precious daughters that they are designated by your twisted version of Jesus to be a second-class citizen 'sheep' consigned to doing the will of their assigned male overseers."

"Jean's words speak with a passion and clarity that needs no elaboration," Weinstein remarks. "I'm eternally grateful to her for providing us with so potent a weapon to use against those who mentally and emotionally raped her daughter.

"Unfortunately, words alone sometimes aren't enough, especially when you're dealing with the fundamentalist Christian factions so deeply rooted at the Academy and elsewhere. Jean's anger and anguish needed to be backed with action and the Foundation immediately demanded a full-scale investigation of the illegal activities of Cadets for Christ. But while we're pushing for a complete ban of such organizations, it's imperative that we keep in mind the human dimensions of this tragic story. A family was torn apart. Hopes and dreams cruelly shattered. A loving mother was deprived of her daughter. Those are the real casualties of the war we're fighting and we must never forget that."

The damage and destruction wrought in the personal lives of honorable and upstanding citizens by fundamentalist Christian incursion in the military is hardly limited to the young and impressionable. As often as not, the tentacles of dominionist zealotry can entangle even the most seasoned and experienced of service men and women and it is on their behalf that the MRFF has launched some of its most ferocious battles.

There is no more egregious example of fundamentalist Christian determination to take out its enemies, no matter how respected and accomplished, than the ordeal endured by an outstanding and dedicated Air Force Reserve pilot by the name of Captain David Horn.

Beginning his career as a civilian airman in 1985, Captain Horn had qualified for his license at seventeen, the youngest age legally allowable to be licensed by the FAA. He would go on to become an Airline Transport Pilot, achieving the highest civilian rating available and being awarded a 'Gold Seal' by the Federal Aviation Administration for his outstanding success as a civilian flight instructor. Horn's military career got underway as Command Post Controller, a position he held for six years before being competitively selected for the most prestigious military pilot training program in the world: Euro-NATO Joint-Jet Pilot Training.

After earning his Air Force wings, Captain Horn spent three exemplary years flying F-16's in the California Air National Guard before transferring to the 349th Air Mobility Wing at Travis Air Force Base in California as a KC-10 pilot. He repeatedly volunteered to fly combat missions in both the Afghanistan and Iraq wars, where he earned, among many other honors, the prestigious Air Medal. By any measure, Captain David Horn had proven himself a tremendous asset to the Air Force Reserve.

That is, until, the fateful day of his return from deployment, during a welcoming ceremony and subsequent debriefing at Travis Air Force Base. It was then that Horn, who professed no particular religious belief, was confronted with an enforced sectarian ritual that had become only too common in the Air Force and one that deeply disturbed him. "Our entire squadron was told to stand and bow their heads for a prayer 'in Jesus' name,'" he recounts. "Since it happened just prior to a meeting to discuss travel pay, participation was essentially mandatory. I was offended by this unwarranted display of religious favoritism, a clear violation of the separation of church and state, and I wasn't the only one. Following the prayer I was approached by one of the enlisted crewmembers with whom I had served overseas, who wanted to know 'How dare they assume I am a Christian?' He had put into words exactly what I was feeling and I soon found out that this was hardly an exceptional occurrence at the base. Specifically Christian prayers, as well as the screening of inspirational videos with a religious theme, happened on a regular basis in the 349th Air Mobility Wing before, during and after its deployment overseas." Understandably upset by the information he had discovered, Captain Horn subsequently submitted a letter in protest to the local paper covering news in surrounding Solano County after having checked with the base legal dept to ensure what he was doing was legal.

It was this simple exercise in freedom of expression that effectively brought Captain Horn's distinguished career and sterling reputation to a sudden and ignominious end. Four days after the letter had been printed, he was handed a copy of a memo written by his Flight Commander and addressed to his Squadron Commander, falsely stating that Horn had failed in a variety of ways to do his duty while deployed in the war zones. Absurd allegations included the patently false charge of failing to complete practice flight simulator sessions, a demonstrable impossibility since there were no such simulators in the forward areas where he was deployed, not to mention the fact that there was no such requirement due to complete this training.

Despite this and other glaring discrepancies, the deliberately inflammatory memo became the primary piece of evidence used to justify a Flying Evaluation Board decision to remove Captain Horn's wings. This, despite the fact that many airmen who had flown extensively with the accomplished pilot testified strenuously on his behalf, even as some of them expressed a fear of reprisal for speaking up in his defense.

But that was only the beginning of his ordeal. The Flying Evaluation Board, with members selected by the Wing Commander, ultimately handed down a recommendation against Captain Horn, charging a "Lack of Proficiency" without ever referencing his actual, official and highly laudatory Proficiency Record. It was a glaring discrepancy duly noted by the Commander of the Air Force Reserve who promptly disapproved the Flying Evaluation Board finding, citing Captain Horn's strong record in three previous evaluations, in all of which he had been graded "Excellent."

"I was grounded for fourteen months during this whole review process," he continues. "I was finally returned to the 349th Air Mobility Wing, only to find out that the more things change, the more they stay the same. The same cast of characters were in place, including the Squadron Command who had headed up the FEB probe that recommended I be grounded in the first place. What they couldn't accomplish the first time around, they tried to pull off in a second round."

This time the kangaroo court aspects of the proceedings were even more ludicrous and surreal. The commander who had initiated the witch hunt was called as a witness, despite the fact that he has never had a face-to-face meeting with Captain Horn. When the Operations Group Commander was called to the stand, he abruptly chose to discontinue his testimony after it was revealed that, as part of the command structure's efforts to besmirch Horn's reputation, he had disobeyed a direct order. Such shenanigans notwithstanding, the board once again recommended a "Lack of Proficiency" judgment against the pilot. For his efforts on behalf of this unvarnished character assassination, the FEB President was subsequently promoted to Squadron Commander just as the previous FEB president who recommended against Captain Horn had been.

But not everyone involved in the shameful episode was willing to turn their tail and run. Captain Horn's competency and dedication were testified to by an impressive array of instructors, evaluators and section chiefs. After having read the FEB transcripts, the 19th Air Force Commander in charge of all Air Force Pilot Training, Major General Irving L. Halter (a 1977 U.S. Air Force Academy classmate of Mikey's), asserted that the case made against Captain Horn did not justify his removal from flying service. Also of note was the fact that the only attorney on the board, a civil and military lawyer with the Air Force Review Board Agency, recommended that he be fully reinstated.

"Despite the fact that this was an obvious fucking attempt to railroad David Horn, pursuant to unconstitutional religious tyranny," Mikey remarks, "it might be tempting for a layman to dismiss all this as the political machinations that inevitably occur in any hidebound bureaucracy. It was abundantly clear that Captain Horn had made enemies. The only question was who and why. They had, up to a point, kept their identities and motives a closely guarded secret. But they couldn't help themselves. They had to let their victim know who his tormenters were. Revealing their reasons was a major element in the satisfaction they derived from ruining an exemplary officer's career."

That revelation came in a chilling confrontation after Captain Horn was summoned to the office of the Vice Wing Commander, an officer who, from the beginning, had enthusiastically participated in the protracted effort to destroy him. "I knew this man socially," David Horn explains. "He and I and our wives had gotten together on numerous occasions. After I wrote the letter decrying the mandatory prayer ceremony at Travis Air

Force Base, they abruptly cut off all association with us, casual and otherwise. I had hardly seen him since, until the day he called me to his office. At
that time he reminded me of the letter I had written years earlier. He told
me that I should use those writing skills to go find a job somewhere else."

"This isn't a question of reading between the lines," Mikey maintains
with palpable anger. "There *are* no lines to read between. Captain David
Horn was summarily drummed out of the Air Force Reserve despite an
outstanding career in service to his country for one reason and one reason
only: because he had dared to challenge the fundamentalist Christian he-
gemony that ruled at the highest levels of Air Force command and control.
The fanatics who occupy those seats of power apparently consider it more
important to purge their ranks of heretics and non-believers than to seek
out, support and maintain those who are best qualified to serve, regardless
of their religious persuasion. That's more than a crying shame. It's a flagrant
criminal act by unconstitutional fundamentalist Christian predators."

The MRFF did its best to make that case. After Captain Horn was permanently grounded as a result of the Flying Evaluation Board's grievously
unjust findings, he sought out the Foundation for legal assistance in his
fight to regain his career and his reputation. Among the many briefs filed
on his behalf, one speaks with distressing detail of the consequences the
pilot subsequently suffered: "Captain Horn has lost an entire career in both
civil and military aviation," it read. "A decorated fighter and tanker pilot,
he was unemployed for months and lost his home as a direct result of the actions taken against him. He now works an entry-level job in an oil refinery
operating pumps. His family has suffered greatly and his marriage has been
severely strained as a direct result of the actions taken against him."

The document concludes with a scathing indictment of its own: "A
corrupt leadership environment that overtly promoted a specific religion—
even producing audiovisual presentations that called non-Christians 'idiots'
and 'fools'—actively blackballed a pilot with an outstanding record and the
respect of those he served with; men and women brave enough to speak out
against this ethically questionable effort despite their fear of reprisal from
the leaders of the 349th Air Mobility Wing at Travis Air Force Base. A
well qualified, combat tested pilot, Captain Horn was removed from service
during wartime because of his expression of his religious perspective outside
work. The perpetrators of this act committed documented crimes against
the Uniform Code of Military Justice, including lying to a commander and

disobeying a direct order in their effort to remove Captain Horn. These crimes and the conflict between Captain Horn's record and the claims against him were made clear to Air Force leadership from the Squadron level all the way to the Secretary of the Air Force, General T. Michael Mosley, before they all ultimately endorsed the unethical and wasteful effort that destroyed Capt. Horn's career and severely harmed his family and future."

There are, apparently, no lengths that fundamentalist Christian fulminators within the military will not go to inflict 'severe harm' to those with the courage to stand up their flagrant attacks on the Constitution. Peter and Jean Baas were only two parents among many who had the fabric of their families torn to shreds by the insidious mind control methods employed by Christian cults such as Cadets For Christ. Captain David Horn was only one example of the thousands who have had their careers and reputations within the armed services savaged by conniving dominionists. But perhaps among the most deplorable incidents of sheer wanton cruelty occurred in the case of Professor David Mullin, Ph.D., whose courage in the face of extremism brought down a particularly ugly stain of vengeance.

Mullin had served with distinction as a professor in the Economics Department of the Air Force Academy for thirteen years, and was a conservative evangelical Christian. It was during his tenure there that he witnessed firsthand the steady encroachment of religious intolerance within the establishment and the systemic abuses of power that followed in train. In retrospect it was hardly surprising: the Academy had been a suppurating wound of Christian extremist infiltration in the armed services long before Mikey Weinstein began his relentless campaign to expose the unconstitutional practices that occurred there on a regular basis.

But Professor Mullin had also taken careful note of other areas of discrimination that had seeped into the very fabric of the school and corrupted its vaunted core values. Suffering from severe pain due to a chronic medical condition, Mullin had been on the receiving end of all manner of bias against the disabled at the Academy. By the same token he had observed firsthand the endemic sexism that had been at the root of the school's shocking and deeply embarrassing sexual assault scandal in 2003.

"There was a pattern of discrimination that reached into all areas of Academy life," explains Mullin, an earnest, thoughtful man who chooses his words carefully. "I experienced it myself as a result of my disability and saw it happen directly to many others, such as a female civilian facility member who was the subject of a whisper campaign suggesting that she was a lesbian simply because she didn't adhere strictly enough to the prevailing gender stereotypes that were being perpetuated by the extreme religious faction prevailing at the institution. When I called attention to the spread of this rumor I was told by my department head that there would be 'consequences' to my action."

It was at the hands of the entrenched fundamentalist faction at the Academy that Mulllin himself suffered the most malignant violations of his rights. "I consider myself to be an evangelical Christian," he continues. "For almost a decade I was an active member of the same Presbyterian church in Colorado Springs. But, as became increasingly clear during my time at the Academy, the Christian clique that controlled the school deemed my brand of faith inadequate. I was subject to sanctions, including marginal performance ratings and the denial of a pay raise as a direct result of my refusal to toe the line of religious conformity."

By the time Mullin joined forces with the MRFF in early 2011, he had compiled an all too familiar litany of constitutional violations regularly committed by the Academy. There were a myriad of examples: "An officially authorized flyer was widely posted by the Officers Christian Fellowship," he recounts. "It stated that 'officers were encouraged to attend,' which was nothing more that a thinly disguised code warning that any absence would be noted by the chain of command to the determinant of your career. Which is exactly what happened to a faculty member, a practicing Buddhist, who courageously raised an objection regarding the flyers. He was promptly denied a well-earned chance to earn his Ph.D., the opportunity instead going to a much inferior candidate."

In another incident, Mullin describes a mandatory faculty meeting at which three instructors were seen sitting together by the department head. They included a person of the Jewish faith, an individual known for his secular humanist views and the woman who had been the subject of the lesbian smear campaign. Following the meeting, the department head summoned the three into his presence and informed them in no uncertain terms that he didn't want the most 'liberal' members of his faculty sitting together.

"At another of these mandatory meetings," Mullins continues, "the

Dean passed out copies of the New Testament and religious literature from the Military Ministries of Campus Crusade for Christ. While I may personally agree with the religious doctrines expressed in this material, it was clear to me that the Dean's actions violated the No Establishment Clause of the First Amendment. The same violation occurred when a faculty member, who, of course, was a federal employee, was authorized to take a year off at half pay to conduct research for a paper that was then published in a journal promoting Christian doctrine. A copy of that paper was then prominently displayed in the front office of the department at the express authorization of the department head."

The unwarranted intrusions also extended into the personal lives of the faculty. "Over the past decade my movements in the main academic building at the Academy were monitored by an officer who is a close ally of the department head," Mullin reveals. "I was repeatedly told through my chain of command that I should not be seen meeting with more than one faculty member at a time. The scrutiny became worse when I was going through a divorce. My department head directed me to see a federal worker who served as a counselor to Air Force Academy employees, who informed me that my marriage was an eternal bond made in heaven. Later when I was about to get remarried, I purchased an engagement ring to be delivered to my office where I could sign for it. Instead the department head gave me the package already opened. It still feels like a deep violation that the man who had done me so much harm had seen this token of my esteem before I had."

A breaking point of sorts came when it was announced that a National Prayer Luncheon event was scheduled to be held at the Academy in early February of 2011. The featured speaker: Marine Corps Lieutenant Clebe McClary, a retired Vietnam veteran who had lost an eye in battle. Endorsed by, among others, Billy Graham and Jerry Falwell, McClary's views of the separation of church and state can best be captured by a snippet from his website, promoting him as "one of the most outstanding, motivational and inspirational speakers in America": "*Clebe McClary continues his service today in the Lord's Army. His life genuinely embodies the vow he took when entering the Marines: Any mission assigned will be accomplished in a superior manner, no matter what the obstacles. For him, USMC will always mean a "U. S. Marine for Christ."* Elsewhere on his site, McClary is quoted as believing that "God is not interested in our 'I.Q.' but our 'I Will.'"

Not everyone was as enthusiastic about McClary's scheduled appearance as the Academy's administrators appeared to be. "Inviting Lieutenant McClary appears to be a step backward in creating a climate of religious respect," warned Interfaith Alliance President, C. Welton Gaddy in a letter to Air Force Academy superintendent, Lieutenant General Michael Gould.

But it was left up to the MRFF, in partnership with Professor Mullin, to actually take aggressive action to prevent the provocative speaker from mounting the podium. Together with three members of the Air Force Academy staff (dubbed John Doe One, Two and Three), who withheld their names for fear of reprisal, Weinstein and Mullin filed a lawsuit in federal district court in Denver, Colorado for a federal injunction to halt the event. It served as a significant moment in Weinstein's long-fought battle against the fundamentalist Christian forces at the Academy. "Over the years we've represented three hundred and forty-one individual clients from the Air Force Academy," Mikey explains. "But Professor Mullin was the first one who ever actually allowed his name to be used in public. He wanted to establish conclusively his identity as a free thinking evangelical Christian and not just a Christian envoy for Air Force Academy fundamentalists. Considering the fucking harassment he was already being subjected to on a constant basis, it was an extraordinarily courageous act."

Weinstein wasn't the only one who thought so. "I am one of the hundreds of MRFF clients in the United States Air Force Academy," one of these anonymous individuals wrote in a powerfully revealing email. "I am a practicing Roman Catholic and am among the many who are just too frightened to be even a so-called 'John Doe' litigant with MRFF. I'm very, very sorry I could not come forward, but doing so would have permanently destroyed my USAF career and I have a family. I know that this is not a valid excuse but it is what it is. I am a client of the MRFF in this Prayer Luncheon event lawsuit because my immediate supervisor told me over 3 weeks ago that my colleagues and I were 'expected' to attend the National Prayer Luncheon. Then something happened that I never thought I would live to see. My immediate supervisor called me at home and asked me if I was one of the unnamed plaintiffs in the lawsuit and did I know of anyone who was. I told him that I was not and did not know of anyone else who was. I should have told him the truth but, again, I was afraid.

"I know that this lawsuit would have been impossible without MRFF, standing up for all of us here at USAFA. From the first moment I called you for help, you have totally been there for me and for my friends who have felt compelled by their military superiors to attend the National Prayer Luncheon. Not attending was billed to us by our commanders as violating [Academy Superintendent] Lieutenant General Gould's decree. Please thank the MRFF lawyers for my friends and me and especially please also thank Dr. David Mullin for coming forward and doing what none of the rest of us had the guts to do. One day I would like to be able to tell him face-to-face how much his 'coming out' meant to all the rest of us who cower in the USAFA shadows because of the Christian proselytizers everywhere."

But Professor David Mullin would pay a steep price in anguish and anger for his decision to step forward and join the MRFF lawsuit. Shortly after news of the filing was announced, his service dog, a two year-old black Labrador named Caleb on whom Mullin depended to help with balance problems and dizzy spells brought on by his illness, began acting sluggishly, breathing heavily and refusing to stand.

Mullin picks up the harrowing account: "I took Caleb to an animal emergency center where blood and other tests showed he had been fed either rat poison or a prescription drug used to thin his blood. It was traumatic in the extreme. I've had him since he was eight weeks old and, in that time, he has become the most loyal and trustworthy of friends." For hours Caleb hovered between life and death. Finally, after three blood transfusions, he began slowly to recover.

"There is no doubt in my mind, nor in Professor Mullin's, that this animal was purposely poisoned in retaliation for the legal action we had taken to halt the prayer luncheon," Mikey remarks, as much in sadness as in anger. "The incident happened on Academy grounds when David briefly left Caleb in his office, a room to which only other Academy personnel had access. But, of course, nobody can prove anything. That's the way these individuals operate: secretly, in the shadows. The fact that someone would try to kill an innocent creature is hard to believe. But I've been facing this fucking enemy for a long time. I've come to understand that they are capable of literally anything."

CHAPTER ELEVEN

JESUS RIFLES

There has historically been a long and deeply unsettling link between the implements of war and the symbols of religious conquest. It was in the year 312 A.D. when Emperor Constantine gazed up into the sky above the pitched battle of Milvian Bridge where he supposedly saw a vision of the cross above the words, "With this sign you shall conquer." Ever since then, crusaders and jihadists and sectarian storm troopers of every description have marched proudly to war under the banners of their respective faiths, killing and destroying in the name of the divinity they worship.

"Symbols have tremendous importance in the psychology of war," remarks Mikey. "Men and women will fight and die for what they believe in, whether it's king and country or some lavish quarter of heaven reserved exclusively for martyrs. A standard carried into combat embodies that ideal, just as the capture of a battle flag historically signals a lost cause. Some of the most difficult and important work we do at the Military Religious Freedom Foundation is to try and disentangle such religious motivations, as personified by signs and symbols, from the reasons we as a nation go to war. It's imperative that the flag we carry before us into battle is the Stars & Stripes, a potent representation of a wholly secular ideal, and not some theological talisman that justifies barbarity in the name of anyone's perception of an angry and vengeful God."

One of the most brazen attempts to transform the weapons of war into tools of religious indoctrination came to the attention of MRFF in late 2009. As Weinstein explains, "Several of our clients, including more than a few active-duty service members in the desert combat zones, alerted us to a situation that, despite the many years I've spent confronting fundamentalist Christian infiltration in the military, made my jaw drop in utter disbelief. The fact that it was clearly an illegal practice wasn't in itself particularly surprising. Regularly trampling the Constitution underfoot is standard operating procedure for these goddamn individuals. I wasn't even especially shocked to learn that this crime had been carried out under the nose of military commanders and policy makers for more than thirty years. The war we're engaged in didn't start yesterday and it won't end tomorrow. No, what really brought this down to new depths of depravity was the circumstances in which it occurred: a war in which the most important victory we can achieve is in the hearts and minds of the populace whose countries we have overrun. The fact that we have done so using weapons essentially sanctified for use in a Christian Crusade is not just seditious. It's breathtakingly stupid. There is simply no more graphic an example of the harm that these religious zealots are willing to put our fighting men and women in—being maimed and disfigured, physically and psychologically, losing arms and legs or, worst all coming back to Dover Air Force Base in a body bag—all in pursuit of their abominable agenda, than to actually engrave their weapons with a naked symbol of fundamentalist Christian dominionist arrogance."

The shocking discovery, which would subsequently go on to make eye-popping headlines around the world, involved Trijicon, an arms manufacturing company with generous supply contracts from the Pentagon. The company, based in Wixom, Michigan, was founded by a South African named Glyn Bindon who had proved his usefulness to the Military-Industrial Complex in a variety of engineering posts at, among others, Grumman Aerospace and the Ford Motor Company, where he was instrumental in developing military applications for new technologies.

But Bindon's most notable achievement came in the early Eighties, when he brought to market a unique gun sight which utilized the radioactive isotope Tritium to create luminous aiming dots that afforded shooters deadly accuracy in precise distance marksmanship with close-in aiming speed. With initial clients that included the FBI, Bindon's manufacturing operation, Trijicon, grew overnight into a major player in the armed services supply industry, landing a $660 million multi-year contract to produce up to eight hundred thousand gun sight units to the Marine Corps, along with additional contracts to provide two hundred thousands of the gun sights to the U.S. Army as well. In all, Trijicon would develop nearly a dozen variations of its state-of-the-art Tritium-lit sighting mechanisms, selling them not just to the military, but also to law enforcements agencies, gun and hunting enthusiasts of every description.

The equipment, known as Advanced Combat Optical Gunsights (ACOGs), may have varied depending on their specific applications, but one element remained constant throughout: next to the model and serial numbers were engraved selected biblical chapter-and-verse references. An example of one such citation, 2COR4:6, alludes to Second Corinthians 4:6, which reads: "For God, who commanded the light to shine out of darkness, hath shined in our hearts, to give the light of the knowledge of the glory of God in the face of Jesus Christ." Other references include words from the books of Revelation and Matthew, as well as the Gospel of John, chapter eight, verse twelve (marked on the gun sights as JN8:12,) which quotes Jesus as saying "I am the light of the world. Whoever follows me will never walk in darkness but will have the light of life."

Given the well-established background of Trijicon and the predilections of its founder, Glyn Bindon, it could hardly have come as a surprise to the arms procurers at the Pentagon that the gun sights they were purchasing by the hundreds of thousands had, in fact, become the means of disseminating strident fundamentalist Christian propaganda. Bindon had made no secret of his own hardcore adherence to Christian dominionism and after he died in a 2003 plane crash in Alabama, the company's corporate heirs, including his son Stephen, enthusiastically carried on the elder Bindon's religious agenda.

"It was there for all to see," Mikey asserts, pointing to the Trijicon website where the firm's fervent mission is stated in no uncertain terms. "Anyone within the vast Pentagon purchasing and supply chain who might have been concerned with this kind of outrageously unconstitutional encroachment can hardly claim that they were kept in the dark."

To the contrary. Amidst the standard boilerplate that comprises Trijicon's "vision" statement on the website is an unambiguous avowal of its agenda under the heading of *Morality*: "We believe," it asserts, "that America is great when its people are good. This goodness has been based on biblical standards throughout our history and we will strive to follow those morals." The website also features a video overview of the ACOGs in which a narrator claims that the Bible inscriptions "are one of the really cool things about this sight."

"Look," Weinstein allows, "there's nothing wrong with a company expressing its core values. If Trijicon's executives believe that the Bible is the source of all morality in America, that's their business. But there was something altogether more fucking insidious at work here and it is explicitly referred to in a section of their statement called *Customers*, which reads, 'We desire long-term relationships with our customers. We will listen and continually improve our products to meet their needs.' You've got to ask yourself whose needs were they meeting by engraving Bible citations on their gun sights? Was that part of trying to continually improve their products? If so, to whose specifications? The bottom line is that it strains credulity to assume that whoever was responsible for purchasing over a million of these essential tools of a soldier's trade had no idea what Trijicon was including as part of its product line."

It's an assertion given added weight by the fact that the firm had been supplying the gun sights to the U.S. military since 1995 and had, in fact, more recently expanded its market to include armed services customers in the United Kingdom, Australia and New Zealand.

A cacophonous international outcry that followed hard on the heels of the MRFF exposé of the decades-long collusion between Trijicon and the Pentagon's fundamentalist Christian faction. Even the Church of England issued a scathing statement condemning the cozy connection. The Foundation's adept handling of the publicity firestorm that had ensued from the revelations was immeasurably instructive and illuminating on many levels. "We had been doing this long enough to realize just what buttons to push to get the story the widest possible exposure," Weinstein reveals. "Trijicon's actions had literally global repercussions and, thanks to the contacts we had developed with the worldwide media, we were able to get out in front of it immediately and tell the story as it needed to be told." To that end, *ABC News* became a de facto partner with MRFF in calling Trijicon and the U.S. military to account, running an explosive series of prime time news stories as events continued to unfold. Not long afterwards, *The New York Times* joined in the fray, publishing in-depth investigative articles that asked some very difficult questions of those responsible for countenancing the practice for so long.

In what was another intriguing element of the fast moving scandal, military spokespersons stumbled over themselves to reach the podium of public opinion with staunch denials of knowledge and involvement. Shortly after the story broke, the Army released a statement insisting that it "was unaware of these coded biblical references until several days ago." The disavowal sanctimoniously went on to claim that, "It is not the policy of the Army or the Department of Defense to put religious references of any kind on its equipment." The Marine Corps was quick to follow, issuing its own shoulder-shrugging statement that it had no knowledge of the biblical references on the gun sights and adding, "We are making every effort to remove these markings from all of our scopes and will ensure that all future procurement of these scopes will not have these types of markings."

That much, at least, had become a forgone conclusion. Central Command head General David Petraeus, who oversaw all U.S. forces in Iraq and Afghanistan, was quoted as saying that Trijicon's practice was "disturbing …and a serious concern for me" as well his field commanders. He told *The New York Times* that there had been considerable discussions within the Department of Defense about how to deal with the Trijicon situation.

In a desperate attempt to contain the quickly spreading debacle, Trijicon president, Stephen Bindon announced that the company, which he had inherited from his father and which had landed untold millions of dollars in lucrative contracts, would immediately cease and desist from turning its gun sights into vehicles for fundamentalist Christian proselytizing. Trijicon would, Bindon promised in a press release, "remove the inscription reference on all U.S. military products that are in the company's factory that have already been produced, but have yet to be shipped." Further, it would "provide one hundred modification kits to forces in the field to remove the reference on the already forward deployed optical sights." While they were at it, Trijicon would also offer foreign forces that had purchased the gun sights "the same remedies."

"Do the math," says Bonnie Weinstein with disdain. "Trijicon sent out one hundred fucking kits to erase inappropriate and illegal scripture passages on how many millions of rifles? That's approximately one kit for every ten thousand rifles. It was nothing more than an absurd and ridiculous face saving effort to control a scandal that was spreading like wildfire."

"Trijicon has proudly served the U.S. military for more than two decades," Stephen Bindon proclaimed in a futile attempt at face-saving, "and our decision to offer to voluntarily remove these references is both prudent and appropriate. We want to thank the Department of Defense for the opportunity to work with them and will move as quickly as possible to provide the modification kits for deployment overseas."

But even then, Bindon could not refrain from defending his company's indefensible action. "Our effort is simple and straightforward," he insisted, with the verbal equivalent of a hand over his heart: "to help our servicemen and women win the War on Terror and come home safe to their families. As long as we have men and women in danger, we will continue to do everything we can to provide them with both state-of-the-art technology and the never-ending support and prayers of a grateful nation."

For its part, the Pentagon did its best to paper over the raging controversy, while at the same time lending aid and comfort to its beleaguered contractor. The Department of Defense, its press secretary announced, "applauds the voluntary actions announced by Trijicon."

But by then, of course, the damage had already been done. "We must ensure that incidents like these are not repeated," warned Haris Tarin, director of the Washington, DC, office of the Muslim Public Affairs Council, "so as not to give the impression that our country is involved in a religious crusade, which hurts America's image abroad and puts our soldiers in harm's way."

Ibrahim Hooper, communications director for the Council on American-Islamic Relations, took a more measured tone, claiming that Trijicon's belated action was a "responsible move that will help reduce or eliminate a potential danger to our nation's military." What he left unsaid was that it was Trijicon itself that had done so much to put our nation's military in danger in the first place.

It was a point Mikey had no such compunctions in bringing to the world's attention. "It's wrong, it violates the Constitution, it violates a number of federal laws," was his trenchant evaluation. "It allows the Mujahedeen, the Taliban, al Qaeda, and the insurrectionists and jihadists to claim they're being shot by Jesus rifles," thereby playing into the hand of "those who are calling this a Crusade." He would go on to reveal that several of the MRFF clients that had initially brought the inscriptions to his attention had been told by their commanders that the weapons equipped with the Trijicon sights were "spiritually transformed firearms of Jesus Christ."

Compounding the outrage was the fact that multiple thousands of these "spiritually transformed firearms" had in fact ended up in the hands of the very allies we were trying so hard to convince of our sincere nonsectarian intentions. Over the course of its investigation, *ABC News* discovered that the U.S. Military, through the Combined Security Transition Command Afghanistan (CSTC-A), had provided over six thousands weapons equipped with the Trijicon sights to elite forces within Afghan National Army. One can only imagine what these presumably Islamic soldiers thought of being given weapons that extolled the sacred texts of a foreign religion. "It's a rallying cry for the Taliban," was how one Al Jazeera reporter characterized Trijicon's unbridled zealotry. "It gives them a propaganda tool. They've always tried to paint the U.S. efforts in Afghanistan as a Christian campaign." Additionally, the Trijicon sights were discovered on the ordnance of such far-flung arm services as the Israeli Defense Force, NATO, and the militaries of Australia and New Zealand.

Those with boots on the ground echoed that outrage sparked by the scandal. Benjamin Busch, was a United States Marine Corps infantry officer who served in Afghanistan and later penned an essay examining the Trijicon episode. "By branding weapons with Christian messages, there is a deep and ugly blending of religion, politics, and bloodshed" he wrote from direct experience. "It has unwittingly painted our government and military with the embarrassing language of 'crusade.' America is largely composed of people who consider themselves Christian, separated by various interpretations of the same book. But I did not go onward as a Christian soldier. I went forth as an American, a Marine. I was sent by my country to fight a threat, with the best intentions of democracy, not theocracy."

"Trijicon's outrageous practice was an unconstitutional disgrace of the highest magnitude," Weinstein would write in the aftermath of the historical controversy, "and an action that clearly gave additional incentive and emboldenment to recruiters for our nation's enemies. It is nothing short of a vile national security threat that, despite our nation's efforts to convince the Muslim world we are not pursuing a holy war against them, our military and its contractors time and again resort to unlawful fundamentalist evangelical Christian practices, even on the battlefield. It has been said that 'civilization is a race between education and catastrophe.' We can now only hope that the United States Congress and The Pentagon will comprehensively investigate how this catastrophe and countless other examples of military religious extremism infiltrates every branch of our honorable armed services. But, at the same time, it's evident that the minds that got us into the mess are not the same minds that can get us out of it. For now, at least we can take solace in Trijicon's affirmation that it will expeditiously remove the Bible verse citations from its scopes. We only hope that the damage from their actions is not yet beyond repair."

Although the precedents aren't encouraging, it's a hope that only history can confirm (and in an interesting historical side note, Mikey's coinage of the term "Jesus Rifles" was officially added to *The New York Times* American lexicographic glossary). But whatever the eventual outcome of the controversy, it was clear that MRFF had taken a major step forward in directly confronting the Christian fundamentalist foes of the Constitution. "We had reached an entirely new level," Bonnie recounts. "It was the big time. Suddenly everything became more intense and extreme. The Foundation was the total focus of our lives. It consumed everything, all the time. We hardly had a moment to catch our breath."

It was a state of virtually perpetual conflict with a vicious enemy that Mikey and Bonnie would soon face in an even more direct and sinister manifestation.

PART FOUR

CHAPTER TWELVE

TROLLING FOR ASSASSINS

Not every battle joined by the Weinsteins and the MRFF is one of their own choosing. Besieged with clients whose cases often have profound consequences in the foundation's ongoing focus on protecting and preserving the Constitution, the MRFF must still be careful to pick and choose which individuals and what cases they will represent. Reputations hang in balance; careers are threatened; lives are at stake. No one with a legitimate grievance against the fundamentalist Christian forces in the U.S. military is turned away. As much as it is their legal recourse to justice, the welfare of these individuals is a solemn responsibility taken on by Mikey and his team. It comes with the territory.

Given the near-constant activity that virtually consumes the Weinsteins every waking hour, it is hardly surprising that there is little time left to look after their own needs. Both Bonnie and Mikey, along with their family, have collectively paid a steep price to take a stand against the unconstitutional onslaught of religious extremists in the armed services. But the time and energy the couple expends for the cause is only part of that price. More telling by far are those wakeful moments that come in the darkest hours of the night, with the realization that there are forces all around them eagerly and actively at work to destroy them.

"The attacks on the house," Bonnie explains, "the anonymous threats over the phone and the Internet; the constant feeling that someone may be watching you. It's hard to try to live a normal life under those conditions. We do our best to carry on with everyday routines, tending to the mundane details of life, but sometimes it's hard to ignore the reality that there are people who fucking hate you and who wish you were dead. There is no way to pretend that they don't exist, especially when they are constantly reminding you of the fact."

That fact is both oppressive and omnipresent in the daily lives of the Weinsteins. Often, their implacable enemies seem incapable of separating their warped concept of America's supposedly divine crusade to bring Jesus to the heathen from the noxious, violent fantasies of wiping Mikey and his family off the face of the earth.

"I am proud wife [sic] of a Green Beret combat soldier," read one recent email that could well serve as a template for such twisted and dangerous obsessions. "He who is a true man of faith, a true Christian father to our children and a true warrior for our Lord and Savior Jesus Christ and USA. In our Bible study on base we know of you and pray and talk of you, Mikey, and your evildoing with MFRR [sic]. We also know that Jesus speak to you to warn you to stop trying to take Christianity away from our military and our USA. USA is and was always a Christian nation meant to bring Jesus to all the world. We know and can see that Jesus does speak to you and will stand up to you and your supporters. Look at how miserable your life is now. We see you on the newspapers and TV. You will never defeat the Lord. Your wife has multiple sklerosas [sic] and will die a painful death all twisted up with pain and bent in agony because of your fighting against Jesus. Your daughter-in-law Amanda's father has bravely chosen Jesus over her because she has fallen to the Evil One you serve. Your sons and daughter Amber will watch helpless as you waste away and slowly die in poverty all alone and forgotten in the further disgrace than you have earned due to fighting Jesus. You will only save them and you if surrender to Lord and Savior Jesus who is the only way and truth and life. Why can't you just see His Love and stop trying to destroy Christians in armed forces?"

Aside from the Weinsteins themselves, no one is more acutely aware of the clear and present danger in which the family has been plunged than Anthony Burnside, founder of the Ronan Group, a world-class security firm that guards and protects the family. With over fifteen years of experience in law enforcement, Burnside has an extensive background in behavioral and abnormal psychology, a skill set uniquely well suited to the services he provides to his high-profile client. His company, likewise, is renowned for its proven information and intelligence sharing techniques, as well as such vital capabilities as threat assessment, risk analysis and what is termed in the security industry as "analytical and operational red teaming." Ronan has provided its executive protection services for major entertainment events from the Grammys to the Golden Globes, serving as security for such high profile stars as Miley Cyrus, Kim Kardashian, Tom Hanks, Lady GaGa, Eminem, Justin Beiber, and a host of others.

In all these respects and more, The Ronan Group is superbly equipped to ensure the safety of a family for whom death threats are an almost daily occurrence. "We assess risk to our clients on scale of One to Four," Burnside explains, "One being the greatest risk. Mikey and his family is Number One all the way." While many of the details of the security shield Burnside provides remain closely guarded secrets, the gruff and no-nonsense bodyguard confirms that the protection he provides is extensive and intensive. "The work that Mikey does and the danger that it puts his family in requires us to stay focused 24/7," Burnside reveals. "We take our work very seriously. It's the least we can do for a man and his family who have put it all on the line to protect the constitutional rights of us all."

Yet, despite the extraordinary level of protection Burnside affords the Weinsteins, there are some threats against which no one can be comprehensively secured. "We don't dismiss anything," says Mikey. "Every attempt at harassment and intimidation is treated as utterly plausible until proven otherwise. But the danger isn't always just physical. There is a psychological element to what we have to endure as a family and that can be the most harrowing ordeal of all."

There is no more stark example of that kind of insidious attempt to ravage the Weinsteins sense of security and peace of mind than the toxic effects of "imprecatory prayer" launched against the family by two of the most extreme leaders of the far right dominionist Christian movement from deep within the military establishment.

To fully understand the execrable effects of this particularly barbaric religious practice, a quick overview of historic scriptural precedents is helpful. Imprecatory prayer is most widely understood to be any petition to God to invoke evil upon or curse one's enemies. It is King David, credited with writing most of the Old Testament Psalms, who is most associated with imprecatory verses such as those that appear in Psalm 55, 69 and, most especially, 109. Language commonly found in such prayers includes phrases like, "may their path be dark and slippery, with the angel of the Lord pursuing them" (Psalm 35:6) and "O God, break the teeth in their mouths; tear out the fangs of the young lions, O Lord!" (Psalm 58:6).

Imprecatory prayers occur with alarming frequency in the Bible, creating an uncomfortable conundrum for those who claim that the scriptures preach only peace and love. According to one thoughtful evangelical theologian, "The question of whether it's justifiable to use imprecatory prayer for circumstances beyond our control today in order to achieve a desired end, as some believe, would require taking these prayers out of context."

"Out of context?" Mikey asks derisively. "Really? You've got to be fucking kidding."

But it's no joke. The violent and blood soaked imagery of these verses make it hard to imagine in what other context they might exist. Indeed, the practice of imprecatory prayer is gaining widespread acceptance in fundamentalist Christian circles as a way of dealing with the enemies real or imagined. "It is time for imprecatory prayers, both ancient and new," reads the exhortation of one notable fundamentalist Christian firebrand. "It is time they rang out across the earth! This present abomination of desolation must be undone!"

Increasing numbers of extremist true believers have, it seems, taken that command to heart. The results have been, to say the least, alarming. During the 2008 presidential campaign, for example, a welter of T-shirts, bumper stickers, hats and even teddy bears began appearing for sale, all featuring the words "Pray for Obama" followed by the Bible verse reference, "Psalm 109:8."

The verse in question reads. "*Let his days be few; and let another take his office,*" but it is instructive and sobering to examine the whole of Psalm 109, among the most vindictive of David's prayers against his enemies. It reads in part: "*Appoint someone evil to oppose my enemy; let an accuser stand at his right hand. When he is tried, let him be found guilty, and may his prayers condemn him. May his days be few; may another take his place of leadership. May his children be fatherless and his wife a widow. May his children be wandering beggars; may they be driven from their ruined homes. May a creditor seize all he has; may strangers plunder the fruits of his labor. May no one extend kindness to him or take pity on his fatherless children. May his descendants be cut off, their names blotted out from the next generation. May the iniquity of his fathers be remembered before the Lord; may the sin of his mother never be blotted out. May their sins always remain before the Lord, that he may blot out their name from the earth.*"

Strong words for a faith that espouses forgiveness and reconciliation, but such was the toxic atmosphere of that political season that "Pray For Obama" merchandise amounted to what one commentator characterized as "trolling for assassins."

But the dark and dangerous use of imprecatory prayers against the perceived foes of Christian fundamentalism had in actuality been in constant use for many months before news stories surfaced about the implied threats to candidate Obama. Among the targets: Mikey Weinstein, his family and their descendants unto the tenth generation.

The prime instigators of this campaign of spiritual blackmail were a pair of former military chaplains whose rage against the MRFF generally and the Weinsteins specifically, had engendered one of the most disturbing and hateful responses the organization or the family had ever encountered.

Formerly an officer with the Navy chaplaincy (and, perhaps not coincidentally, an Air Force Academy graduate), Gordon Klingenschmitt first came to public attention in 2006 by claiming that he sacrificed a sixteen-year career and a military pension that is worth a million dollars because he was targeted for praying publicly in Jesus' name in his official capacity. The facts of his case were far different than his feverish accusations of persecution for his fundamentalist Christian faith. In actuality, he was charged with disobeying a direct order and subsequently drummed out of the Navy for attending a political rally in front of the White House in March 2006, dressed in his Navy uniform in direct violation of military regulations. An Air Force officer for eleven years prior to his Navy stint, Kligenschmitt had also been part of an intense lobbying effort to force the Bush Administration to sign an executive order authorizing military chaplains to pray "in the name of Jesus."

Norm Holcomb, a retired Navy chaplain who was Klingenschmitt's superior would later reveal the truth behind the voluble chaplain's specious claims of discrimination. "I was the dishonored ex-chaplain's supervisor for two years," Holcomb would write to each member of the Kentucky House of Representatives which had passed a resolution lauding Klingenschmitt for his "service to God, country and the Commonwealth of Kentucky." "I found him to be totally untruthful, unethical and insubordinate," Holcomb continued. "He was and is contemptuous of all authority and the issue of prayer had nothing at all to do with his dismissal from the Navy. He disobeyed the lawful order of a senior officer. I am sure that you understand that Navy regulations forbid any of us, regardless of rank or position, to appear in uniform in support of any political or partisan event.

"We have been relatively quiet regarding our ex-chaplain's untruthfulness and lack of honor," Holcomb continued, "because we are embarrassed that one of our own could display such behavior in the name of our Lord. We wanted to spare all concerned the embarrassment associated with his dishonesty. However, it now seems that it would be wrong for those of us who know the truth to remain silent."

After being found guilty in a court martial, the rogue chaplain fired off a rambling screed to Secretary of the Navy Donald Winter, accusing Navy officials of "raping" him because he had filed a whistleblower complaint alleging that his civil rights were violated. Shortly afterwards Klingenschmitt sent an email to Vice Admiral John C. Harvey, head of the Bureau of Naval Personnel, requesting a cash settlement in exchange for dropping his complaint.

Weinstein lent his weight to the battle, writing, "The shocking revelation of this blatantly extortionate demand letter for payoff money from Klingenschmitt to senior U.S. Navy leadership paints a crystal clear picture for all the world to see. That shamefully irrefutable picture is none other than one of a morbidly hypocritical 21st Century Judas Iscariot lustfully eager to betray his boundlessly self-professed piety, proselytizing ministry and missionary zeal for Jesus 'for the right price' to be paid to him by the United States Navy."

In April of 2006, MRFF, in conjunction with American United for Separation of Church and State, called for an investigation into Klingenschmitt for continuing to represent himself as an active-duty Navy chaplain while trying to raise funds for a new Internet endeavor called PrayInJesusName. On the site he posted a photograph of himself dressed in a Navy uniform and referred to himself as "Chaplain Gordon James Klingenschmitt."

The bogus holy man retaliated by posting a demented disclaimer defending his right to call himself a chaplain, insisting that he had a current endorsement as a "Chaplain and Evangelist to America" from the Chaplaincy of Full Gospel Churches (CFGC).

"I should have sent Klingenschmitt a fucking fruit basket," Mikey remarks wryly. "He really put that organization under our microscope." What the MRFF found was a fundamentalist Christian cabal extreme even by prevailing standards of religious fanaticism. "This is a so-called chaplain endorsing an agency founded by a retired fundamentalist Christian Army colonel and chaplain named James Ammerman," Weinstein continues. "Incredibly, the CFGC is authorized by the Department of Defense to provide the ecclesiastical endorsement required for all military chaplains, with several hundred of its chaplains and chaplain candidates, currently serving in various branches of the armed services. What's astonishing is that an individual with Ammerman's views would be allowed to endorse *anything*. This is a man who is genuinely convinced that the United States government is planning to turn over sovereignty to the United Nations. He believes that there are secretly hidden throughout the United States, especially in inaccessible part of national parks, foreign troops ready to take over. He believes that there is a contingent of Russian tanks in the Great Smokey Mountains under United National control. He believes that Holloman Air Force Base in New Mexico has been given to the Russians and that Fort Bliss in El Paso has been given to the Germans. He is virulently anti-Semitic and has expressed hatred for Roman Catholics, Muslims and even mainstream Protestant groups. He has advocated the assassination of such public figures as Barack Obama, Hillary Clinton, Joe Biden and Christopher Dodd." He draws a deep breath. "Holy shit! Do I really need to go on?"

But Weinstein's revelations regarding a clearly dangerous and deranged man, who has been selected by the military to appoint its chaplains, tells only part of the story. Ammerman has also made numerous public statements all but advocating the overthrow of the government, which he claims was founded by the Illuminati and satanists. He has also "suggested," in speeches before frenzied followers, that elected officials be arrested and executed.

Once Mikey began his investigation of the Chaplaincy of Full Gospel Churches and its leader, he and his family became a prime target for Ammerman's ire. In one particularly noxious speech before his accolytes he described how Weinstein became a "madman" because one of his sons "got saved" at the Air Force Academy. "Mikey," he told the frothing crowd, "was a graduate from there and became a lawyer—a real estate lawyer—and he's a multi-millionaire and he's getting other Jews to give him money to stamp out the name of Jesus throughout this nation. But one of his two Jewish sons got saved up there and he's been a madman ever since. He should come—and I pray God will enlighten him and say your son's not on the road to hell any longer, and if I get a chance to meet him, I will say, 'Do you know how happy you ought to be? One of your sons is on the road to heaven.' Now, he might slug me because he'd turned into a madman at that point, but I'll take a lick for Jesus. In fact, if he broke my neck and I died, I'd be in the instant presence of Christ, and I'm sure Jesus would have a little smile on his lips when I reported in."

Mikey wasn't smiling. "I was enraged," he admits. "Over the course of all this time, fighting all this shit, I developed a pretty tough hide. I take a lot of comfort in knowing that I give as good as I get, if not better. But this was about my family and the lies being told cut to the heart of our identity, of our heritage. How *dare* anyone, no matter how unhinged, talk about my sons like they were pawns in some game of religious brinkmanship. I was as fucking angry as I had ever been, and I've been pretty angry…you can ask any of those who have to live with me."

But Weinstein hadn't reached the tipping point, not yet. That didn't come until Klingenschmitt, feeling the hot breath of the MRFF at the nape of his neck, lashed back with an incendiary email to his extensive mailing list, followed by a posting on both YouTube and his PrayInJesusName website.

"Let us pray," Klingenschmitt intoned on an audio recording posted on the internet, "Almighty God, today we pray imprecatory prayers from Psalm 109 against the enemies of religious liberty, including [Americans United for Separation of Church and State head] Barry Lynn and Mikey Weinstein, who issued press releases this week attacking me personally. God, do not remain silent, for wicked men surround us and tell lies about us. We bless them, but they curse us. Therefore find them guilty, not me. Let their days be few, and replace them with Godly people. Plunder their fields, and seize their assets. Cut off their descendants, and remember their sins, in Jesus' name. Amen."

"He was calling down fire from heaven against me and my family," Weinstein recounts. "When I pulled up this malevolent video on the computer Bonnie happened to be walking by and was drawn in by the sound of a boson's whistle that this maniac uses to open every prayer. She just stood there, transfixed and in shock. We didn't for a minute think the God he was petitioning for death and destruction, if he actually existed, was even listening to Klingenschmitt. That's not what worried us. What concerned us infinitely more were those who followed Klingenschmitt and Ammerman and their ilk, the fringe element who might take the vile imprecatory prayer as an invitation to take up God's vengeance on their own. These men, by their base, odious and irresponsible actions, had directly endangered the people I loved the most, the ones I would lay down my life for. CNN had it right when it characterized their activities as 'trolling for assassins.' They had to be stopped."

"It's difficult to articulate the effect of all this hatred directed toward us and our family," Bonnie reveals. "Everyone likes to think that they're a good person, that they deserve the respect and dignity afforded to all human beings. But when you find out that there are those who are nightly on their knees, praying for you and your loved ones to suffer and die in the most extreme and horrible fucking way imaginable, it shakes your faith in human nature. You don't look at people the same way; with trust and respect. Everyone becomes a potential threat. That's an excruciating mindset to have to overcome. It's another battle we fight every day."

In September 2009, Mikey and Bonnie Weinstein filed a lawsuit in Dallas County, Texas, headquarters of the Chaplaincy of Full Gospel Churches, against Gordon Klingenschmitt, Jim Ammerman and their organization. "We didn't take legal action through the Military Religious Freedom Foundation," Mikey explains. "It wasn't about the Foundation. This time it was personal."

The lawsuit sought an injunction restraining the defendants from "making further terroristic threats" or "encouraging, soliciting, directing, abetting, or attempting to induce others to engage in similar conduct or to harm Plaintiffs or their family.

"Make no mistake," the complaint continued, "Klingenschmitt is not appealing to the Lord. He is appealing to the defendant's followers, using biblical quotes as a code, urging the defendant's followers to acts of imminent violence…Defendant's conduct was intentional and reckless, their conduct has been extreme and outrageous, and plaintiff have suffered severe emotional distress as a result of that behavior."

"There wasn't one word of exaggeration in our lawsuit," Bonnie avows. "After the imprecatory prayer was made, the threats on our lives increased exponentially. It was as if suddenly we were on the hit list of every fundamentalist Christian crackpot in the country, of which there are clearly a great number. We lived in an atmosphere of palpable and well-founded fear for months while the case wound its way through the courts."

For their part, Klingenschmitt and Ammerman tried to subvert the course of justice through a variety of legal technicalities, but ultimately to no avail. On March 18, 2011, the Fifth District Court of Appeals handed down its decision, ruling on Kligenschmitt's argument that Texas had no jurisdiction in the case: "In accordance with this Court's opinion of this date, the judgment of the trial court is affirmed. It is ordered that appellees Michael L. Weinstein and Bonnie L. Weinstein recover their costs of this appeal from appellant Gordon Klingenschmitt."

"We had won an important preliminary procedural legal victory," Bonnie affirms, " but in a larger sense we had struck a blow against the forces of hatred and intolerance being allowed to incite violence and provoke murder." She pauses for a moment to gather her thoughts. "I'm so proud of all that Mikey and I have accomplished. But it's been at the extreme cost of a normal life and a secure future. That's a trade-off no one should have to make. There is a very real toll that comes with this work. The Danish philosopher Søren Kierkegaard once said that, 'We live our life forwards, but we only understand it backwards.' In my best moments, I know in my heart and with every fiber of my being that defending the Constitution is the right thing to do." She pauses, leaving a silence that is as expressive as a primal scream. "It doesn't cost a lot," she continues at last. "It costs *everything*."

CHAPTER THIRTEEN

"I'M DONE WITH HIM"

If there is any tried and true aphorism that best applies to the work of Mikey Weinstein and his team at the Military Religious Freedom Foundation, it may well be "What goes around, comes around."

"The deeper down you drill into the morass of unconstitutional fundamentalist Christian influence in the military," Weinstein explains, "the more you realize that it's essentially the same group of people—utilizing the same tactics to the same end—who are behind the conspiracy. Which is not the same thing as saying that their influence doesn't continue to exponentially expand. They are very effective at seeking new recruits and enlarging their network of operatives. In some respects they have succeeded in making the armed services the career of choice among the hardcore dominionists in this country who are looking for the most direct way to advance their agenda. But it is the high-ranking elite, the same revolving cast of usual suspects, who are calling the shots. And they tend to congregate in locales that have historically provided a safe haven for their illegal activities. One such location is the Pentagon in Washington, DC. The other is the U.S. Air Force Academy in Colorado Springs, Colorado. These are the viper's nests, the lairs where they can operate with the most impunity and where their power is most concentrated. Of course, their tentacles extend far and wide, but it's at the Air Force Academy that they can shape the minds of the young almost at will and it's at the Pentagon that the brute power of that will is being exercised. It's not surprising that the work of MRFF is often concentrated in the midst of these two enemy camps."

Nor is it surprising that two of the most explosive examples of rampant fundamentalist abuse that MRFF has come to expose would be centered at these vital hubs of military command and control.

The first was launched when the Foundation received a letter in the early spring of 2010, written by Muslim military personnel and Department of Defense employees at the Pentagon. The request for assistance, the correspondence explained, was "a matter that concerns all Americans."

"We are dumbfounded," the letter continued, "that the Pentagon's Chaplain's Office has invited Mr. Franklin Graham to be the guest speaker at the National Day of Prayer at the Pentagon on May 6, 2010.

"Seven years ago, the Pentagon Chaplain's Office invited Mr. Graham to speak at the Pentagon, dismissing the concerns of the Pentagon Muslim worship community, as well as those of the Muslim community at large. At that time, the Pentagon chaplain claimed a lack of knowledge of Mr. Graham's opinions on Islam and Muslims. The current Pentagon chaplain made the same claim and dismissed our concerns by stating that Mr. Graham's comments are old news.

"That anyone serving in the Pentagon now could claim a lack of knowledge of Mr. Graham's very public, negative comments about Islam and Muslims stretch the limits of credulity. Mr. Graham never retracted his previous bigoted statements and, as recently as December 2009, in a CNN interview with Campbell Brown, Mr. Graham reiterated his negative views of Islam and Muslims by stating, "But there are millions of wonderful Muslim people. And I love them. I have friends that are Muslims and I work in those countries. But I don't agree with the teachings of Islam and I find it to be a very violent religion."

"The bigoted viewpoints repeatedly expressed by Mr. Graham, without retraction or apology, contradict not only Department of Defense policy but also our overall national policy, as articulated by President Obama. Once again, we hope and pray that the Pentagon Chaplain's Office will reconsider its invitation to Mr. Graham and instead invite more inclusive and honorable clergy persons to speak at the Pentagon."

"It was a cry from the heart," contends Mikey. "Those who had courageously signed their names to this document had done so out of a genuine love for this country and an understanding of its constitutional protections that frankly exceeded the comprehension of their superiors. The fact that Franklin Graham is rabidly anti-Islamic is hardly a headline grabber. Unfortunately the fact that the Pentagon would countenance his appearance and implicitly endorse his message of hate is also, sadly, nothing new."

Son of Billy Graham, the man dubbed "America's Pastor" by popular acclaim, Franklin Graham has done little since being designated the heir apparent of his father's mantle to promote the somewhat more arguably evenhanded tone of the elder Graham's ministry. Instead, he has become spokesman-in-chief for the growing hatred and mistrust of Muslims in this country and abroad. In the aftermath of the 9/11 attacks, he was quoted as referring to Islam as "a very evil and wicked religion." "True Islam cannot be practiced in this country," Graham told CNN's Campbell Brown, in a stunning display of religious hubris and ignorance. "You can't beat your wife. You cannot murder your children if you think they've committed adultery or something like that, which they do practice in these other countries." He then compounded these willful misconceptions during the controversy that exploded around the proposed construction of a mosque near the Ground Zero site, blithely asserting the absurd conjecture that "Muslims will claim now that the World Trade Center property is Islamic land." Islam "is a religion of hatred," he told *Time Magazine*. "It's a religion of war."

Graham, in fact, seemed to be doing everything in his power to fan the flames of sectarian rage, once again reflecting directly and accurately the very Crusader image promulgated by the jihadists. While touting the humanitarian intentions of his organization's charitable work in Iraq, he made sure to underscore his true intentions. "I believe as we work, God will always give us opportunities to tell others about his Son," he was quoted as saying. "We are there to reach out to love them and to save them, and as a Christian, I do this in the name of Jesus Christ."

While his father made a point of offering his spiritual insights to presidents both Democratic and Republican, Franklin made no secret on which side of the political divide he stood, and of the pernicious religious presumptions that came with the territory. "I think the president's problem is that he was born a Muslim," he told CNN. "His father was a Muslim. The seed of Islam is passed through the father like the seed of Judaism is passed through the mother. He was born a Muslim, his father gave him an Islamic name." He would later make the absurd and inflammatory assertion that President Obama "has allowed the Muslin Brotherhood to become part of the U.S. government and influence administration decisions. The Muslim Brotherhood is very strong and active in our country. It's infiltrated every level of our government. We've brought in Muslims to tell us how to make policy toward Muslim countries. And many of these people we've brought in, I'm afraid, are under the Muslim Brotherhood."

"Clearly the man is a loose cannon," says Mikey, "a poster child for lunatic, bigoted sectarian hatred. But the really frightening aspect of his unhinged statements is how many in the military effusively agree with him and are anxious to give him a platform to spew his rants. And there is no more perfect a vehicle for disseminating this filthy, bigoted bile than the Pentagon's National Day of Prayer event."

The law formalizing the annual observance of a day of national prayer was enacted in 1952, with constitutional challenges being mounted regularly ever since. Association with any number of extreme Christian fundamentalist front organizations has just as regularly sullied the event's weak-kneed non-sectarian status. There is perhaps no more glaring example than the National Day of Prayer Task Force (NDPTF), a private organization headed by Shirley Dobson, wife of Focus on the Family founder and ardent fundamentalist Dr. James Dobson.

It has long been an accepted practice that the honorary chairman of the NDPTF would also be selected as the keynote speaker for the Pentagon's observances. Such a long-standing affiliation has turned the NDPTF into a de facto "official" sponsor of the National Day of Prayer, a reality underscored by the Pentagon Chaplain's Office use of promotional materials supplied by the NDPTF.

"There's only one problem with this cozy little setup," Mikey asserts. "It's fucking illegal. To begin with, it violates the Department of Defense's Joint Ethics Regulation, strictly prohibiting endorsement of a non-federal entity or, for that matter, bans any attempt at providing a selective benefit or preferential treatment to any organization."

And the National Day of Prayer Task Force is hardly any organization. "It has comprehensively exclusive restrictions and blatantly sectarian requirements," Weinstein explains, "that make all NDPTF affiliated events exclusively fundamentalist Christian in scope, message, and nature. To begin with, all NDPTF volunteers must subscribe to a 'Statement of Belief,' an oath that universally excludes not only all non-Christians and non-religious, but, in point of fact, even many Christians themselves. It reads in part, 'I believe that the Holy Bible is the inerrant Word of The Living God. I believe that Jesus Christ is the Son of God and the only One by which I can obtain salvation and have an ongoing relationship with God...I believe that those who follow Jesus are family and there should be unity among all who claim his name...I commit that National Day of Prayer activities I serve with will be conducted solely by Christians..."'

This fundamentalist Christian pledge of allegiance is backed up by another document the NDPTF has also produced known as the "Official Policy Statement on Participation of 'Non-Judeo-Christian' groups in the National Day of Prayer."

"The National Day of Prayer Task Force was a creation of the National Prayer Committee," it read in part, "for the expressed purpose of organizing and promoting prayer observances conforming to a Judeo-Christian system of values. People with other theological and philosophical views are, of course, free to organize and participate in activities that are consistent with their own beliefs."

"Look," Weinstein allows, "of course the NDPTF has every right as a private organization to organize exclusively Christian events and to prohibit the participation of non-Christians. But the Pentagon Chaplain's Office absolutely cannot endorse or provide a selective benefit to a private entity. That is an unequivocal matter of U.S. military law, indeed U.S. Constitutional law. Inviting Franklin Graham, the NDPTF honorary chairman, to spew his heinously hurtful and hateful rants against the entirety of the religion of Islam was an illegal, not to mention immoral and inhuman act."

But even with so firm a grasp on the obvious illegality of Graham's appearance, coupled with the heartfelt plea of the Pentagon's Muslim service personnel, there was no guarantee that Weinstein and the MRFF could halt the momentum that built up around the impending event. "There was an already established tradition in place here," Mikey explains. "This is the way it had been done for a long time and anyone who knows the military knows the impacted power of tradition. The Pentagon's entrenched fundamentalist Christian faction was not about to give up and go home without a major confrontation. If we were going to stop this outrage we were going to have to move quickly and decisively."

To that end, Weinstein promptly jumped the bureaucratic cue and went straight to the top, sending a letter to Secretary of Defense Robert Gates and copying all three military service secretaries, all five members of the Joint Chiefs of Staff and President Obama. In no uncertain terms it demanded, "that the Pentagon Chaplain's Office immediately rescind its invitation to Mr. Graham and choose a more appropriate and inclusive speaker for this high profile event."

Events were moving quickly, thanks to MRFF's timely intervention. Knowing full well that their demand for a withdrawal of Graham's invitation would fall on deaf ears without a credible threat to back it up, the Foundation's legal team swung into action, preparing a temporary restraining order to stop the NDPTF event at the Pentagon. Prospects for the case were immeasurably aided by the decision, just a few days earlier, of U.S. District Court Judge Barbara Crabb in Wisconsin, declaring the National Day of Prayer itself to be unconstitutional. The event, her decision reads in part, "goes beyond mere 'acknowledgment' of religion because its sole purpose is to encourage all citizens to engage in prayer, an inherently religious exercise that serves no secular function in this context. In this instance, the government has taken sides on a matter that must be left to individual conscience."

"We had the wind at our back," Weinstein recounts, "but at the same time we knew we had to keep pushing as hard and as fast as we could. Everyone at the Foundation was working feverishly and the excitement and tension was very high. The event itself was only weeks away and we had to turn a very large and very cumbersome ship around in very short order." To that end, the Foundation began preparing for a major media push, laying out the issue, and the clear and present dangers behind it, in the starkest possible terms. In a subsequently published *Washington Post* editorial titled *Why We Object to Franklin Graham's Islamophobia*, Mikey began by stating the obvious: "Let's just face it: Franklin Graham is an Islamophobe, an anti-Muslim bigot, and an international representative of the scourge of fundamentalist Christian supremacy and exceptionalism.

"I often wonder," Weinstein continued, "how painful it must be for U.S. citizens of the Muslim faith to hear Graham's universal, Father Coughlin-esque condemnations of Islam. Indeed, and how much worse still for the grieving families of recently fallen American servicemen of the Islamic faith.

"...Islamic fundamentalists must cherish Graham as a propaganda tool. For terrorists, jihadists and insurrectionists, Franklin Graham is the gift that keeps on giving. His rejection of Islam can be likened to having an acute case of fundamentalist Christian Tourette's syndrome; the only good Muslim is a Christian-converted Muslim."

In the end, the combination of a swift and savvy media blitz, a looming federal court threat and passionate and closely argued defense of the Constitution directed at policy makers who could actually effect change, won the day. With the Foundation's attorneys virtually on the steps of the Alexandria, Virginia courthouse about to file Graham's invitation to speak was withdrawn. It was a moment of unalloyed triumph, or as Mikey characteristically put it, "Fuck, yeah!"

"As much as anything," Mikey later allowed, with all due modesty, "I think our reputation preceded us. The fundamentalist Christians in the Pentagon knew the kind of havoc we could wreak if we put our minds to it. The Franklin Graham affair was so obviously an egregious constitutional violation that the handwriting on the wall was clear enough for even them to read. We had gained a major victory and at the same time, learned an important lesson. It was vital to go in with every fucking gun blazing. We had to intimidate, to overpower. Sadly, it was the only language they understood."

Yet, even then, while a significant battle may have been won, the war raged on. In the less than a year after the decision declaring the National Prayer Day unconstitutional, it was unanimously dismissed by a federal appellate court.

"The battles for constitutional protection never end," Mikey acknowledges. "The important thing, the only thing, is that you keep on fighting, with every last damn ounce of energy at your command."

The next clash of arms in that fight would follow hard on the heels of the Franklin Graham victory, when the long-festering issue of fundamentalist Christian proselytizing at the U.S. Air Force Academy once again erupted. While the controversy over unwarranted sectarian influence at the institution continued to make headlines into the late summer and early of 2011, the impetus for MRFF's renewed action to curtail Christian fundamentalist coercion at the institution reached back to 2005 and the earliest days of Weinstein's struggle with the Academy.

It was then, in response to Mikey's explosive revelations of religious abuses at the school—especially those perpetrated by the then-Commandant of Cadets, Brigadier General Johnny Weida—that administration officials announced that an investigation would be launched to look into the charges. Heading up the inquiry was a retired Air Force Colonel and 1976 Air Force Academy graduate, who the Pentagon named as the on-site

Department of Defense and United States Air Force's Inspector General in the matter under the purview of the Pentagon's Secretary of the Air Force Inspector General's office.

While the subsequent report duly criticized Weida for his fundamentalist Christian overreach, there was no question that the investigation was little more than a whitewash, papering over the pervasive problem of continual, unconstitutional proselytizing at the Academy, by insisting "the climate does not involve overt religious discrimination." It was as if, by simply propagating the lie with enough conviction, the Academy assumed it would be taken for truth.

Mikey would live to fight another day, but the officer who had played an important part in the probe was not about to let the matter rest, subsequently mounting an offensive and highly personal smear campaign against Weinstein, the one man who had dared to stand up against the fundamentalist Christian cabal that had for so long held sway at the Academy.

In his ire, the officer would go so far as to create a slew of fictitious documents, including a mock Department of Defense form he titled the "Hurt Feelings Report" to be filled out by a "Whiner." He would, at considerable effort, go on to fabricate false news stories, using the logos and internet links of *The New York Times* and *The Washington Times* to plant outrageous, disgusting and defamatory stories about Weinstein and his family.

Given the doubts that such libelous actions cast on the officer's objectivity, to say the least, Weinstein demanded that a new investigation into the toxic religious atmosphere at the Academy be immediately launched, this time under the auspices of an officer not quite so blatantly biased.

In the meantime, Academy cadets were continuing to flood the MRFF with requests for representation. By early September 2010, the Foundation had assembled enough evidence to go public with the allegations of over fifty cadets, together asserting that they were being subjected to extreme pressure to conform to the school's program of active Christian fundamentalist conversion. One email written by an anonymous MRFF client suffices to tell the tale of the disintegrating atmosphere pervading the Academy: "I keep 'Christian' books and 'Christian' CDs in my room," the message read, "so others will be fooled and leave me alone and not suspect that I'm not actually with the USAFA 'Christianity is the Only Way' program here, even though I consider myself to be a Christian."

The Academy moved quickly, issuing a press release in an effort to contain the damage brought on by MRFF's newest revelations. "Mr. Mikey Weinstein of the Military Religious Freedom Foundation (MRFF), claimed that the Academy has allowed a private religious group to promote improper Christian proselytizing at publicly accessible Academy facilities," the release read in part. "Upon learning of this allegation, Lieutenant General Mike Gould, USAFA Superintendent, directed an immediate review of the claim. To date, the allegation is not substantiated."

"It was a bald-faced lie," Mikey maintains. "The so-called 'Climate Study,' which had been uncovered by intrepid *Colorado Springs Independent* investigative journalist Pam Zubeck, actually reported that three hundred and fifty-three cadets, almost one out of every five survey participants (nearly fifty percent of the minority faith Academy cadets) reported having been subjected to unwanted religious proselytizing, and twenty-three cadets—thirteen of whom were Christians—reported living in fear of their physical safety, being pounded because of their religious beliefs."

Lieutenant General Gould, the Academy Superintendent, responded with a mixture of mystification and indignation. The findings, he claimed in an interview with the *Air Force Times*, "don't do me any good unless I can find out why certain people are feeling like they aren't free to practice their religion, or someone feels they are being harassed."

On hearing Gould's obfuscating evocations, Bonnie's response was direct and unvarnished. "What kind of fucking idiot is this guy? People who are being harassed don't go to their harassers to complain. That's just plain stupid."

Weinstein could have provided reams of material informing Gould just what many cadets, faculty and staff under his command were actually feeling—fear, intimidation, humiliation, anger and, especially, danger—but he was never afforded the opportunity. In early October, MRFF was specifically barred from attending a Climate Survey briefing being held at the Academy, a briefing that had been called to answer charges leveled at the Air Force Academy by the foundation in the first place.

The MRFF hit back with everything it had, issuing a blistering statement that directly called Gould to account for the exclusion. "MRFF's victim-clients are enduring horrific and unconstitutional systemic religious oppression at the Academy," the statement read, "the very same systemic oppression which Gould is dishonorably trying to 'spin' to the media as being either trivial or nonexistent. It is, of course, obvious why Gould barred

MRFF; he cravenly wanted to silence all opposition and dissent to his farcical briefing. He wanted no avenue of inconvenient and contrary communication available for those for whom MRFF alone speaks. Gould and his command at the USAF Academy will neither now nor ever speak for MRFF's clients who are being tormented and afflicted on a daily basis. The U.S. Air Force Academy craves and enforces brutal silence among those it unconstitutionally torments. What does MRFF think of Gould and his fellow USAF Academy oppressors? Confucius said it best: "To see that which is right, and not to do it, is cowardice."

"We did what we could to sound the alarm," Mikey would later reflect. "Gould and the Academy had absolutely no right to exclude us from any briefing on an issue that was of clear and urgent concern to us. We had rock solid legal standing to drag them into court but we decided to hold back for the moment. Our concern was for our clients and there was a sense that if we pushed too hard at that juncture we might be endangering them. We decided to step back and wait for another shot. We knew that, sooner or later, this crisis was gong to rear its ugly head again."

That eventuality came sooner than expected. Six months after the Gould cover up, the Air Force announced that it would be conducting yet another review of the religious environment at the Academy. The intent was clear: the 2010 Climate Review, and the attendant exclusion of MRFF from any deliberations, had left behind a putrescent cloud of mistrust and suspicion. A new investigation, no matter how cursory, might serve to offset the storm of bad press the Air Force had received in its handling of the matter.

The new review proved not only cursory in the extreme, but a foregone conclusion virtually from the beginning. Headed by retired Air Force General Patrick Gamble, a former Commandant of Cadets, with an investigative team that included a former Academy dean and two former Academy department heads, the work of interviewing, assessing and evaluating took all of five days in early April. It was barely enough time to speak with a handful of faculty and staff members, with only about a hundred cadets agreeing to participate in the process, in large part due to the fears of those who had not volunteered that their interviews would not and could not be kept confidential. There was simply no guarantee of confidentially in the process. Cadets who had actually experienced noxious fundamentalist Christian pressure tactics simply refused, for good reason, to get involved.

Not surprisingly, Gamble's report painted a picture of enlightened tolerance, sweet harmony and brotherly love in every corner and crevice of the Academy. The institution was, in fact, an exemplar of spotless virtue.

"Who knew?" commented Mikey with withering sarcasm.

"Cadets' acceptance of those with different beliefs is *exceptional*," the findings claimed with a straight face. "USAFA should be recognized for its institutional leadership in this area. We found widespread agreement that everyone throughout the chain of command has been given and is giving appropriate guidance with respect to official neutrality, not only among religions, but also between religious and non-religious beliefs. Cadets expressed a near-uniform belief that they can (and do) make their own choices to participate—or not—in religious activities, without repercussion. Reports of actual pressure to participate were rare and easily resolved by simply expressing that the invitation or speech was unwelcome. Cadets are not unduly stressed about possible pressure to join or conform to a religion, and the majority clearly feels empowered to deal with unwanted approaches. Across the board, cadets disavow that any favoritism or retribution would accrue based upon religious or non-religious affiliation…We found no evidence in our interviews at any level that anyone fears for their physical safety based upon their religious beliefs or non-belief."

So it went, on and on, in an interminable palaver of evasion, equivocation and outright deception. The response to the whitewash of those within the institution with firsthand experience of religious repression can best be summed up by an email from one of over two hundred Academy cadets who had turned to MRFF for help.

"If any of us gave even the slightest indication that we weren't one of their number," the cadet revealed, "our lives would be even more miserable than they already are due to the fact that we are all living lies here. Despite the Cadet Honor Code we all lie about our lives. We have to.

"Just one example of many I could talk about is Gen. Gamble saying in his report that a polite 'no, thank you' to Christian religious proselytizing is just fine and dandy. It is not for at least two reasons. First, if you try to be polite and say 'no thanks' to them they *never* stop asking you repeatedly to reconsider. Second, you know that eventually you are going to get them mad at you by always 'politely declining.' I and many other cadets have seen and experienced this over and over again. This is why there is a large group of USAFA cadets (larger at least than the size of the group that Gen. Gamble says he interviewed) who pretend to be evangelical Christians in order to just be left alone."

Along with pointing out just how far Weinstein's beloved institution had fallen in its principles and practices, these sentiments resoundingly echoed the experiences of an Academy graduate who had gone on to teach at the school and who knew first hand exactly how deep the deception in the Gamble Report actually went. Asking that his name and rank be withheld to protect him from retaliation, he wrote: "I am convinced more than ever the leadership at my beloved USAFA is only dedicated to fluffy, empty statements when it comes to dealing with the need to tolerate and respect beliefs different than those of the dominionist 'Christians' that hi-jacked our institution over twenty years ago...The consequences have been devastating to the lives of hundreds and hundreds of outstanding cadets, officers, enlisted, and civilians. The fact that the USAFA leadership sees anyone who wants to uphold the establishment and practice clauses of the First Amendment, which is part of the Constitution we swore or affirmed to defend, as trying to undermine the institution's goals is ludicrous and cowardly.

"As a cadet in the early 1990s, I saw blatant evangelization by the officer and cadet minions of the New Life Church and other dominionist organiza-tions. Back then I was too immature to understand the seriousness of the problem, and I just wanted to survive the rigors of USAFA. On active duty I have run into dominionists in every assignment, and I finally woke up when I read what the Weinstein family and other fine individuals had to put up with."

Another courageous individual who stepped forward to refute the Gamble Record was Air Force Academy Economics Professor David Mul-lin, who had direct experience with the length to which the fundamentalist Christian faction at the institution would go when his devoted service dog was poisoned. Mullin, who had meet with Gamble's team, issued a statement shortly after the report was made public: "Rather than taking seriously the cries of victim of religious discrimination," Mullin wrote, "Gamble listens and believes the perpetrators. What kind of a police force is effective if they only ask criminals if they are committing crimes? Gamble is flat-out wrong in stating that he had a good representation of participants. When you can-not guarantee anonymity, you cannot expect victims to come forward. So the composition of participants is strongly biased toward the perpetrators of religious discrimination. Gamble was forewarned by me and others of this, which he totally ignored. Gamble's report is the perfect image of an ostrich's head in the sand. When your head is in the sand, you see no evil and hear no evil."

Despite the fact that the Academy was systematically blocking the Foundation from any access to the institution, its staff or cadet corps, Weinstein and his team continued to push for reforms. Through a Freedom of Information Act request in late 2010, they succeeded in getting nearly three thousand pages of documents, primarily emails, made public. What was immediately apparent from the data dump was that the Academy had engaged in a comprehensive and prolonged practice of ignoring, stonewalling and trying to discredit the MRFF and its work.

A glaring example came from an email string in September of 2010, in which an aide to Lieutenant General Gould sent a message offering to direct emails from Weinstein and the MRFF into a subfolder of in the Superintendent's mailbox inbox, "given the volume of MRFF emails you get."

"Best solution would be to block them from reaching my machine," Gould shot back within minutes. "I'm done with him."

In another egregious example from September 2010, Weinstein forwarded a message to Dean of Faculty Brigadier General Dana Born. Born sent the email to others at the Academy with the note, "hate to forward these—not worth the time usually you will spend reading it." In response to another urgent correspondence to Born, the Dean this time copied Chaplain Colonel Robert Bruno, forwarding a message he had already sent to Lieutenant General Gould. "Mikey," it read, "is clearly trying to undermine your and our vision of institutional pride."

Weinstein, Bruno replied, "may be suffering from attention deficit syndrome: no one is listening or responding, but we'll continue maintaining the high road and doing the right thing."

The "right thing" in this case seemed to be to adopt a tone of righteous indignation when confronted with evidence that MRFF's legitimate constitutional challenges were being routinely ignored. In a written statement, Academy officials insisted that the institution "respects all organizations dedicated to the principles of integrity, truthfulness, religious respect and religious freedom...We seek to work constructively with these groups to continue fostering religious respect at the Air Force Academy."

Despite the suffocating sanctimony, it was painfully evident that the Academy was actually working round the clock to subvert those "principles of integrity, truthfulness, religious respect and religious freedom."

"Each of these experiences in confronting the Academy has taught us the same lesson," Weinstein concludes. "Whether it's Gould or Gamble, the faces may change but the evil that Air Force Academy Professor David Mullin so eloquently describes remains the same. The only way to ever change the 'climate' at the Academy is to eradicate the fundamentalist Christian infestation that had taken root at the deepest levels of the institution. The same applies to the Pentagon. The mindset that had gotten us into this national security crisis was the not the same one that could get us out. This is a question of an entrenched leadership that will do anything to protect itself and carry on its unconstitutional sectarian crusade. MRFF does the best it can in attacking the symptoms, but the fatal disease will continue to metastasize until and unless America as a nation rises up to take back its military."

The urgency with which Weinstein delivers these words only serves to underscore the extraordinary work his foundation continues to accomplish. And that work was about to take on an astonishing new dimension that would have extraordinary implications not simply for America, but for the whole human race.

CHAPTER FOURTEEN

NUKES, NAZIS, AND NORWAY

"I have been often accused of wild exaggeration," Mikey remarks in one of his more reflective moments. "I've been told that I need to tone down the fucking rhetoric, to 'go along to get along,' to seek compromise and accommodation in order to achieve my goals, to be a kinder and gentler Mikey. According to that logic, the forces I'm fighting against are ultimately sincere individuals motivated by their honest and good faith religious convictions to carry out what they believe they've been called by God to accomplish in order to bring about His reign and rule on earth. I need to respect where they're coming from, make allowances for their earnest spiritual convictions and find a way to work out our differences in a civil and mutually supportive dialogue.

"Well, fuck that," his eyes flash with a quick, wicked gleam, his defiant words spoken half in provocative jest and half in deadly seriousness. "These people are out to destroy everything I hold near and dear; the most basic principles on which this great nation was founded; the precious freedoms that brave men and women fought and bled and died to preserve; the charge that has been solemnly laid on my people to 'never again' let religious intolerance become a tool of totalitarian genocide. For these causes I give no quarter and I ask no quarter. These enemies of civilization know that I won't stop until I have dragged them out from under the stinking rocks ey cowardly hide into the blinding light of day. And I know that stop at literally nothing to achieve their ends. That includes mass

He leans back to gauge the effect of his uncompromised claim. "The fact that those fundamentalist dominionist Christians are willing to kill to achieve their twisted agenda is a fact of history. And I'm not just talking about the Holocaust, the Inquisition or any of the other abundant examples across two thousand years of fundamentalist Christian savagery. What I'm talking about happened in Oslo, Norway and on the idyllic island of Utoya on July 22, 2011, when over seventy innocent people, most of them teenagers, were systematically slaughtered by a man who believed with utter fundamentalist conviction that he was doing God's sovereign will."

By evoking the horrifying bombing and massacre carried by Norwegian Christian terrorist Anders Behring Brievik, Weinstein lays bare the lethal chaos that religious extremists are only too eager and able to inflict on an unsuspecting world. "I wonder," he says with withering insight, "what Brievik's bleeding victims would have thought about entering into a 'constructive dialogue' with the monster who gunned them down in cold blood? I wonder if they would have thought I was exaggerating the threat posed by fundamentalist Christian zealots who unleash hell on earth in order to bring about a blood drenched Armageddon? I wonder if the parents of those slaughtered children would think that I was going too far in trying to warn the world of the deadly danger it was facing by these radical Christian extremists?"

Weinstein's anguished questions are more than mere rhetorical flourishes. In point of fact, he *did* raise a warning, years before the tragic events in Norway, regarding both the perverted ideology that fueled Brievik's actions and the individuals that spouted these repugnant tenets, specifically that odious tenant of fundamentalist Christian faith that espouses total war against Islam.

The link can be found in the repellent fifteen hundred page manifesto the mass murderer posted on his website in the run up to his rampage. There among his toxic incitements to a sectarian war to save Christian civilization from the Muslim hordes, Brievak cited, often and at length, a pair of primary influences for his doomsday manifesto, both of whom Mikey had previously faced down in a successful attempt to put a stop to their hateful ideology within the U.S. military.

The confrontation began in early 2007 with a lecture delivered at the Joint Forces Staff College in Norfolk, Virginia. The event was part of the institution's "Islam Elective," a course open only to American military and national security personnel. Foreign students attending the college, including those from allied Islamic nations, were not allowed to attend.

The cordially welcomed speaker for the session was Brigitte Gabriel, founder of extremist right wing Christian conclave Congress for Truth and the author of a particularly vile Islamophobic tract titled *Because They Hate*.

The tenor of Gabriel's remarks can best be captured by the question and answer period that followed the talk. Responding to the query, "Should we resist Muslims who want to seek political office in this nation?" Gabriel replied: "Absolutely. A practicing Muslim who believes the word of the Koran to be the word of Allah, who abides by Islam, who goes to mosque and prays five times a day, cannot be a loyal citizen to the United States of America. A Muslim sworn to office can lay his hand on the Koran and swear to tell the truth and nothing but the truth fully, knowing that the same Koran that he is swearing on justifies his lying in order to advance the cause of Islam. When we are faced with war and if a Muslim political official has to make a decision either in the interest of the United States or Islam, that Muslim in office will always have his loyalty to Islam."

When asked for her advice to Americans alarmed at a mosque being built in their community, she asserted, "Find out who owns the deed to that mosque. Is it a Saudi foundation...some Islamic sheik outside of the United States of America? Write those names down. Call the F.B.I. in your local community. Turn the names in. Are these people on the most wanted list? Do they have links to terrorism? This is how we can help our government as citizens."

A year after Gabriel's incendiary appearance at the Joint Forces Staff College, three men who billed themselves as "ex-terrorists" were invited by the Air Force Academy and paid $13,000 each to speak at the 50th Annual United States Air Force Academy Assembly on the topic "Dismantling Terrorism: Developing Actionable Solutions for Today's Plague of Violence." One of them was Walid Shoebat, who had previously been given top billing at such hardcore fundamentalist venues as Tim LaHaye's Pre-Tribulation Research Center conferences and John Hagee's Christians United for Israel events. Shoebat was accorded great acclaim at these dominionist Christian strongholds despite that fact that his professed status as a former terrorist who had come to see the error of his ways was a claim widely disputed by academics and terrorism experts alike. So dubious was the fabrication, in fact, that the FBI had refused to even dignify Shoebat's story with an investigation.

Both Gabriel and Shoebat were also featured talking heads in a fear mongering anti-Muslim documentary titled *Obsession: Radical Islam's War Against the West.* "I know that the U.S. Department of the Navy uses the film," asserted Gregory Ross, co-writer and director of *Obsession,* "and that it has also been shown on Capitol Hill on many occasions in order to educate politicians."

It was just that kind of "education" that Mikey and the MRFF were doing everything in their power to thwart. Having caught wind of the Air Force Academy's plans to invite Brigitte Gabriel to speak, the Foundation launched a furious protest, and in February of 2009, the Academy rescinded the invitation under pressure.

But it didn't stop there. After repeated demands for equal time to counter the virulent tide of anti-Muslim preaching that had swamped the Academy, school officials were eventually forced to allow Mikey, along with MRFF stalwarts as advisory board member Reza Aslan and board member former Ambassador Joe Wilson, to speak to the cadets in an attempt to repair at least some of the damage inflicted by the strident sectarian rhetoric that had been unconstitutionally countenanced by the constitutionally-challenged Academy's administration.

"That might have been the end of it," Mikey reflects with palpable sorrow. "We had done our best to counter the hatred and bigotry spewed by these agents of intolerance. But tragically, we were too late to totally stop the spread of their destructive influence." He pauses to take a deep, steadying breath. "Walid Shoebat and Brigitte Gabriel are two of the primary anti-Muslim extremists who are quoted at length in the manifesto of Anders Behring Brievik. Shoebat is cited fifteen times and a link to a forty-five minute video featuring Brigitte Gabriel is provided to provoke further incitement. We may have silenced them for a time, but their voices were heard loud and clear by a murderous man on a violent and unyielding crusade to save this twisted fundamentalist version of Christianity and the means to enforce his murderous intentions."

Bombs and assault rifles can be very effective in carrying out the lethal agenda of fundamentalist zealots. But their determination to impose their noxious creed hardly stops with a lone gunman, no matter how well armed. It was a warning Mikey would sound with conspicuous success as he took on one of the most egregious examples of what amounted to a silent coup by the Christian fundamentalists to seize control of America's vast armory.

That warning had its origins in a recent appeal for representation that was made to the MRFF by thirty-one United States Air Force nuclear missile launch officers at Vandenberg Air Force Base, a key facility one hour north of Santa Barbara on the California coast. Twenty-nine of those who came to the Foundation were professing Protestants and Catholics. In addition to the participating instructors and students at Vandenberg, active duty nuclear missile launch officers from various other sites sought MRFF client status. Banding together as a courageous group, they called attention to a mandatory training program for newly arriving officers at this key nuclear missile launch training facility, an insidious attempt at subverting established ethical guidelines within the military that stands as an outrageous example of the incursion of religious indoctrination into the very heart of the armed services establishment.

As subsequently confirmed by pioneering investigative journalist Jason Leopold of *Truthout* (for which Weinstein serves as a member of the Board of Advisors), Air Force Chaplains conducted the Nuclear Ethics and Nuclear Weapons training sessions during the launch officer's crucial first week of arrival at Vandenberg. Such sessions were held under the auspices of 381st Training Group and 392nd Training Squadron. These units are responsible for preparing every Air Force Space and Missile Officer to assume their crucial nuclear missile launch duties, and takes place prior to their being stationed at one of three Air Force bases to guard the country's Intercontinental Ballistic Missile (ICBM) arsenal. If called upon to do so by the President, these are the very men and women who would launch nuclear-armed Minuteman IIIs. The officer who initiated and led the "nuclear ethics presentation" was Air Force Chaplain Capt. Shin Soh.

The U.S. Air Force nuclear missile launch officers that contacted the MRFF provided as evidence of unconstitutional religious bias in the ethics curriculum a PowerPoint presentation and over 500 pages of other material used in the program. The pernicious content of the presentation came primarily in the form of the forty-three pages that comprised the PowerPoint display, broadly titled *Ethics*, with a provocative subheading that read *Who Are You When No One Is Looking?* The instruction purported to offer "five ethical principles for service to the Air Force" specifically regarding nuclear warfare. The presentation then proceeded with an in-depth examination for St. Augustine's famous Just War Theory, which listed as 'qualifications" for morally defensible warfare, "To avenge or to avert evil; to protect the innocent and restore moral social order" and "to restore moral order; not expand power, not for pride or revenge."

Among the ostensibly ethical questions contained in the PowerPoint program, missile officers were asked: "Can you imagine a set of circumstances that would warrant a nuclear launch from the US, knowing that it would kill thousands of non-combatants?" Another blatantly religious query posed to the trainees was, "Can we train physically, emotionally and spiritually for a job we hope we never have to do?"

The answer to such questions, according to the PowerPoint slides, could be found in numerous examples of characters from the New and Old Testament who fought "just" wars. One example given was that of Abraham who "organized an army to rescue Lot." God also supposedly motivated "Samson, Deborah and Barak to fight and deliver Israel from foreign oppressors," and claimed that "David is a warrior who is also a 'man after God's own heart.'"

The New Testament citations included that of Timothy 2:3, in which, according to the PowerPoint, "Paul chooses three illustrations to show what it means to be a good disciple of Christ." One of them was a soldier, who must "be willing to put up with hardship." Romans 13:4 was quoted to the effect that, "In spite of personal blemishes, God calls *the emperor* to be an instrument of justice". The PowerPoint slide also highlighted a passage from the Book of Revelation that attempts to explain how Jesus Christ, as the "mighty warrior," believed some wars to be just. It goes on to assert that there are "many examples of believers who engaged in wars in the Old Testament" in a "righteous way" and notes there is "no pacifistic sentiment in mainstream Jewish history."

The training material next posed the question, "Can A Person of Faith Fight in a War?" and laid out a series of propositions that cut to the heart of a United States Air Force nuclear missile officer's sworn duty to obey orders. "Can we exercise enough faith in our decision makers, political and military, to follow through with the orders that are given us?" read one of the most incriminating PowerPoint slides.

"This is as clear a case of treasonous subversion as could possibly be imagined," Weinstein insists. "Do we really want those individuals to whom we have entrusted the most fucking destructive weapons ever conceived by the mind of human beings making a decision, based solely on personal religious principles, about whether or not to obey a direct order? Put aside for the moment the fact that no other theory of just war from any other religious perspective was ever offered, the assumption being that every U.S. Air Force missile launch officer at Vandenberg was a de facto Christian adherent whose ethical concerns could be addressed by a direct appeal to Biblical quotations. These seditious actions reach far deeper than that. Good order and discipline is not subject to religious qualms or second thoughts. These brave men and women are given this awesome responsibility in the expectation that they will faithfully carry out their orders without having to ask 'What Would Jesus Do?' The fact that the preponderance of the Vandenberg nuclear missile launch officers who sought help from the Foundation were, in fact, practicing Christians only underscores the fact that this kind of indoctrination is beyond the pale even for those who acknowledge a spiritual dimension to their lives. This is a shocking example of coercive fundamentalist Christian tactics in a realm where clear, unambiguous lines of responsibility must be drawn. The bottom line is that the higher calling to which these individuals are answerable is that of our nation's duly constituted authorities, not some supreme being, however such an entity might be defined. That way lies fucking madness, as history has so amply proven."

In the case of the Vandenberg Air Force Base nuclear missile launch training program, history would prove something else as well: that what goes around, comes around. As if the clearly unconstitutional religious incitements didn't go far enough, the PowerPoint presentation also included slides that highlighted quotes from a former member of the Nazi Party and SS officer, Wernher Von Braun, widely considered to be the father of the U.S. space program.

But Von Braun was hardly being cited for his scientific expertise. Instead he was being specifically referenced as a moral authority, a horrifying assertion considering that this top Nazi scientist, a highly-decorated SS major, used Jewish slave labor selected from concentration camps, as well as captured French anti-Nazi partisans and civilians to help construct the V-2 rocket at the Peenemunde facility on the north German coast. It was from that site that rockets were launched which were responsible for the death of thousands of British civilians in the final months of the war.

The training material evoked Von Braun's disingenuous words after his surrender to American forces in May 1945. "We knew that we had created a new means of warfare," the scientist told his interrogators, "and the question as to what nation, to what victorious nation, we were willing to entrust this brainchild of ours was a *moral decision* more than anything else," Von Braun went on to sanctimoniously claim that, "we wanted to see the world spared another conflict such as Germany had just been through and *we felt that only by surrendering such a weapon to people who are guided by the Bible could such an assurance to the world be best secured.*"

As a key participant in a top-secret military program known as Operation Paperclip, Von Braun was one of the most important Nazi scientists recruited after World War II. According to Operation Paperclip documents, such scientists "were secretly brought to the United States, without State Department review and approval; their service for Hitler's Third Reich and SS memberships, as well as the classification of many as war criminals or security threats, disqualified them from officially obtaining visas."

Nevertheless Von Braun and about five hundred other Nazi scientists went on to work in the classified program developing advanced guided missile and ballistic missile technology in military installations in New Mexico, Alabama and Texas.

According to Mikey, "the notion that the words of a known Nazi SS rocket scientist would be used to explain the philosophical nuances of a 'just' war not only strains credulity, it defies belief. By the same token, this is not just an egregious example of the tone-deaf ignorance so often displayed by the Air Force, a service branch under the direct control of the Department of Defense, on matters of the constitutional separation of church and state: it is a glaring instance of the American military's own moral and ethical blindness. That willful disregard for the sensibilities and sensitivities of the men and women under its command is horrifically heightened by the content of this outrageous exercise in religious indoctrination, one which wretchedly asserts that war, especially nuclear war, is both ethical and part of 'the natural order' of man's existence on earth.

"Astonishingly," he continues, "the training presentation grotesquely attempts to justify that unconscionable concept that blatantly asserts that 'war is good because Jesus says it is.' It does so by specific textual references of allegedly supportive Bible passages from the New Testament Books of Luke, Acts, Hebrews, Timothy and, finally, even Revelation. If this repugnant nuclear missile training is not constitutionally violative of both the 'no religious test' mandate of the Constitution and the First Amendment's No Establishment Clause then those bedrock legal principles simply do not exist."

He is not the only one who thinks so. "There is no way in hell this should have been pressed as a mandatory briefing to everyone in the basic missile class," read an email from a highly placed senior Air Force officer, who requested anonymity for fear of reprisal. "It presumes all missile officers are religious and specifically in need of Christian justification for their service. Whoever approved this, along with the Training Group Commander at Vandenberg, should be fired instantly for allowing it."

The officer's incisive email went on to point out that if the Air Force was indeed sincere in wanting to help people with their moral justification for serving as nuclear missile launch officers, then it should have arranged discussion times with chaplains from faith groups appropriate to the individual trainees. For those who professed no faith, a talk moderated by a professor, counselor or ethicist would have been called for. "If you're already good with your role and duty as a missile officer," the email concluded with unsubtle scorn for the program, "then you're welcome to hit the golf course or gym."

But the bold action of the U.S. Air Force nuclear missile launch officers in contacting MRFF was once again only the tip of the iceberg. As the Foundation, in conjunction with *Truthout*, continued its investigation into the training program at Vandenberg Air Force Base, it was discovered that such abuses of authority and constitutional violations had been going on for years. Another Air Force officer and MRFF client stepped forward to tell his story to *Truthout's* Jason Leopold, once again on condition of anonymity. His shocking claim was that, while being trained as a missile officer in 2001 he vividly recalled how the chaplain leading the session on the ethics of launching nuclear weapons asserted that, "the American Catholic Church and their leadership says it's ok in their eyes to launch nukes."

It was the kind of outrageous claim that, it seemed, was regularly being put forth by those in command positions within the Air Force Training Groups tasked with educating the nuclear missile launch officers. And it wasn't long before another of these brave individuals stepped from the shadows to enlist the help and guidance of MRFF.

One of them was former Air Force Captain Damon Bosetti, who attended missile officer training in 2006 and was stationed at Malmstrom Air Force Base in Great Falls, Montana. It was there, he told the Foundation, that he and his colleagues had taken to sarcastically calling the religious section of the ethics training the "Jesus loves nukes speech." Bosetti, who would go on to be represented by MRFF, unequivocally stated his belief that the intent of quoting Bible passages was to make officers feel "comfortable" about launching nuclear weapons, a process that included signing a legal document stating they had "no moral qualms" about "turning the key" if ordered to do so. The document in question, written by the Department of the Air Force, Air Education and Training Command states in part, "I will perform duties involving the operation of nuclear-armed ICBMs and will launch them if lawfully ordered to do so by the President of the United States or his lawful successor."

Bosetti, who left active duty in the Air Force in 2010, revealed that officers were immediately presented with the three-page document to sign after the end of the training session on nuclear ethics. "I think the average American would be and should be very disturbed to know that people go through training where the Air Force quotes the Bible," Bosetti warned. "This type of teaching sets a dangerous precedent because no one above you is objecting. It shifts the group definition of acceptable behavior more and more off track."

As Mikey clearly explains, the combination of fundamentalist Christian propaganda and the pronouncements of a Nazi scientist utilized in explaining to nuclear missile launch officers why launching nuclear weapons is an inherently Christian act represents a new low, even for the U.S. military. "Leave it to the United States Air Force to find a way to dictate the 'ethical' value of nuclear war and its inevitable role in the 'natural order' of humanity's existence, to its missile launch officer trainees by merging unadulterated, fundamentalist Christian end times Armageddon doctrines with the tortured biblical endorsements of a former, leading Nazi SS official," he wrote.

In a signal victory for the MRFF and its ongoing efforts to halt religious extremism whenever and wherever it is found, the exposure of the unconscionable Christian-themed ethics training program through *Truthout*, at last compelled the Air Force to take long overdue action. According to a statement released by David Smith, chief of public affairs of Air Education and Training Command at Randolph Air Force Base in Texas, the Nuclear Ethics and Nuclear Warfare "has been taken out of the curriculum...The commander reviewed it and decided we needed to have a good hard look at it and make sure it reflected views of modern society."

Smith went on to admit that the ethics training program had been in place for "20-plus years" and offered belated assurances that it would be "given thorough scrutiny" and "folks will be appointed to look at what we have and determine its utility and if they think its useful to continue having an ethics course they will develop a new course."

While acknowledging that the decision by the Air Force to pull the ethics course material was a "great victory for the constitution," Mikey was also quick to point out that generations of U.S. Air Force nuclear missile launch officers had already been subjected to this unconstitutional infringement on their First Amendment rights. "We are not going to commend the Air Force for doing something they should have done a quarter-century ago," Weinstein insisted. "It's an outrage and a deliberate attempt to torture and distort our Constitution when the U.S. Air Force mandatorily teaches its nuclear missile launch officers that fundamentalist Christian theology is inextricably intertwined with the 'correct' decision to launch nukes."

Only too predictably, the MRFF's action to compel the Air Force to withdraw the missile launch officer's specious ethics training prompted howls of outrage from the mouthpieces of the extreme right. Conspicuous among the list of the usual suspects were ultra-conservative talk radio tub-thumper Michael Savage, who during an on-air rant on his nationally syndicated program *The Savage Nation*, the day after the decision was announced, claimed that if it weren't for the Christians he "hates," Weinstein would have been cremated in a concentration camp oven as in Nazi Germany. Insulting both of Mikey's parents, mocking Mikey's family name and calling MRFF a "sham" organization, Savage repeatedly bleated, "why do you hate Christians, Mr. Weinstein?" It was a canard which conveniently oft-stated the fact that nearly every one of the nuclear missile launch officers that had brought the original complaint to the MRFF were, in fact, professing, practicing Christians.

Such libelous fabrications aside, when all was said and done, MRFF would chalk up a major win against the dark sectarian forces of intolerance by thwarting what amounted to a dominionist conspiracy to indoctrinate those whose fingers were on the nation's nuclear trigger. "We had threatened the Air Force with what amounted to a major class action suit on behalf of the U.S. Air Force nuclear missile launch officers," Weinstein explains. "We also did everything we could to garner as much public attention as possible. We wanted to make sure they knew we weren't bluffing."

The results were nothing short of historic. According to *The Washing-*

ton Post, "The reversal marks a victory for the Military Religious Freedom Foundation, a watchdog group that provided the documents to *Truthout* and that has waged a series of battles, legal and otherwise, to preserve the separation of church and state in the services."

Not surprisingly, the story generated massive attention worldwide, including the front pages of leading newspapers in Japan, perhaps the nation with the most compelling historical reason to be concerned about just who has control of America's nuclear capabilities. The use of a horrific photograph of the ravaged faces of Hiroshima and Nagasaki atomic bomb casualties to illustrate the dubious ethical suppositions of the PowerPoint presentation drew the totally justifiable outrage of the Japanese public and government officials alike. *Truthout's* exclusive exposé, meanwhile, became the most viewed story ever published by the website, with over a million views in little more than a week.

Without question the Military Religious Freedom Foundation had won a major victory, all the more so when, soon afterwards, a total of forty-two Air Force ROTC instructors approached the Foundation seeking assistance in scrubbing any and all fundamentalist Christian bias in the ethical training course *they* taught to their young charges.

But it didn't stop there. Shortly after the ethics course taught to nuclear missile launch officers was suspended, Texas Republican Senator John Cornyn sent a letter to Secretary of the Air Force Michael Donley demanding an explanation for the action.

"Our military services, like our nation, are comprised of people representing all faith," Cornyn opined. "However, that fact does not preclude military chaplains from teaching a course on Just War Theory—a theory that has been a part of moral philosophy and the law of war for centuries— merely because it has historically been predicated on religious texts...The Air Force personnel who have taken this course for the past 20 years have been free to determine, according to their own consciences, whether they accept or reject the premises of Just War Theory."

"The Senator can put as much lipstick as he wants on this pig," Weinstein retorts. "That doesn't change its porcine proportions. There was an undeniable element of coercion to this course, one that determinedly advocated a deliberate fundamentalist Christian agenda. But don't take my word for it. Ask the sixty-nine additional nuclear missile launch officers, sixty-one of whom are themselves Christians, that have subsequently sought out the help of MRFF to repudiate Cornyn's odious contentions. They need our help for a very simple reason: Article Eighty-Eight of the Uniform Code of Military Justice states quite clearly that, 'Any commissioned officer who uses contemptuous words against the President, the Vice President, Congress, the Secretary of Defense, the Secretary of a military department, the Secretary of Transportation, or the Governor or legislature of any State, Territory, Commonwealth, or possession in which he is on duty or present shall be punished as a court-martial may direct.' These brave military men and women are prevented from refuting Cornyn's specious argument by pointing out their own experience with the outrageous bullying tactics of the ethics regimen. The Military Religious Freedom Foundation, on the other hand, is not, and we intend to give them the bold, action-oriented voice they deserve."

There is no question that shutting down the nuclear missile launch officer's mandatory ethics course, with all of its fundamentalist Christian trappings, represented a major victory for the MRFF. But the enormous dimensions of that victory would only become clear when a truly groundbreaking memorandum from the desk of General Norton Schwartz, Chief of Staff (Commander) of the Air Force, was written in the weeks after the Vandenberg Air Force Base revelations became public. The magnitude of the General's directive to the global United States Air Force forces under his command were immediately and unequivocally clear from the subject line of this extraordinary document: *Maintaining Government Neutrality Regarding Religion.*

"Leaders at all levels must balance Constitutional protections for an individual's free exercise of religion or other personal beliefs and its prohibition against governmental establishment of religion," General Schwartz continued. "For example, they must avoid the actual or apparent use of their position to promote their personal religious beliefs to their subordinates or to extend preferential treatment for any religion. Commanders or supervisors who engage in such behavior may cause members to doubt their impartiality and objectivity. The potential result is a degradation of the unit's morale, good order, and discipline.

"Chaplain Corps programs, including activities such as religious studies, faith sharing, and prayer meetings, are vital to commanders' support of individual Airmen's needs and provide opportunities for the free exercise of religion. Although commanders are responsible for these programs they must refrain from appearing to officially endorse religion generally or any particular religion. Therefore, I expect chaplains, not commanders, to notify Airmen of Chaplain Corps programs.

Our chaplains are trained to provide advice to leadership on matters related to the free exercise of religion and to help commanders care for all of their people, regardless of their beliefs. If you have concerns involving the preservation of government neutrality regarding religious beliefs, consult with your chaplain and staff judge advocate before you act."

Weinstein's immediate response put the memo into its monumental historical context: "General Schwartz deserves significant kudos and comprehensive congratulations for being *the* most senior Pentagon official to date to ever send this strong a mandate of Constitutional religious compliance to our United States armed forces members. While MRFF wishes that such a letter had been sent by the Chief of Staff of the Air Force a very long time ago, the old adage 'better late than never' most certainly applies. While this letter may not be a home run, it *is* a damn good line-drive single to potentially start a rally of Constitutional religious freedom compliance, which has been scandalously lacking in the entire Defense Department for decades. General Schwartz has the U.S. Air Force at least now 'talking the talk.' Whether the USAF can 'walk the walk' will depend upon many factors, not the least of which is whether *anyone* in the Air Force is *ever* punished for violating its clear mandates of Constitutional recognition for *both* the No Establishment Clause and the Free Exercise Clause of the Bill of Rights' First Amendment."

To help ensure that the Air Force would indeed "walk the walk," the MRFF was forced to take the unprecedented step of paying for a large billboard in Colorado Springs, Colorado, which quoted General Schwartz's watershed directive in its entirety. The reason for this extraordinary step was simple and compelling: the Air force Academy was doing everything in its power to bury the General's edict.

"We had made the astonishing discovery that USAF Academy Superintendent Michael Gould had flat out refused to distribute General Schwartz's directive to *all* Academy personnel—cadets, faculty and personnel at the 10th Air Base Wing station at the Academy," Mikey explained. "His insubordination came despite our repeated demands that he obey orders and make everyone at the Air Force Academy aware of Schwartz's critically important memo. We had no choice but to display the directive in the most conspicuous and public manner possible." The large billboard was erected at the heavily trafficked Colorado Springs intersection of Woodward and Lexington, where it could be viewed by over 100,000 passing motorists and pedestrians on a daily basis.

As a result of Gould's ludicrously transparent and revelatory refusal to distribute the USAF Chief of Staff's religious neutrality directive to all Academy personnel, staff, cadets and government contractors, MRFF's client load at the Academy shamefully and precipitously skyrocketed from two hundred and ninety seven to three hundred and forty one in a little more than a week. Since Gould would not spread this critically important message of religious neutrality generated by his boss, General Schwartz in the Pentagon, MRFF was compelled, yet once again, to do Gould's duty for him.

"This was the one way we could make sure the message got out," Weinstein explains. "With this billboard displaying Gen. Schwartz's desperately needed demand for religious equanimity, MRFF will give voice to the voiceless who suffer from horrendous religious oppression and tyranny every day under Gould's control at the Constitutionally-challenged U.S. Air Force Academy. Speaking as President and Founder of MRFF, Gould's willful, abject failure to do that which is clearly his duty is one of the most vulgar expressions of betrayal and deceit I have ever encountered."

The tactic worked brilliantly. A mere nineteen hours after the billboard went up, the Academy administration at last distributed General Schwartz's directive. But even then its acquiescence was grudging and incomplete. Only the Academy's Cadet Wing, but not the faculty or the personnel of the 10th Air Base Wing, saw the memo. When questioned as to the timing of their tardy and grudging action in light of the very public rebuke represented by the billboard, an Academy spokesperson brushed it off as a "coincidence." "If anyone is either naïve or stupid enough to believe *that* 'coincidence,'" Weinstein retorted with withering scorn, "then they would immediately be qualified to replace Academy Superintendent Michael Gould at his post."

The importance of Weinstein's words are clear. General Schwartz's memo represented a significant victory for the foundation, just as Gould's obfuscation represented yet another example of the implacable resistance from these enemies of the Constitution. Simply put, Weinstein and his allies have no time to rest on their laurels. There are always other battles to be fought in the never-ending war against religious intolerance, harassment and infiltration by fundamentalist Christian extremists into the highest circles of America's military establishment.

A CALL TO ACTION

It has been over three years since that fateful night on Father's Day, 2008, when a quiet suburban Albuquerque neighborhood was stirred by the frenzied barking of dogs, warning of intruders bearing a searing message of hate.

In that time, Mikey and Bonnie Weinstein and their children have endured a near constant barrage of threats and imprecations, financial crisis and turmoil, both public and private, that have tried and tested the bonds of their love and their commitment to the high ideals which are so integral a part of their shared heritage. In that crucible, they have forged an indissoluble link of love and common purpose that has only grown stronger through the trials they have together faced.

"I sometimes wonder, if we had to do it all over again, whether I would change anything," Bonnie reflects with characteristic candor. "Everyone has regrets, of course, but the thing we don't have is the luxury of choosing the life we want to live. We take what comes and do the best we can. Looking back, I'd have to say I'm grateful that an important part of our lives was about directly confronting injustice and intolerance, and of helping its victims. We have been able to make a real difference in the lives of so many others, and that gives great meaning to our own lives. For all the hardships we've suffered, that's something I wouldn't trade for all the security and predictability in the world. We've been given a great responsibility, to stand up for those who are being persecuted, and with that responsibility comes hardship and suffering. I've learned to accept that we have created a legacy and set an example for others to follow. What more could you ask?"

"I'm proud of my parents," says Curtis Weinstein, wasting no words in his typically straightforward manner. "They've done a lot of good things that matter to a lot of good people." With at least two more years of Air Force service before him and a posting in Stuttgart, Germany in the offing, Curtis can count many of his Air Force colleagues among those who offer their support and encouragement for the work of the Weinsteins'. "People come up to me," he reveals. "They let me know they believe in what my mom and dad are doing. That means a lot to me."

It also means a lot to his older brother Casey, now out of the service, but still with direct links to the military through his job overseeing marketing for a large company that provides technical expertise to the Air Force. "The vast majority of the men and women wearing that uniform are good and decent and caring individuals," he asserts. "They can see what my mom and dad are standing for, and the need for real and lasting change in the military. That kind of affirmation has actually opened doors for me in my career. And I think that, sooner or later, it's going to make the difference in bringing about the changes we all want to see." He pauses in reflection. "Sure," he adds after a moment, "there are things I wish my parents didn't have to deal with; the threats, for example, and the stress of it all that weighs so heavily on my mom and dad. The hate that some people carry around with them is shocking. Even though, after all this time, you get a little numb, and once and in a while it still shakes you up.

"Then there's the financial insecurity," he continues. "They put everything they had into building the Foundation, just at the time when they needed to be putting more away towards their retirement. That takes courage and hope, that more people will join the cause. I admire that tremendously, but I also worry for their future."

The unequivocal admiration and encouragement shown by their children has also been increasingly echoed by a growing number of those who acknowledge and applaud the Weinsteins' work. It has come in the form of a number of prestigious recognitions and awards from a wide range of organizations, beginning with *Forward*, the nation's preeminent Jewish publication, which named Mikey one of the 50 Most Influential Jews in America. He has also been honored with the Rabbi Marshall T. Meyer Risk-Taker Award from the distinguished civil rights organization, Jews for Racial and Economic Justice, as well as receiving a nomination for the JFK Profile in Courage Award. Americans United for the Separation of Church and State named Weinstein the organization's first-ever "Person of the Year" in 2011 and he has been singled out by the legendary Southern Poverty Law Center for his work on behalf of Muslims serving in the U.S. military. Weinstein was also the recipient of the Pacific Palisades Democratic Club's 2010 Anne Froehlich Political Courage Award and was awarded the Albuquerque Community Foundation's "Giraffe Award" for "sticking his neck out" as an "individual who takes personal or professional risks to stand up for his or her beliefs and make a difference."

In the spirit of such illustrious recognition from a full spectrum of social, political and religious allies, the MRFF has established its own form of acknowledgement and gratitude, giving back with its annual Thomas Jefferson Award for Civil Rights Activism, now in its sixth year of celebrating those who have stepped forward in defense of the principles on which the Foundation was established. MRFF also recently initiated the John Adams Award for Pro Bono Legal Support, to honor the tireless work of its truly stellar legal team.

Weinstein has also become the indispensible "go-to" expert on the ever-evolving issues linking religion and the military. He and other MRFF spokespersons have appeared on every major cable and terrestrial TV news network, as well as a plethora of Internet news outlets and international radio programs. Among the many: *The Rachael Maddow Show*, ABC's *Nightline*, Fox News, ShockNet Radio, Austrian National Radio, Humanist Network News, *Army Times*, *Navy Times*, American Muslims Today, Religion News Service, *To The Point*, *Market Place*, Radio Islam, Pagan News Wire, *TruthOut* and *Alternet*. Extensive print media coverage and profiles include major articles in *The Associated Press*, *The New York Times*, *The Washington Post*, *The Los Angeles Times*, *The Denver Post*, *The Guardian*, TIME, *Foreign Policy Review*,and many other national and international newspapers and periodicals, ranging from the cover of *Harper's* to even the cover of *Hustler*. It was *Harper's*, in fact, that dubbed Weinstein the "Constitutional Conscience of the Military."

Even the U.S. military establishment has been forced to acknowledge Weinstein's towering stature as the foremost proponent for freedom of—and from—religion within the armed services. In its ongoing, if routinely disingenuous, attempts to present an evenhanded public image, the military establishment had been obliged time and again to concede Mikey's expertise. He had represented the MRFF in a panel debate alongside military chaplains at a U.S. Army War College Strategy Conference on faith in the U.S. military in 2011. He has additionally been asked to speak to students at a number of the U.S. military's educational institutions and events, including the U.S. Air Force Academy's National Character and Leadership Symposium; the Air Force JAG School; the Air Command and Staff College, and the U.S. Army War College.

But there is one honor that, more than any other award or accolade, points out the truly global scope of the work of the Weinstein's and the Military Religious Freedom Foundation. In October of 2009, MRFF was officially nominated for the Nobel Peace Prize. The nominator, who wished to remain anonymous, is the only Christian in the upper chamber of the national parliament in a country that is counted as a close ally of the United States. Shortly thereafter, another anonymous Qualified Nominator submitted a second official nomination for MRFF to receive the prize. Yet again, in 2010, for the second consecutive year, the Military Religious Freedom Foundation was officially nominated, this time for the 2011 Nobel Peace Prize, which had the most competitive field in the history of the award, with two hundred and fifty one nominations, of which only fifty-four were organizations.

"Obviously, I'm deeply moved by these nominations," remarks Mikey. "But more than even bringing increased recognition to the work we're doing, they point out the growing international awareness that the well-being of the entire planet hinges on the integrity and honorable intentions of the United States military. It goes without saying that we have created the most powerful and lethal armed force in the history of humankind. That reality demands a concurrent adherence to the vital constitutional principles that guide our secular democracy. We must not, we cannot, allow that power to fall into the hands of Christian fundamentalist dominionists who believe that the Bible instructs them to eradicate all nonbelievers as a prerequisite for the second coming of Christ and the establishment of his millennial rule and reign. In a nuclear age, this is, purely and self-evidently, a matter of the survival for the entire species. I can't make it any plainer than that and it's tremendously gratifying to know that, after all these many years, the message is finally, *finally*, beginning to get through.

"Look," he concludes, with a patience borne of long struggle. "I'm one man, with one wife and one family and one foundation. I'm immensely proud of what we've been able to accomplish, but the fact is, we can only do so much by ourselves."

"When I learned of the first two Nobel nominations in 2010," Bonnie interjects, "it was completely surprising and also extremely gratifying. But what came along with it, and with the third nomination the following year, was a sobering moment of clarity. What I realized was that it didn't just cost a lot to earn such an honor. It cost *everything*. We have dedicated our lives to this overwhelming important cause of protecting and defending the Constitution. But, in a very real way, we've also *sacrificed* our lives. We're not going to have those peaceful and prosperous golden years that everyone strives and saves for. That opportunity vanished in 2005 when, as pissed off parents, we started the foundation. Unless and until we get more support, it's not coming back again."

"Bonnie is right, of course," Mikey concurs. "In hindsight, we have had to give up so very much to carry on this cause. But there are rewards, too. Maybe they're less tangible than a vacation home and a comfortable retirement account or a steady paycheck, but they have tremendous significance of their own. A friend of mine, a good man now in his eighties and very affluent, recently told me that he wished he had done more with his life, that he had stood for something greater than himself, that he had made a difference. That's what we've ultimately done, knowing full well that the mission of the Military Religious Freedom Foundation, and of the courageous men and women who have joined its ranks, is far, far bigger than any single one of us. Yes, we have sacrificed 'a lot,' but some of our clients have paid the greatest cost to ensure the liberties enshrined in this nation's Constitution. Nine of them in fact, have been killed in action in Iraq and Afghanistan. Each of them had distinguished themselves in battle, winning silver and bronze stars, Purple Hearts and other tokens of our nation's esteem. We can do no less.

"I began this book by declaring that its purpose is to save lives. That has never been truer than it is today and the lives we are trying to rescue from the vise grip of unconscionable, unconstitutional fundamentalist Christian extremism, could very well encompass the entire population of the planet.

"Despite what is said by those who want to silence me, I'm not a wild-eyed fanatic, an irresponsible doomsayer, a hater of Jesus Christ, an enemy of God, a puppet of the Antichrist or a field general in Satan's army. I know very well that sincere people of faith, especially those who practice the Christian faith, understand what I'm trying to do and support the foundation and me. So very many of our clients are professing Christians, but it goes deeper than that." He smiles broadly, with genuine pleasure. "Recently Amber's boyfriend proposed to her. He's an Air Force Academy graduate, the sixth one in our family, and is currently in Air Force jet pilot training. In a way, it kind of brings the whole story full circle. Amber was subjected to an extreme example of fundamentalist sectarian hate with the attack on our home. Now, a practicing Christian, who has taken an oath to support and defend the Constitution against all enemies foreign and domestic, will become her partner in what I hope will be a very long and gloriously happy life together."

"Look," he continues, "I'm an American citizen who loves his country. I took a solemn oath to support and defend the Constitution of this country. The best way I can do that is to follow what the renowned historian Howard Zinn once said: 'Dissent is the highest form of patriotism.' I want to pass that value on to generations yet unborn. I'm guided in that purpose by the great men and women who came before me and who stood up to tyranny and oppression wherever they encountered it. You can go as far back as the Roman poet Juvenal, who famously asked '*Quis custodiet ipsos custodes?*' Loosely translated from the Latin, it means, 'Who will guard the guards?" It's a question that echoes down through the ages of history. The way Voltaire put it has enormous resonance for me: 'No snowflake in an avalanche ever feels responsible.' Whatever else I may or may not be, I have no intention of being a snowflake.

"In our own time Dr. Martin Luther King, Jr. wisely advised us that, 'In the end we remember not the words of our enemies, but the silence of our friends.' He also said 'There comes a time when silence is betrayal.' That time is now.

It's my duty to speak, loudly, clearly and consistently, into that silence and it's a responsibility I still take seriously to this day, with great pride and even greater humility. I value any support that comes my way, or to the MRFF, more than I can say. But if, in the end, it's just me and my wife and my family standing at the barricades, then that's where you'll find us. That's where we belong." He pauses, and leans forward, his bright eyes burning. "It's where we all belong."

LETTERS

Dear Mikey Weinstein,

Your support during my deployment was professional, the most prized blessings I received. As a Muslim minority fighting the war against terrorism abroad, you knew the problem that I was facing; unjust discrimination and unbelievable mistrust among those who I am teaming up with. It will be beyond any regular U.S. Citizen to understand the hardship that all religious minorities endure, especially Muslim American soldiers. Mikey you did understand all of this and completely felt my emotional pain.

I have no parents in the United States to have them complain on my behalf. Furthermore, even if they were living in states, they would most likely not know where to go or whom to trust and talk to as they're first generation immigrants and countless roadblocks would confront them.

Mikey what you did was what a loving father would do for his own kid. When I was so distraught and seeking help you replied immediately. That reply give me confidence and got my self-esteem back.

The psychological game that I was undergoing due to my Muslim faith was harsh. U.S. taxpayers ignore what it is like to face the backlash from other soldiers when we hear on the news that one criminal with a Muslim background committed an act of terrorism in the United States. Combat teamwork and morale would lose its meaning and once you asked for an explanation the reply would be that we're soldiers first. When you're discriminated against you will feel it no matter how much the other side covers it up.

Mikey understands it all and I am so glad and thankful to have people like him and the Military Religious Freedom Foundation in our society.

Words are never good at expressing the true depth of the heart's feelings. I find mere "thank you" so inadequate. Nonetheless, there is no other way to tell you how much I appreciate your being there for me in my time of need.

Thank you my friend. From the bottom of my heart,
(U.S. Army Soldier's name, rank, MOS, combat unit and installation withheld)

***

UN-AMERICANS FIGHT FRANKLIN GRAHAM !

What kind of wine has Mikey Weinstein been drinking? As an anti-Christian Jewish supremacist and as the president of the Military Religious Freedom Foundation, he's doing all he can to create an anti-Jewish backlash and help bring about the predicted endtime Holocaust of Jews that'll be worse than Hitler's. Neither Falwell, Hagee nor any other Christian initiated this prediction. But Weinstein's ancient Hebrew prophets did. In the 13th and 14th chapters of his Old Testament book, Zechariah predicted that after Israel's rebirth ALL nations will eventually be against Israel and that TWO-THIRDS of all Jews will be killed! Malachi revealed the reasons: "Judah hath dealt treacherously" and "the Lord will cut off the man that doeth this." Haven't evangelicals generally been the best friends of Israel and persons perceived to be Jewish? Then please explain the hate-filled back-stabbing by David Letterman (and Sandra Bernhard, Kathy Griffin, Bill Maher etc.) against followers of Jesus such as Sarah Palin and Michele Bachmann. Weinstein wouldn't dare assert that citizens on government property don't have freedom of speech or press freedom or freedom to assemble or to petition the government. But God-hater Weinstein maliciously wants to eliminate from government property the "free exercise" of religion – especially by evangelicals – a freedom found in the same First Amendment. Significantly, this freedom was purposely listed FIRST by America's founders! And Weinstein wouldn't try to foist "separation of church and state" on strongly-Jewish Israel, but he does try to foist this non-Constitution-mentioned phrase on strongly-Christian America. In light of Weinstein's Jewish protectionism and violently anti-Christian obsession, Christians in these endtimes synagogues ye shall be beaten." Maybe it's time for some modern Paul Reveres to saddle up and shout "The Yiddish are Coming!"

PS – Some, like Weinstein, are so treacherously anti-Christian they will even join hands at times with enemies, including Muslims, in order to silence evangelicals. It was Weinstein, BTW, who put pressure on the Pentagon to dis-invite Franklin Graham from speaking there on the National Day of Prayer!

PPS – Weinstein is an echo of the anti-Christian, anti-American Hollywood which for a century has dangled every known vice before young people. We seriously wonder how soon the lethal worldwide "flood of filth" (global harming!) that Hollywood has created will engulf and destroy itself and help to bring to power the endtime Antichrist (a.k.a. the Man of Sin and the Wicked One)!

***

Mikey,

I wanted to reach out to you and thank you for the advocacy that you, Chris Rodda and Military Religious Freedom Foundation engage in. The critical work that MRFF does for our brave men and women in the Armed Forces—irrespective of faith (or none at all) cannot be emphasized enough.

I speak to you as a proud American and a practicing Muslim. I am also the son of Jewish father and a Catholic Christian mother. Religious freedom, tolerance and pluralism are not just lofty concepts for me—it's deeply personal. I also have family members and colleagues who are Muslim Americans and have served honorably for decades to defend our nation.

MRFF is important because it fights everyday to ensure that people of all religious orientations (or none at all), including Muslim Americans, can serve our nation with the dignity and honor so many other Americans aspire to do everyday. Several thousand Muslims soldiers serve proudly, honorably and effectively in our armed forces everyday as our top soldiers, analysts, translators and more. Unfortunately the sad reality is that after 9/11, because of pernicious fears, misperceptions and dangerously persistent innuendos about Muslim Americans these contributions are largely overlooked.

During yesterday's Senate hearing on Muslim American civil rights, held by Sen. Durbin, a lot of the stories about Muslim American contributions to our nation were about individuals serving in our armed services. The stories were extremely compelling and personally moved me, as they did for many other people attending and participating in the hearing.

At the same time, I could not help but think of the persistent uphill battles many of these very same service members must be facing on account of their faith. Like Mikey and others at MRFF, I have personally heard heart-wrenching stories directly from our Muslim American service members of the discrimination they face.

And that's why MRFF is so important—it fights to ensure that the tight-knit brother and sisterhood we call the United States military is open and welcoming to Muslim Americans. With MRFF in their corner, Muslim Americans can also ensure they are treated equally as any other American soldier proudly serving our nation. They also help to maintain the necessary unit cohesion and morale that's so important to effectiveness on the battlefield. In that regard MRFF does our nation a double service by protecting our nation's values and its military readiness.

I highly encourage our military service members, including our Muslim military men and women, to learn more about MRFF and support the great work they do. They are an invaluable asset to our soldiers and our nation.

Thanks,
Government and Policy Analyst
Muslim Public Affairs Council

***

That you hold man-sanctioned sheepskin in such high regard betrays your humanist ideaology. You are a tremendous fool-all this time you've believed intellectualism and education is what makes a man. You've been so enamored by high-brow propaganda as
   to be motivated to suck an education out of the government.

No wonder you're such a paranoid loser. What you hold in high-esteem is worthless when you are confronted by a bully alone, late at night. Did your brains help you any then? Of course not-those kind of things take balls. Coward.

(name and location withheld)

***

I wish I had the words Mikey. I wish I had the vocabulary to express how deep my thanks goes to you, MRFF, and everyone you call "client", for standing up at great risk to their career to support our Constitution. In my 25+ years of service I've never seen, nor heard of, a General Officer regardless of status or position, put into words our obligation to Religious Equality, and I've NEVER seen a 'directive reminder' to support our Constitution.

The highest Air Force authority has (FINALLY) stated loud and clear for all Airman to hear—Support and Defend the Constitution! General Schwartz has reminded every Air Force member from the youngest new Airman to the seasoned Officer, our Oath is REAL, our duty to the Constitution is not an option, and Service Before Self means putting the greater good of our Constitution before a personal spiritual belief.

While our Chief of Staff is now viewed as a "trend setter" in DoD, we all know what made this possible—YOU. Truly a great victory for you Mikey, a great victory for MRFF, and even greater victory for all who serve in the greatest military on earth.

I salute you Mikey.

Thank you.

(name withheld)

***

you f*****g piece of shit jew and your stinking jew woman and inbred jew childrun and jew-lover traiter daughterinlaw deserve to torture die you filth jew liberil america hating jesus hating basterd Lord willing none of us will have to wait long america is too good for dirty jew scum of your family and your commie foundasion

(name and e mail address withheld)

***

Dear Reader,

If you want something done right, sometimes you just have to do it yourself. For Mikey Weinstein, that "something" is safeguarding the Constitutional religious freedom of America's soldiers, sailors, marines, and airmen when the government programs intended to do so fail. I am one of hundreds of thousands of service members who frequently have our Constitutional right to be free from government establishment of religion violated by mandatory participation in religious rituals. Others face employment discrimination (try being a chaplain if you don't belong to an state-approved religious group—a job requirement in explicit violation of our Constitution's No Religious Test Clause), difficulty getting promoted, religious insults from peers and superiors, and even physical assaults. The vast majority of complaints come from Christians who feel they work in a hostile environment because they aren't "Christian enough" for their commanders. Using the official reporting systems (Equal Opportunity, Inspector General, the chaplains, etc.) frequently results in reprisals, breaches of confidentiality, and suppressing the complaint. The Military Religious Freedom Foundation was founded by Mikey Weinstein to fill this void for religious minorities who have no reliable institutional protections for their religious liberty.

Following our deployment to Iraq, where I was awarded the Combat Medical Badge and Purple Heart for multiple concussions from nine IED blasts, I was frequently required by my commander to attend unit religious activities. I attempted to resolve the problems by speaking with him directly, speaking with our Equal Opportunity representative, and explaining how this violated my conscience to our unit chaplain. None of this stopped them from sending me, almost monthly, to obediently participate in state-orchestrated rituals. Desperate to stop these command-enforced religious practices, this unconstitutional establishment of religion, I contacted the Military Religious Freedom Foundation in 2007.

Asking nothing in return, Mikey Weinstein and a team of brilliant lawyers dedicated their time, effort, and funding to fighting these Constitutional abuses our military overlooks. They helped me when nothing else worked. Mikey has given himself 100% to fighting this much-needed political battle on behalf of those who fight our military battles abroad. But Mikey needs your help to continue advocating for the religious liberty of our troops. Please consider showing your support with a contribution to the Military Religious Freedom Foundation.

Respectfully,
Spc. Dustin Chalker (recipient of the Combat Medic Badge and the Purple Heart)

***

To MRFF
  you bunch of egg sucking dogs have no business sticking your fucking

nose in religious beliefs. Join with the egg sucking CAIR and fight against Graham. We will not be safe until Cair and people like you are eradicated like cockroaches from the land of the USA. Islam and everyone supporting Islam is evil. Accept it. You are trying to take over the USA. Not without a fight. we have had it.

***

Dear MRFF,

I wish I had known about this organization when I was in the U.S. Navy. I was a Master at Arms (MP) and was deployed to (name withheld), and was harassed more by my ship mates for religious reasons than by the detainee's almost everyday. This was because I was not and am still not christian or any denomination there of. I am an American Indian and I believe in what my ancestors have believed in for more 10,000 years. And for this I was harassed.

Anyways Congratulations on the Nobel Nomination.

You are the voice I wasn't allowed to use.

(name withheld)

***

Mike, you are so off base. YOU want all Christians DEAD? I read your comments. YOU are what is wrong with this country. Are you closet Muslim? Do you hate our country so much? There was NEVER anything that said there was to be a separation of church and state!!!!!!! Just freedom to practice any religion. You want to force your evil views on all people. Yes Christians believe the Bible and for your information, you and your organization are helping fulⅅll prophecy by condemning Christ and His followers. But, whether you believe or not, YOU are still going to burn in Hell!!!!!!!!!!!!!!!!! I wish all you people would leave my country, (I am a native American, so I have every right to this country, YOU have zero rights to this land) People like you are ushering in Islam for everyone. I bet you voted for the pretender and chief, Obama the liar. Congratulations, you are anti-

American, pro-evil, anti-Semitic, anti- Christian and just plain stupid. May God forgive you, for you know not what you do I will stand for Jesus and lay my life down for His word, me and 38 million other fanatics

***

Mikey,

being the liberal that you are the very people who wish to recognize you are already apoligetic! about wahwhat?? typical demo-krap for brainz and the bain of ther 21 century. thank GOD the assholes will be out of ther system at the next election. so the nigger fucked up again, oh!oh!oh! it was THE BUSHGUY!!?? why can-not niggers take the responsibility for their own fAILURES. WE GAVE THEM FREEDOM AND THEY SRTTILL WANT TOO TAKE THE ELEVATOR INSTEAD OF THE STRIRS LIKE ALL THE RST OF US??!! WAS JUDAS QUEER? have fun out there with the wet pantiez pull-pussy and all her wqueer friend,. by the way; leave the queers alone in the military... some of my besss frenzz are queer. tell those weak rectums too make another sociual; disorder, like fill the well/hole NIGGER.god bless america,yours in christ,support my troops. your buddy

***

Spare a Jew from the grave, and he will insult the military that saved him.

Spare a nigger the whip, and he'll turn to insult the man who made the whip.

the lesser need to understand that they're made that way. We must cultivate enough knowledge in those who are beneath men that their mouths only open to say "yes sir!" in the full bloom of joy that comes with appreciating their role. This requires a firm but caring attitude; without that, they'll never be led to know that God has a natural hierarchy in which we all play a part.

the problem is, it's difficult to convince some creatures that their part in God's plan involves an oven...sometimes only a physical reminder will suffice.

I'm hoping that all jews at the air force academy receive this reminder when McClary thunders truth from the rafters.

The air force always was, and always will be, the vanguard of the Christian front.

(Anonymous)

v/r,
(name withheld)

***

Aloha,

I happened to catch a portion of Michael Weinstein's interview with Dan Rather. I was unable to watch the entire program but fortunately have a DVR so was able to record it to view later.

As a United Methodist Clergyman I am well aware of some of the tactics of the fundamentalist groups in their aggressive attempts to "win souls for Jesus Christ." I find that most of them are driven by hate and intolerance. I feel that their homophobia is simply the tip of the iceberg of their agenda. I resent the fact that this sort of hate mongering is going on in the U.S. military which is funded by the tax dollars of ALL Americans. I have heard these fundamentalists referring to making the U.S. a "Christian Nation" and it scares the hell out of me!!

The only thing that scares me more that a fundamentalist Muslim is a fundamentalist Christian!!

Please know that I support you in you efforts and wish you every success.

Sincerely,
Rev. J.E.B.

***

Dear MRFF:

I am proud wife of a Green Beret combat soldier who is true man of faith, a true Christian father to our children and a true warrior for our Lord and Savior Jesus Christ and USA. In our bible study on base we know of you and pray and talk of you Mickey and your evildoing with MFRR. We also know that Jesus speak to you to warn you to stop trying to take Chrisianity away from our military and our USA. USA is and was always a Christian nation meant to bring Jesus to all the world. We know and can see that Jesus does speak to you and will stand up to you and you supporters. Look at how miserable your life is now. We see you on the newspapers and tv. You will never defeat the Lord. Jesus wills it all. Your wife has multiple skluroses and will die a painful death all twisted up with pain and bent in agony because of you fighting against Jesus. Your daughter in laws Amber's father has brave chosen Jesus over her because she has fallen out to the Evil One cause of you and whom you serve. Your sons and daughter Amanda will watch helpless as you waste away and slowly die in poverty all alone and forgotten and further disgrace than you have earned now due to you fighting Jesus. You will only save them and you if surrender to Lord and Savior Jesus who is the only way and truth and life as John 14:6. Mickey, you are so wicked evil as is your lying MFRR and your family and all those you try to get to join up to fight Jesus. Bit Jesus still loves you all. Why can't you just see His Love and stop trying to destroy Christians in armed forces? If you can't do it for you do it for your wife and children and USA.

(name and location withheld)

***

Mikey Weinstein:

Thank you for your presentation at the Army War College. Particularly helpful and, frankly, surprising to me was your distinction between evangelicals and fundamentalists. So many people fail to recognize the distinctions and nuances and, e.g., the huge range within Protestant Christianity.

I'm ordained in the same denomination as your fellow panelist, Chaplain Kenneth Bush. Both he and I are members of a chaplain endorsing agency. We lamented the departure of certain groups (such as some you described) that left NCMAF (National Conference on Ministry to the Armed Forces, the endorsing agencies' organization) and went off and formed their own organization, a competing one in effect, that they think will better serve their purposes.

On the other hand, our endorsing commission does have to intervene at times when one of our chaplains experiences discrimination by very liberal Protestant chaplain supervisors, e.g., who object to any expression (even somewhat privately) of opposition to ending Don't Ask, Don't Tell, or to directives to hold joint "general Protestant" services (especially if sacraments are involved) with Mormons or Christian Science chaplains and so on.

Anyway, I've heard about some of your experiences at the Air Force Academy. I regret what happened, but view the perpetrators more as naïve, thoughtless, lacking self-reflection, etc. than as cunning, intentionally callous, or whatever. I felt like saying to you: "But Mr. Weinstein, they mean well. They just don't understand. Give them a break!"

Now I see you as less "out to get people" than I'd imagined, and I'm glad for that. I deeply regret the false statements about your organization and the threats against you personally.

I served as a Pennsylvania Army National Guard chaplain for 22 years. I did everything I could to help the non-Protestants, including any number of practicing Jews. They were very appreciative. Rabbi Mark Shook here in St. Louis is a fellow volunteer police chaplain and personal friend, now just retired as senior rabbi at Temple Israel, but still a chaplain, occasional public radio guest commentator, and adjunct instructor for Judaism courses at Saint Louis University.

(name withheld)

***

Dear Mikey:

"When one proudly dons a U.S. military uniform, there is only one religious symbol; the American flag."

Dear Schlemazel – a tallit is a "religious symbol." When you designate the American Flag as a "religious symbol," you are akin to the Islamic Brotherhood waving their [Egyptian, Syrian, Palestinian, Lebanese, Saudi, Pakistani] banners calling for worldwide Islam
domination.

"There is only one religious scripture; the American constitution."

Schlemiel – you, who insist on separation of church and state, are doing a bang-up job of equating a STATE document such as our Constitution, to a "religious scripture."

"Finally, there is only one religious faith: American patriotism." ~ Mikey Weinstein

Nudnik: AMERICAN PATRIOTISM is NOT a "religious faith." PATRIOTISM denotes our NATIONAL IDENTITY and our NATIONAL ALLEGIANCE. "Religious faith," is each and every American citizen's PRIVATE, PERSONAL, INTIMATE, and SACROSANCT

relationship to GOD.

Tell me "MIKEY," did you study Torah and Talmud? Did you chant a Torah portion at your Bar – Mitzvah, or did you spout an editorial from Der Forvaard? Were your parents so assimilated, so embarrassed of their Judaism, too eager to shed their 6,000 year-old

Heritage?

"Mikey" was named one of the 50 most influential Jews in America by the Forward, one of the nation's preeminent LEFTIST SOCIALIST Jewish publications." [big surprise] On which side of the Jordan River do you stand, "Mikey," on the issue of Eretz Yisrael

being goaded by the schvartze, to revert to 1967 borders in exchange for some bullshit goyishe promises of a Peace Plan?

When I read the article on Fox News about the "Military Religious Freedom Foundation" breaking the balls of the Air Force over references to the Bible, I knew IMMEDIATLEY that the founder of the MRFF would be a leftie Jew.

Refer to The Chumash, our "ancient" Hebrew Bible upon which Western Civilization was founded: Was David a WARRIOR? Did DEBORAH THE PROPHETESS not inspire Barak to lead his troops to victory?

(name and e mail address withheld)

***

Know Jesus, know Peace. No Jesus, no peace. Know Weinstein, know satan. No

Weinstein, no satan. (Colossians 2:15)

(name withheld)

***

11. Mr. Weinstein, my cadet roommate (cadet name and rank withheld) told me last night that one of his friends and classmates was in a class yesterday afternoon in Fairchild when another cadet in the class by the name of (cadet name and rank withheld) was telling people in the class that the only reason that Military Religious Foundation put up the billboard was to attack Christianity at the Academy. Another cadet challenged that statement and the cadet who said it responded by saying that you only put the billboard up because "It's a Jewish thing, a money thing. He's just crucifying Christ again for the same 20 pieces of silver." I'm sorry to pass this on. I am not Jewish. I am Catholic and face the same pressure to convert to being a "complete Christian" all the time. All I can say is that none of us knew anything about General Schwartz's letter until sometime on Wednesday morning which is the day after you put the sign up in the Springs. Thanks for all you do for all of us here at the Academy. If you want to hear more my class schedule is very tough today and I have alot of GR's and some papers due but my cell number is (cadet's cell number withheld). What the leadership has done with General Schwartz's letter is real messed up. We see the lies. They hate you guys here. But many of us don't.

(USAF Academy cadet's name, rank, title and Cadet Squadron withheld).

***

now you make the air force get rid of even sharing the love of Jesus? america needs to be rid of plotting jew lawyers like you mikey Whinerstein

(name withheld)

***

Greetings.

Please pass along my heartfelt thanks to the Founder and President of the Military Religious Freedom Foundation, Michael L. "Mikey" Weinstein for standing up for what is right.

I spent twenty years on Active Duty in The Unites States Army and I was forced to attend military functions over and over again where I had to listen to them give official Benedictions and Invocations taking about their lord and Savor Jesus Christ. I complained over and over again to no avail. I always attempted to talk to the Chaplain and ask that they not do this and I was continually ignored over the years.

Now, I fight a constant battle with all the Veterans Organizations that I participate in to keep their religious beliefs and practices out of these organizations. Here again they hold meetings and meals and continue the same sort of thing that I had to endure in the Military.

- W. H.

US Army Retired

Life Member of: the Disabled American Veterans (DAV),

The Retired Enlisted Association (TREA), The Veterans of Foreign Wars (VFW),

The Noncommissioned Officers Association (NCOA),

American Veteran Association (AMVETS) &The Korean War Veterans Association

And a current member of the American Legion.

***

Dear Military Religious Freedom Foundation:

Thanks for making people of faith look like quacks, and mindless creatures. IF you think you have done favors for the military you are fooling yourselves. In combat there are few atheists, and few who wouldn't like to have faith in something. When the going gets tough it would be incredibly naïve to think the end is hopeless and not stand and fight for all your beliefs. Boo to you and your organization. I pray one day you will have the faith to look up and see redemption before it is too late. I stand for Jesus Christ, I live for Jesus Christ, and I will die preaching for Jesus Christ. To do otherwise would be betraying the one who made this country great! Think I am wrong? Remember we are all created equal, with unalienable rights endowed by our creator. The whole point of our very existence. We will be praying for you folks. We hope you realize that a truly religious Christian fanatic will die in your place rather than let someone of another faith kill because they want to force their beliefs on the rest of the world.

(name withheld)

***

Dear Mikey Winstein:

Read article on Fox News relative to your having an Air Force military program that included reference to scriptures, both Old and New testament, at least temporarily suspended. Dorks like yourself and the mentally and spiritually challenged persons, assuming you all are persons, do not know what the hell you are talking about. there is no "separation of church and state" in the constitution, nor was that Jefferson's intent in the Danbury letter. One of these days you derelicts of society are going to literally crap in your drawers when King Jesus, who incidentally is and will come back as a warrior, actually comes back, and if you are not ready, I pitty your sorry derrieres

(name and e mail address withheld)

***

I am a soldier in the United States Army. I was raised as a Southern Baptist. Today I was attending graduation practice for my AIT graduation. When we arrived at the chapel where the ceremony is taking place in, I saw the plan for graduation included a prayer. When we reached that part, we were told we were required to bow our heads and cross our hands in front of us. I immediately pointed out that not only is a prayer at a public ceremony un-constitutional, but to force someone to give the illusion of religion when the individual does not believe in any religion is blatantly wrong and very illegal. Instantly the rest of my platoon groaned and said to suck it up, stop com-plaining, etc. I stood my ground while the sergeant in charge said the same thing, albeit more politely. When I sat down, I immediately emailed Mikey Weinstein of the Military Religious Freedom Foundation about the incident. He quickly responded to my email with his phone number. I went into the bathroom to make the call. However, partway through a sergeant came in and told me to get off and come outside the bathroom. My call remained connected, and the sergeants berated me for jumping the chain of command, although where consulting a lawyer violates the chain of command was never pointed out. I was then sent to see my company commander and 1st SG. I told them my issue and was again told it was unfounded. I was told that if I did not bow my head and clasp my hands that I would be subject to UCMJ punitive action. As I refuse to compromise on my beliefs, the idea that my military career could be cut short due to standing up for my beliefs frightened me. I was told I could do it or call the inspector general. When I returned to the chapel, I asked my cadre if I could call IG. He told me to wait until after practice. I was then again ridiculed by my peers, however I stood my ground. Shortly thereafter, my commander came to me and told me that bowing was now suddenly "optional" and that I could remain at attention. Mr. Weinstein moved remarkably fast on this, and I believe that my cadre's knowledge that I already had a lawyer from the Military Religious Freedom Foundation in the loop is what caused them to change their blatantly unconstitutional order. My fear of punishment for standing up for my beliefs is gone, and knowing how quickly the MRFF can move to help soldier's whose rights are violated gives me a high level of confidence. Their work to get the numerous promotions of religion in the military out is a great service to the entire armed forces.

(U.S. Army Soldier's name, rank, military unit and military installation withheld)

***

More Graphics:

He was guilty as sin, just like you. Tried, convicted, sentenced, appealed, denied. When jew money bought him a Clinton style pardon, white justice stepped in. Are you ready?

***

Mikey,

I have used your material in many of my columns for the Florida Jewish Journal. The Military Religious Freedom Foundation is a national treasure because it does what no other organization is doing. Keeping an eye on the continued separation of church in state in the military is crucial to the future of our country. Given your background and education you are the perfect person to be in charge. Thank you for bringing the mess at the Air Force Academy to light and for all your other work. I look forward to your South Florida appearance on November 15th. I hope to be with you.

Bruce
Rabbi Bruce Warshal is Publisher Emeritus and columnist for
the Jewish Journal.

Dear Rabbi Bruce:
Thank you for your awareness and advocacy of the Military Religious Freedom Foundation. The Columbus Jewish Foundation, like you, is strongly supportive of Mikey Weinstein's efforts. It's lonely out there: most Jewish organizations, including ADL, appear to be oblivious to what MRFF is up against. Please keep up the good work.

Jackie Jacobs, Executive Director
Columbus Jewish Foundation
L'shana tova from
your Columbus Jewish
Foundation Family

***

Dear MRFF,

Succinctly, I'd like to say: The only thing countries in the history of the world that protect and defend the idea of religious freedom are ones who's predominate constituency is Christian.

If you succeed in ridding the military of ministers who influence all for

Christian ends, you will have yourself to thank once your posterity lives under a religion you don't choose. Look at Europe which is heading towards Islamic rule. They are being overrun by a religion which will eventually out-number and so impose its religious perspective on the whole even through a democratic system.

The bottom line is this: If Jesus wins it is better for everyone. So you might as well surrender now and find forgiveness and grace from him or be very disappointed once you die and face him on terms that will not be favorable. Besides, your religious freedom this side of eternity depends on it. Oh wait, you won't be around when your great, great, great grand children have to learn Arabic to read the Koran. So you don't care.

Turn to Jesus now while you can or you posterity will suffer. Sorry to be so bold but I hope it makes you think a little and so causes you to turn from this nonsense. Christianity is the only thing that allows you to put forward this ridiculous organization.

Let me give you and illustration: You are like a little girl I once saw on a bus sitting in her grandfathers lap holding an ice-cream cone. She dropped the head of the cone on the floor and began to cry. When her grandfather said, she would get another one soon, she turned up and smacked him in the face because soon was not soon enough. Even though everything she had was attributed to her grandfather, she disrespected him and did it in ignorance. Here is the punch line: the Christian God is the only reason why you can complain, why you can have the wonderful education the Air Force academy affords, why America is so great. Yet instead of thanking him and worshiping him, you smack him in the face. Please know he is humble and patient even with your foolishness. But know this, the day is coming when you will realize how foolish you've been. I pray not. I pray not. Please understand I do not relish your demise. I pray for you to come to Jesus and surrender before it is too late.

***

Just wanted to tell you how much I admire what your organization is doing. I wish it had existed (or if it did, that I had known about it) during my years as an Air Force officer (dates withheld). In what should have been some of the best years of my life, I was routinely shunned and made to feel a pariah for no other reason than that I did not consider the bible to be a true story.

I never tried to push my atheist beliefs on others, never really cared what others thought. But because I answered honestly when someone directly asked me if I believed in evolution, I was made an outcast in a very closed community.

The military in the 90s (and I would guess still today), in particular the Air Force, had become a large scale Christian cult. Every meeting would begin with a Christian prayer. Every event that would happen was some sort of sign from Jesus, and it was up to us to interpret it somehow. I remember my general, a two star, discussing the "don't ask, don't tell" policy to the wing by holding up a bible and stating "THIS is my policy", to a rousing ovation.

Most of all I was concerned about the conception of Islam as an "evil" religion, and the idea that the U.S. was a Christian nation in a holy war with Islam over the people of the middle east. I have no doubts whatsoever the influence this played on President Bush's decision to go to war with Iraq 7 years ago.

Anyways, I just wanted you to know how much I admire what you are doing. Eventually, common sense and reason always wins out.

Sincerely,
(name and rank withheld)

***

INDEX